Bc

The Psychological Study
of Object Perception

The Psychological Study of Object Perception

*Examination of methodological problems
and a critique of main research approaches*

ARILD LIAN

*Institute of Psychology, University of Oslo,
Blindern, Oslo, Norway*

ACADEMIC PRESS · 1981
A Subsidiary of Harcourt Brace Jovanovich, Publishers
London · New York · Toronto · Sydney · San Francisco

ACADEMIC PRESS INC. (LONDON) LTD.
24/28 Oval Road,
London NW1

United States Edition published by
ACADEMIC PRESS INC.
111 Fifth Avenue
New York, New York 10003

Copyright © 1981 by
ACADEMIC PRESS INC. (LONDON) LTD.

British Library Cataloguing in Publication Data
Lian Arild
  Examinations of methodological problems and a
  critique of main research approaches.
  1. Environmental psychology   2. Man — Influence
  of environment
  301.31   BF353   80-41629

  ISBN 0-12-447850-6 ✓

Phototypeset by Dobbie Typesetting Service, Plymouth, Devon, England
and printed by T.J. Press, Padstow, England

Preface

The perception of material objects is generally considered to be the main subject matter of the psychology of perception. Various forms of psychophysical methods have been used to inquire into this matter. The adequacy and prospects of single methods have been discussed, but no one seems to have argued, on grounds of principle that psychophysics prohibits an analysis of perceptual activities related to objects in the environment. In this book, however, I shall promote an argument in this direction.

There may be several reasons why research workers have not advanced a similar critique concerning the application of methods to the type of problems formulated in the area.

Firstly, the interdependency of the method and the research problem has but recently been acknowledged by a few writers in psychology. For a long time research workers have tended to assume that there exist general methods — in particular the methods of psychophysics — which are appropriate for the studying of almost any question that can be asked concerning man's perception of the external world. In consequence the subject matter or the phenomena studied by way of these methods has been taken for granted or considered to be well known. For example, no one has seriously discussed what is meant by "the perceiving of a material object".

I have set out to reconsider more thoroughly the method–problem relationship in the psychology of perception, and I have asked what assumptions will have to be made concerning the subject's apprehension of the environment in psychophysical experiments on perception. What does it mean to say that theoretical statements are based on studies of *attentive* organisms? Does the assumption of a certain awareness constitute, on the one hand, a prerequisite for the method, and on the other, a constraint with respect to the type of problem which can be studied by way of the method in question?

These questions are both challenging and delicate. Their discussion tends to be time-consuming and should perhaps be avoided if one is aiming at a high publishing rate. Thus I have the impression that concern with such questions is not often encouraged in Western universities or research centres. At least such questions are, for the most part, evaded during research apprenticeship.

At the University of Oslo, where I have worked most of the time since my graduation in psychology, the situation may have been a different one. Here young researchers have been encouraged to raise fundamental problems and to make clear the basic presuppositions of various procedures in their field of research.

This situation has to a great extent depended on the teaching and writing of Professor Per Saugstad, a researcher and scholar who has promoted a thorough-going analysis of the foundations of psychology as a science. He aroused my interest in the field of perception, and he called my attention to the need for a more critical discussion of the object concept in psychology.

In particular Saugstad has made me aware of the interdependence of research problem and method in psychology. Moreover, he has stressed that perception should be studied in the wider context of development and adjustment to the environment, and that perception should be considered as a form of activity. These are important points of departure for the present work.

My task has been to show which are the prerequisites of some common methods used in the study of perceiving activities, and to relate these prerequisites to general descriptions of perceptual events, in particular to the so-called object constancies. It is my contention that these prerequisites prohibit an analysis of perceiving activities related to objects, and that contrary to common opinion therefore, the so-called constancies in perception have no clear empirical basis. What then can be said about the events that are generally assumed to be the subject matter of the psychology of perception? The question calls upon more detailed discussion of the concepts of "perceptual identity" and "material object".

This book is the result of rewriting my doctoral dissertation (Mimeograph, Univ. Oslo) on the matter. I have cut down the length by omitting two chapters of the original dissertation, i.e. one chapter on the constancy ratios and one chapter on the distinction between localization and identification. I have also cut down parts of other chapters, and thus omitted a discussion of "the modes of appearances of colours and the doctrine of the unity of colour and visual direction" and a discussion of Festinger's theory on the role of efference in visual space perception.

In the present book, however, I have added a discussion of the concept of a sense modality, and I have analysed more thoroughly the prerequisites of psychophysical procedures. The concepts of "perceptual identity" and "material object" are now discussed in separate chapters. Some of the recent philosophical literature on identity is included in the former discussion, and computer programs for the recognition of objects are examined and argued about in the chapter on the object concept. Lastly, I have added an examination of some studies of perceptual activities by infants. The work, however, still retains some of its historical emphasis in the way that it highlights some classical issues, for example, the relation of Emmert's law to size constancy.

I want to reiterate my thanks to Saugstad for his encouragement and stimulating criticism. I also want to thank Harald Martinsen and Ernst Ottem for having patiently listened to me when I needed someone to talk to about my work. They have also gone over some of my arguments with me, and they have helped me to correct and to improve upon them.

Lastly, I want to thank members of the adjudicating committee to whom the dissertation was submitted. In particular I want to thank Professor I. K. Moustgaard and Professor R. J. Hirst for their critiques and examinations of the dissertations by the official disputation 19 December, 1974.

Oslo, December 1980   *Arild Lian*

Contents

1

Introduction

1.1 The problem of method in the psychological study of object perception

This book deals with psychological studies of the perception of objects in the environment. In such studies psychologists have generally inquired into the conditions under which we become aware of the colour, size, form, orientation or location of an external object. The limitations of this field of research depend on the definitions of the terms "perception" and "object".

In general, the method and subject matter of a science are closely related. Therefore, to define the psychological study of object perception, we must also specify a set of research methods or procedures. We claim that the characteristics of the method should be included in the definition of one's subject matter. Conversely, we also claim that a method of research involves a subject or type of research problem. Hence method and subject matter cannot be defined independently of each other.

To study object perception psychologists have used various methods or procedures. In the main these have been psychophysical methods. Some studies have been made in accordance with classical procedures in psychophysics, and some have been made using various adaptations of these procedures. The question is whether the perception of objects, considered as a subject of research in psychology, can be properly defined in relation to psychophysical methods?

Psychophysics has been developed with a view to treating a particular type of problem in science. Moreover, the use of psychophysical methods rests on a number of presuppositions which limit the applicability of these methods. Certain preconditions must be met in order that psychophysical data can be properly analysed by the researcher. Some of these preconditions are trivial ones; others are not. Thus there may be subtle preconditions which are rarely spelled out, yet tacitly assumed by most research workers, and these may be the preconditions which serve to limit the scope of psychophysics. In Chapter 2 we shall deal with some basic preconditions of psychophysical experiments.

Traditionally, psychophysics is said to be concerned with measurements of the sensations, and the relationships between sensations and physical stimuli. Moreover, sensations or "sense data" such as brightness, hue, pitch etc. have been contrasted with the perception of objects and events in everyday life. From the days of H. L. F. von Helmholtz many psychologists have involved themselves in comprehensive discussions of the relationship between sensation and perception.

The Gestalt psychologists claimed that object perception obeyed certain laws of organization, and that such perception could not be reduced to sensations. Instead of psychophysical analysis they proposed a phenomenological method for the study of object perception. This method, however, could not easily be defined, and thus it did not gain general acceptance among other psychologists.

On the other hand, a psychophysical approach to perception has had its adherents up to the present day. J. J. Gibson asserted that psychophysics could still be said to deal with the perception of objects and events in the environment. However, he made it a condition that psychophysical variables should be specified in terms of margins, ratios, densities, flow patterns, etc. It has been said of Gibson that he advanced a form of perceptual psychophysics.

Yet, we think it may be possible to specify certain preconditions underlying a psychophysical approach to perception, and these preconditions are probably independent of whether variables are specified as simple measures of physical energy (as in classical psychophysics) or as ratios between such measures (as in perceptual psychophysics). For the former a psychophysical approach involves the specification of a discriminatory task in relation to a particular environmental setting. The question is what perception of this setting must be assumed, explicitly or implicitly, in order to instruct a human subject to perform the task? This perception must be considered as part of the essential preconditions of the method, not as a subject of experimental analysis.

In this book it will be shown that many research workers may have tacitly assumed their approach to object perception, indicated by the way subjects have been set discriminatory tasks in their experiments. Thus perceptual characteristics have been included in the presuppositions underlying the procedure, and therefore we must ask whether the research problems studied are formulated independently of these presuppositions? It will be argued that assumptions regarding the research problems have been included in the *a priori* basis of the procedure, and that the research workers, therefore, have tended to beg the questions concerning the characteristics of object perception.

Our criticism applies to a tradition of research, not merely to individual studies of object perception. Thus it is our contention that a psychophysical procedure prohibits an analysis of the perception of material objects in the environment.

In the psychological study of object perception a general problem of method is acknowledged. At present, therefore, it may also be difficult to formulate exactly problems of research in the area.

1.2 Communication between subject and experimenter in psychophysical studies

In a psychophysical experiment the subject and the experimenter must be able to communicate about certain properties of the environment. As a rule, these properties are explicitly mentioned in an instruction. The subject may, for example, be told to compare the colours of two objects, or the orientation of two lines in the field of view. Hence the subject and the experimenter must be able to communicate about colour and orientation.

It is important that the discriminatory task can be properly understood by the subject. Otherwise communication will be inadequate. As pointed out, however, the discriminatory task is set for the subject in a particular environmental setting and perception of this setting may easily influence the communication between subject and experimenter.

In general the subject's perception of the setting forms a basis for an understanding of the discriminatory task. However, there is no independent way of ascertaining the subject's perception of the setting. Therefore a certain aspect of perception will be presupposed as part of the common understanding of the discriminatory task.

In the present work "understanding" will as a rule be used in relation to a certain task which is set for the subject. Moreover, the subject's understanding, which is presupposed in the instruction, also involves an aspect of the perception of the environmental setting.

1.3   The concepts of "perceptual identity" and "material object"

The subject's understanding of the stimulus situation determines what appears for him as identical parts or events in this situation. The experimenter, however, cannot ascertain the perceptually identical colours, orientations or forms in a certain stimulus situation merely by appealing to what is supposed to be the subject's understanding. Rather the experimenter needs a set of rules by which he can assess the identities and differences between events which are included in his system. In other words, the psychologist needs to specify the procedures by which he can define a "perceptual identity".

In psychophysics lack of discrimination has been advanced as a main criterion of identity. At the same time procedures for the study of sensory discrimination are well specified in psychophysics. However, the use of a "lack of discrimination" criterion excludes from consideration the type of perceptual identity which seems to involve the recognition of an object. It also excludes from consideration the type of identity which can be described as "permanence amidst change", yet in the study of object perception these identities have been discussed extensively by the researchers.

In philosophy there exists a comprehensive literature on identity statements about objects. Part of this literature will be examined, and it will be argued in this connection that identity statements generally presuppose knowledge of a certain change in the perceiver's interaction with the environment. Hence *the activity of perceiving* must be taken into account in order to define perceptual identities. The question is, what type of reference system is needed to give an adequate description of perceptual activities?

The concept of a material object will also be examined. In the literature notions of identity have been closely linked with the notion of an object. Although we may specify an object in terms of its physical properties, the object is ordinarily considered as something more than a collection of properties. In perception the object is said to occur as an integrated psychological unity. Again we shall raise the question of a reference system for dealing with such a unity.

1.4   Outline of the book

This book gives a methodological examination of some well-known studies of object perception. Since these studies may be said to represent a general psychophysical approach to perception, we shall start by discussing the scope and subject matter of psychophysics, and the *a priori* conditions underlying the use of psychophysical methods.

Thus Chapter 2 provides a basis for the examinations which will be put forward in Chapters 6, 8, and 9.

The concepts of perceptual identity and material object are treated separately in Chapters 3 and 4. Against this background we shall scrutinize some common formulations of the so-called perceptual constancies. In the research literature the constancies are said to involve perceptual entitites which remain constant under transformation of the "proxminal stimulus". In Chapter 5, therefore, we ask, what is it that is supposed to remain constant in the perceptual constancies?

It will be shown that traditional formulations of constancy involve two types of problems which tend to be confused by researchers. One type of problem refers to the psychophysics of certain perceptual attributes, and the other type of problem refers to the identity of an object under transformation.

In Chapter 6 we examine some experiments of Katz, Gelb and Hsia on the constancy of achromatic surface colours. Modern writers often refer to these experiments as "classics". Also in this chapter we deal with some "classic" as well as some more recent studies on the perceptual reliationship between illumination and the dimensions of the achromatic surface colours.

The rest of the book is mostly concerned with the problem of the perception of space and the spatial attributes of objects. As an introduction to this part of the book Chapter 7 is devoted to an examination of Poincaré's notion of a *displacement group*. Thereby we shall call attention to the complex relationship between space, object and locomotion in perception.

Chapter 8 is concerned with studies of size constancy and the size–distance relationship. Helmholtz once formulated a set of preconditions which must be fulfilled in order to study visual size discriminations. A description of these preconditions will serve as a further basis for our examination of studies of size constancy and the size–distance relationship. In this chapter we shall also give a discussion of Emmert's law, and we shall reconsider the classical issue of the relationship between the size–distance invariance hypothesis, size constancy and Emmert's law.

Studies relating to the perception of form and the form–orientation relationship are examined in Chapter 9. Discussion of a few studies of infants' perception of form and orientation are included to give a thorough exposition of methodological problems which are common to all studies in the field of form perception. Lastly, we shall critically examine the stimulus concept which is presented in the works of Gibson and Johansson, and we shall compare the position taken by these two researchers with a so-called neo-Helmholtzian position in psychology. In our opinion, the differences between the two positions have been exaggerated in the literature. We shall also call attention to the similarities between the approaches taken by Gibson and Johansson on the one side and the approach taken by the neo-Hemholtzians on the other.

Due to our concern with the perceptual constancies and the invariance hypothesis, the book has an historical emphasis. However, the methodological problems we discuss are relevant to classical as well as modern research works in the area. Therefore, an examination of some recent research trends are also included in the present work.

It goes without saying that this is a critical book. We are, in fact, questioning the foundation of most of the psychology of perception. To make our position clear, we have taken up parts of the philosophical debate on identity in perception, but our critique derives its main support from a thorough analysis of experimental designs and empirical data. Moreover, we think that the development of a new and adequate theoretical framework for the study of object perception will take place in psychology, and whenever possible we shall indicate new approaches.

2

Psychophysics

2.1 The concept of a sense modality and the scope of psychophysics

In our opinion there exists, in the various cultures of the world, a comprehensive knowledge of perception and the things we perceive. The psychologist studying perception should take some of this knowledge into account, and while delimiting the scope of his inquiry, he should be able to introduce new systems of reference that innovate general cultural knowledge in the area. The establishment of a perceptual science along these lines is most clearly illustrated by the history of psychophysics. Yet psychologists may have rendered discrepant accounts of the objects of psychophysical research and hence of its scope of inquiry. Consequently, attempts have been made to extend psychophysics beyond limits which are probably determined by basic preconditions in its establishment as a science.

We tend to put the blame onto Fechner for some of the confusion about the task of psychophysics. He proclaimed psychophysics as ". . . an exact theory of the functionally dependent relations of body and soul or, more generally, of the material and the mental, of the physical and the psychological worlds" (1966, p.7). Psychophysics is generally dated from the publication of Fechner's work (1860). The psychophysical problem, however, is much older. Yet philosophical concern with this problem hardly explains why systematic research in this field started around 1860. The reason for this relatively late start is to be found in the fact that psychophysics was linked with classical physics and thus had to await some early progress in optics and acoustics. These branches of physics also defined a frame of reference for the new science.

Moreover psychophysics has always dealt with the senses and their discriminatory capacities. Therefore, the establishment of psychophysics as a science depended on definitions of the sense organs that also served to delineate its field of research. A certain knowledge of the senses has been available since ancient times, but this knowledge did not suffice to found a new field of research. It was 19th century science that provided the groundwork for a study of the senses, and which defined a more limited scope of psychophysics than is commonly recognized by present-day psychologists. Going back to the beginning of the physiology of the senses, we shall ask how pioneering researchers conceived of a sense organ and its function.

Knowledge of the senses will to a great extent depend on knowledge of the nervous system. Thus Bell and Magendie's discovery that sensory and motor nerves are different preceded some of the main contributions made to the physiology of the senses during the 19th century. This discovery has since become fundamental to most theories of the senses and has given rise to the common assumption that sensory and perceptual events can be studied independently of motor activities.

Once sensory nerves could be separated from motor nerves the time had come to categorize them and to describe their functions. In his *Idea of a New Anatomy of the Brain*, Bell (1811, 1869) proposed that each sensory nerve has its own specific energy and can respond only with its own individual quality. Johannes Müller (1838) gave formal status to this proposition which has later become known as *the doctrine of the specific energies of nerves*. It is Müller's name which is associated with this doctrine, and we shall therefore consider some principles set forth in the first section of his *Handbuch der Physiologie der Menschen*. Our quotations will be taken from Dennis (1948) who presented an English version of excerpts from this handbook.

Firstly Müller stated that "external agencies can give rise to no kind of sensation which cannot also be produced by internal causes . . . ." (p.157), and that "the same internal cause excites in the different senses different sensations . . . in each sense the sensations peculiar to it" (p.159). Likewise "the same external cause also gives rise to different sensations in each sense, according to the special endowments of its nerve" (p.159).

Müller's text was full of instances which gave support to these principles. For example, he carefully described how the stimulus of electricity may give rise to a bright flash of light when applied to the eye and to a sensation of sound when applied to the ear.

By way of implication of the first three principles Müller maintained that the senses can only inform the organism of their own states, not of external objects. In this way each "nerve of a sense seems capable of one determinate kind of sensation only, and not those proper to the other organs of sense; hence one nerve cannot take the place and perform the function of the nerve of another sense" (p.165).

To explain the perception of the external world Müller took the position of a representational theorist. The sensations were considered as representations, not images or eidola of the external objects. However, the reliability of perception called for a separate principle. He thus stated that "the nerves of the senses have assuredly a specific irritability for certain influences; for many stimuli, which exert a violent action upon one organ of sense, have little or no effect upon another" (p.162). This principle of specific irritability was rephrased by Sherrington as the concept of *adequate stimulus*.

Müller purported to distinguish the notion of specific irritability from the notion of specific energy. The former may be said to refer to a functional relation between the sense organ and the environmental flux of physical energy; the latter, on the other hand, referred to the *content* of the nerve.

What is the content of the sensory nerve? Müller said it was a certain energy. That term, however, caused much bewilderment among later research workers, for they tended to think that in a physical sense all sensory nerves are equal: the impulses transmitted along the auditory nerve do not differ considerably from the impulses transmitted along the optic nerve. Boring remarked that ". . . when he (Müller) called the nervous essential an energy, he must have been influenced by such doctrines as the vis viva and the vis nervosa in his choice" (1942, p.71). But it is quite clear from Müller's text that "specific energy" was supposed to be a psychological term. Thus he pointed out one place where quality would do as an alternative term for energy. He even said that ". . . the sensation of sound — is the peculiar 'energy' or 'quality' of the auditory nerve; the sensation of light and colours that of the optic nerve; and so of the other nerves of a sense" (p.163).

For centuries Western culture has treated light and colour as one modality of sensations mediated by the eye, and sound as another modality mediated by the ear. Thus the term "modality of sensations" has been used with reference to a class of sense experiences. H. L. F. von Helmholtz suggested that such experiences can be divided into modalities according to qualitative criteria. Light and colour experiences were said to fall in uninterrupted continua in such a way that intermediaries could be found between any two colour or light experiences, either chromatic or achromatic ones. These experiences were, therefore, classified into one modality of sensations. Discrete qualities of sense experiences, such as a particular hue of colour and a particular pitch of sound, for which no intermediates could be found, were to be placed in separate modalities. Moreover, a sense organ was defined with reference to a particular modality of sensations, hence the hues of colour were mediated by one sense organ, and the pitches of sound by another.

As long as Müller merely equated the "specific energy of a nerve" with a particular modality, he was unable to innovate cultural knowledge in the area. He could only ascertain that the nerve considered *was* the nerve for a sense. Contributions to the study of the senses required independent definitions of the modalities, i.e. definitions which add something to cultural knowledge by relating sensations of light, colour, sound etc. to new systems of references. At the time Müller published his work such systems had been introduced by theories of the kinetic energies, the mechanical vibrations of solids and liquids, and the undulatory motions of the ether. Thus physics provided the discoveries that enabled Müller to distinguish a principle of irritability from a principle of specific energy. Assuredly, both principles rested on cultural knowledge about the modalities, but the former presupposed in addition new systems of reference according to which one could identify a colour stimulus, a temperature stimulus, and a touch stimulus.

Cultural knowledge or common conceptions of sound and colour were maintained and refined in science. However, one can also say that specification of the sound stimulus in physics served as a redefinition of the auditory modality, and specification of the stimuli for light and colour served as a redefinition of the visual modality. We can say that a sense modality was no longer defined by qualitative criteria alone, but also with reference to specifications of physical energy.

Notice that the subdivisions of classical physics coincided for the main part with common distinctions between the sense modalities. Considerations of the conditions for sensations of touch, warmth and cold, light and colour, and sound have given rise to the studies of mechanics, heat, optics and acoustics. Research in these areas had direct bearings on conceptions of the sensory functions. Thus we might say that classical physics introduced new ways of dealing with the modalities, at least in so far as it gave strict rules for the use of concepts such as heat, light, colour, sound, etc.

From the point of view of a representational theorist, however, physics was not concerned with the sensations *per se*. Light was commonly considered as a subjective representation created by the mind, and to distinguish this representation from the agent represented, the researchers introduced the term "lux" for the former and "lumen" for the latter. In accordance with the principle of primary and secondary qualities, the sensation was also said to be caused by the external agent. In other words, a sensation produced by light was considered as the internal effect of an external agent acting on the eye of an observer. Likewise the sensations which belong to other modalities were considered as internal effects of external agents.

Nonetheless, physical definitions of external agents were initially based on concommitant variations that involved an observer. A good example is Newton's demonstration of the refractive powers of light in which a pencil of rays passing through a wedge prism gives rise to the various hues of colour. Physical variables were thus introduced by reference to a sensory system of an observer. That is to say that cultural knowledge of the sense modalities formed a prerequisite for classical physics. Yet, however, when independent systems of references were established for dealing with light, sound, etc., physics no longer needed support from common conceptions of the modalities. Once heat, for instance, was defined with reference to the kinetic energy of atomic structures, mechanics no longer needed to be directly concerned with warmth, cold and touch as defined by general cultural knowledge. Instead physicists became concerned with the motions of bodies, whether these bodies constitutes molecules, atoms or merely material points. Detector systems other than the human skin receptors were introduced to the study of such motions which henceforth were declared as independent of an observer. In consequence it was also possible to break down the original subdivisions of physics, and its relationships with the modalities were no longer clear ones.

According to Ronchi (1957), modern physics was compressed into two studies: the physics of matter and the physics of ether. He pointed out that in this state of affairs optics no longer seemed to be an autonomous science. Yet one could still distinguish between three receiver–detector systems for studying light in physics, namely:

    (a) photoelectric cells,
    (b) photosensitive emulsions,
    (c) eyes.

According to Ronchi, there was nothing "optical" about the characteristic reactions or processes of (a) and (b) which indicated that they had absorbed radiation. The term "optical", he contended, always implied some reference to eyes. The process of detection, which had such an important function in physics, was supposed to exercise an influence also on classification and terminology. Ronchi, therefore, suggested that this process should be the subject matter of three sister sciences, which he called:

    (1) photoelectricity,
    (2) photography,

(3) optics.

We may add that the ear similarly represents one of the receiver-detector systems which are available for the study of the transmission of mechanical energy in various media. This means that the ear serves as a basis for delimiting acoustics as a branch of mechanics, and thus the term "acoustical" implies some reference to the human auditory system.

The point to be stressed is that definitions of light and sound are based on interactions between external agents and the particular receiver-detector systems used by the physicists, and since knowledge of light and sound is possible only by way of certain interactions, we are inclined to equate these interactions with the modalities themselves.

In early optics the researcher made direct use of his own eyes for the purpose of detecting radiated light energy. This means that initially the visual system of the researcher constituted the receiver-detector system. Definite prescriptions for the observation of light and colour were laid down. Hence early optics depended on some knowledge of the perceiver, i.e. of the function of the visual system in the perceiver.

In the long run, however, the visual system was considered as a most unreliable instrument, and hence the physicist did not place much confidence in the eye as a measuring device. He thus proceeded to define a "standard" observer, by way of which he made explicit assumptions regarding the ordinary characteristics of the eye or ear.

Though physicists did not state it explicitly, light was thus considered as a *department of interactions with the environment*. Sound was similarly considered as another department of interactions. In other words, the modalities could be defined in such a way as to innovate cultural knowledge and yet to maintain common distinctions between light, sound, cold, warmth and touch.

On this basis we can now rephrase some of Müller's statements about the "specific energies" of nerves. Instead of saying that the sensory nerve can only inform us of its own state, we can say that the nerve mediates a certain type of interactions with the environment. The nerves of other senses mediate other types of interactions. Rather than contrasting the state of a nerve or the quality of a sensation with the perception of external objects, it should be emphasized that the type of interaction is severely restricted and does not form the basis of all possible knowledge about the external world.

The contributions of the physical sciences made possible a systematic investigation of the senses. Psychophysics and the physiology of the senses both developed from the physical sciences. In particular, psychophysics has been closely related to physics. Thus it may be hard to distinguish, for example, optics and acoustics from the corresponding parts of psychophysics. Ronchi defined optics as the science of vision. He could similarly have defined acoustics as the science of hearing. What is the difference between optics considered as the science of vision and the psychophysics of vision, and what is the difference between acoustics and the psychophysics of hearing? The physical definitions of light and sound served as the frame of reference for psychophysics as well as the individual branches of physics.

Yet physics and psychophysics have generally pursued different goals and have set different objectives for research. Psychophysics turned its interest on the observer's part in maintaining the various kinds of interactions with the environment. The organism was supposed to contain a number of sensing devices that subserved these interactions, and the psychophysicists considered as their task the exploration of the capacities or functions of these devices. Assessment of borders or limits to sensory discriminability became important, and the concept of a sensory threshold was highlighted by the researchers.

The point is that sensory capacities rather than psychophysical correspondences were considered as the main subject matter for research in psychophysics. Once the psychophysicist accepted certain specifications of the visual stimulus in optics and certain specifications of the auditory stimulus in acoustics, he also accepted (1) the physical definitions of the two sense modalities, and (2) a set of psychophysical correspondences (hue–wavelength, pitch–sound wave frequency etc.). We do not deny, of course, that psychophysicists have been able to demonstrate additional correspondences, particularly by calling attention to more subtle aspects of colour and sound, and to relations between simple measures of the visual stimulus. These other psychophysical correspondences have also been ascertained within the general framework of optics and acoustics. Thus we can say that the two branches of physics have provided systems of reference for psychophysics. To borrow terms from Kuhn (1962) we can also say that the physics of the last century formed a "paradigm" for psychophysics, and that most of contemporary research on the senses is to be considered as "normal science".

It should be emphasized that the physical definitions of the sense modalities rest on certain assumptions concerning the perceiving organism. These assumptions were not well specified. However, they must have been concerned with the organism's ability to make abstractions and to be aware of particular aspects of the environment. In other words, each of these definitions presuppose a particular organism–environment interaction. Therefore, to study a visual capacity, the researcher must ascertain that his subject is capable of interacting with the environment in certain ways. On this assumption, variations in the wavelength of light stimulating the eye, for example, will be reported as hue differences by the subject. If hue differences are not reported, the psychophysicist will tend to blame his subject rather than refuting the hue–wavelength relationship. Therefore it is important to know the circumstances under which psychophysical data can be considered as valid. Such circumstances are rarely stated explicitly in the literature. In the following sections we shall call attention to some of the critical circumstances which are mostly taken for granted by the researchers.

Firstly, we want to dwell a little more on the scope of psychophysics. To estimate the capacities of a sense organ certain reference values of discrimination are needed. The concept of an absolute sensory threshold was introduced. This concept will be discussed in the following sections, particularly in Section 2.4. More important perhaps was the definition of a "standard" observer in several fields of psychophysics. The use of a standard observer reference in psychophysics heavily restricted the admissibility of individual differences among subjects.

Psychophysical variables, particularly in the field of colorimetry, have been defined with reference to a "standard" observer. A distinction is generally made between physical and psychophysical variables. The wavelength of radiant energy and the amount of energy at each wavelength are physical variables, and as put by Evans: "From these physical variables and the known properties of the visual response system are derived three psychophysical variables, which serve to determine, among other things, whether or not two given light stimuli will match visually if viewed under stated conditions" (1964, p.1467). Here "properties of the visual response system", which can be demonstrated under "stated conditions", means the performance of a standard observer. In this case definition of a standard observer made possible the calculation of the trichromaticity chart in the CIE system.

Variables have also been defined with reference to a standard observer in photometry. For example, the definition of physical brightness includes a set of visibility constants which refer to the matching performance of a standard observer under specified conditions of viewing.

In short, therefore, the standard observer means a fixed reference for the specification of stimulation in an experiment with human subjects. A specification of stimulation in relation to known response characteristics is an essential aspect of experimental control in psychophysics.

In addition, the reference to a standard observer implies a certain precondition which must be met in order that psychophysical data can be properly analysed. The notion, one can say, means a particular observer–environment relationship which cannot be maintained without attentive abilities on behalf of the observer. Hence the standard observer, whether or not seen as an ideal non-human observer, must be equipped with cognition or understanding. A certain understanding of the environment is implied by the response characteristics of the system.

The use of a standard observer reference means that essential conditions for the performance of this observer have been reproduced. Also it must be assumed that the standard observer and the experimental subject perceive the environment in essentially the same way. We shall say that the two must understand the stimulus situation in a similar way. Unless the experimenter can make this assumption, a proper analysis of the response data cannot be made.

2.2 Psychophysical experiments: description of a prototype

In the preceding section psychophysics was said to be concerned with the assessment of sensory capacities. The procedures or methods used in such assessment vary a great deal, and already Fechner has devised a set of alternative "psychophysical methods". Yet these methods share certain characteristics which can be used to describe a prototype of several psychophysical experiments.

The description of such a prototype serves a particular purpose in this work. Firstly, we want to show at this point how the procedure and the research task go together in psychophysics. Secondly, we want to take this prototype as a point of departure in examinations of experiments which deal with object perception (see Chapters 6, 8, and 9). The question is whether an experiment on the constancy of size, for example, can be understood as an attempt to determine a particular discriminatory capacity, or is such an experiment liable to a different interpretation?

The prototype of psychophysical experiments may be conceived of as an ordinary procedure for the calculation of a sensory threshold. It does not show the technical and statistical refinements of many experiments in the area, yet it represents in a general sense psycho-physical procedures, and it provides a point of departure for the type of examinations mentioned above. Firstly the prototype will be described as a generalized procedure; then we shall select a particular experiment to show more specifically what can be the object of such a procedure. We also want to show specifically how an analysis of the response data rests on assumptions concerning the subject's understanding of the stimulus situation.

In its most simple form an experiment in psychophysics includes (1) an independent variable, (2) a dependent variable, and (3) a discriminatory task or instruction. We shall first give some general remarks on each of the three parts:

The independent variable is, in this case, also called the psychophysical variable. Such a variable, we have said, can be derived from physical specifications of environmental events and response characteristics of an observer. The point is that the independent variable in psychophysics either has an explicit reference to the response characteristics of an observer, or it presupposes a particular organism–environment interaction in the form of a selective awareness of colour, sound, etc.

Sometimes the researchers seem to have been contented with a physical or metrical specification of the variable. In such cases we presume that a certain reference to the organism is implied by the fact that the radiation from an object or the object itself is called a stimulus. Thus when a luminous source or an energy range is specified in physicalistic terms only, this range can usually be related to certain limits of discriminability. It may, for example, be a supra or near threshold range. An external object may also be specified metrically, while its position relative to the sensory surface of a subject is roughly taken for granted. As a rule, however, psychophysical research problems require specification of the independent variable in relation to certain response characteristics of the organism.

The dependent variable constitutes a set of response alternatives. These alternatives may or may not be arranged in a ranking order, i.e. the variable can be specified for different levels of quantification. Quite frequently, however, the dependent variable in psychophysics includes two mutually exclusive response alternatives such as "yes/no" or "left/right" or "in front/behind". In such cases the dependent variable is but a nominal scale, since the response alternatives, for example "yes/no", are not given a ranking order. In the various methods of scaling variables of higher quantification levels have been used (see Torgerson, 1958).

In the case of a nominal arrangement, the researcher may still define a ranking scale from the relative frequency of the use of one of the two response alternatives, and in this way he may systematically relate the subject's responses to the independent variable in the experiment. He thus presents the response data in the form of a psychometric function (see Fig. 1). (The function is ordinarily called a psychometric one in order to distinguish it from other functions relating "subjective magnitudes" to physical magnitudes.) Since the psychometric function is also a cumulative one, a certain measure of its despersion is usually taken as definition of a sensory threshold.

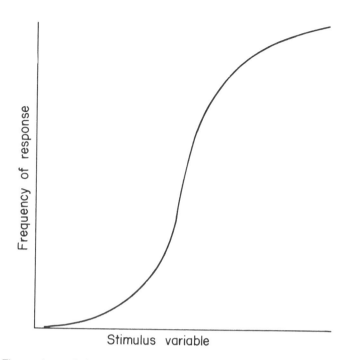

Figure 1 The psychometric function.

This procedure means that both the independent and dependent variables can be related to a particular discriminatory task. One way of expressing this is to say that each of the response alternatives represents a certain understanding of environmental events included in the independent variable. The use of two mutually exclusive response alternatives means that the discriminatory task involves an active choice on behalf of the subject.

As an example we shall consider an experiment by Blakemore (1970) in which points on the longitudinal horopter were determined for a particular angle of symmetrical convergence.

Firstly we should say a few words about the concepts of retinal disparity and the longitudinal horopter. Objects in the plane of fixation which lie on the Vieth–Müller circle are imaged on corresponding points in the two retinas. That is to say the objects are imaged in the same geometrical position on the nasal retina of one eye and the temporal retina of the other. The Vieth–Müller circle, passing through the fixation point and the nodal points of the eyes, defines the locus of objects which are imaged with zero absolute horizontal disparity in the two retinas. If an object is not located on the Vieth–Müller circle, it will be imaged with some absolute disparity, defined as the difference in the angle of azimuth, by the two eyes. Objects inside or nearer than the Vieth–Müller circle have some convergent disparity, whereas objects outside this circle have some divergent disparity. Relative disparity is defined as the difference in absolute disparity between two objects in the field of view. It can be said that the longitudinal horopter is a kind of subjective Vieth–Müller circle, the locus of objects that appear to lie in the same position in the field of the two eyes. The longitudinal horopter is part of the total horopter (see p.33).

Blakemore made use of a stimulus array which is shown in Fig. 2. In this array there is a fixation point F and two black targets on a white background. The one target is presented only for the left eye directly

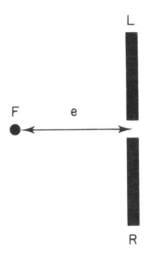

Figure 2 Stimulus display in binocular view of subject. Target L is presented to the left eye and target R to the right eye. F: fixation point (from Blakemore, 1970).

above the fixation point or at some eccentricity at the same height in the visual field. This target is continuously visible for the subject. The other target is presented for the right eye only and positioned below that for the left eye with a gap of 8 minutes of arc between them. The right eye target was briefly exposed while its lateral position was varied from trial to trial. Presentation of this target followed a modified method of limits (the staircase method).

The subject was instructed to tell whether the flashed lower target appeared to lie to the left or to the right of the upper target, i.e. he was given a forced-choice between two response alternatives.

A psychometric function could now be drawn from a count of the relative frequencies of "to the right" responses for different relative disparities. Blakemore, however, referred to this function as a frequency-of-seeing curve. The position which was judged as "to the right" 50% of the time was said to be the position whereby the two targets appeared to lie in the same visual direction. This position, therefore, was said to define a point on the horopter. Blakemore did not measure the disparity thresholds in this experiment. A quartile deviation or an s.d. in the frequency-of-seeing curve could be taken as a measure of the threshold.

Now to consider further the independent variable for this particular experiment. Relative disparity may be said to constitute an interactional aspect. It refers to a spatial relationship between the stimulus targets and the eyes of the subject. This relationship is a dynamic one since it is being maintained by a proper adjustment of the eyes. Therefore, a measurement of relative disparity always rests on an assumption of particular response characteristics of the eyes. (For an analysis of the gross movement characteristics of the eye, see Southhall, 1937, pp.170–186.)

The discriminatory task involves a judgment of relative direction. To ascertain whether the subject is able to perform this judgment, the experimenter and the subject should first be able to communicate about relative direction. Such communication requires a common understanding of the spatial framework. Evidently, Blakemore made in this experiment the tacit assumption that the upper and the lower target appeared for the subject at the same distance. In this case, therefore, identical distance or the front-parallel plane was implicitly assumed to form a spatial reference for estimations of relative direction. The reference need not be mentioned in the instructions. For competent users of language this reference is implied by the formulation of the task. Moreover, the reference must be assumed to be part of the general acceptance of understanding of the spatial framework. This general acceptance of understanding is to be looked upon as a prerequisite for the experiment; it, in a manner of speaking, validates the procedure. The spatial reference included in the assumed mutual understanding cannot be ascertained by the response data. Rather the analysis of these data always rests on the assumption of the use of a certain reference and hence of a mutual understanding.

One might say that the subject in this experiment is assumed to perceive the targets at equal distances, since this is how he can most efficiently compare them with respect to direction. Thus a certain perception might be said to form an *a priori* basis of the method. However, the procedure involves a communication between a subject and an experimenter. Therefore, we prefer to speak about a mutual understanding of the spatial framework or stimulus situation as a prerequisite for the method.

2.3   Perceptual organization as part of the preconditions of psychophysics

The spatial framework in which the targets appeared for the subject in Blakemore's experiment may be said to constitute an example of *perceptual organization.* In general such organization has been considered as an accomplishment of the perceiver, and particularly the Gestalt psychologists have studied the principles according to which perceptual organization can take place.

In Blakemore's experiment, however, perceptual organization was not a subject of empirical investigation; rather the organization of a spatial framework made up a precondition for the discriminatory activity which was studied. This is no unique case. Requirements of organization are mostly unstated, yet tacitly assumed in traditional works on psychophysics.

Colour discrimination requires spatially located test-fields or surfaces. Hering (1907, 1964) pointed out that a reliable comparison of two coloured fields can only be made if the two appear side-by-side in the same superficial configuration. Localization in three-dimensional space, he said, belongs to the secondary circumstances which influence colour judgements. Thus he added that:

> . . . a completely reliable comparison of two colours is possible in case these secondary circumstances, even if they are not excluded, are at least the same for both colours. Therefore both colours, except for their being side-by-side, should appear localized in precisely the same way and each of the two colours should be so completely homogenous that they show no internal variation and are seen not at all as belonging to a specific external object but only as independently existing plane or space-filling qualities.   (1964, p.12)

This mode of appearance of coloured fields is another example of a perceptual organization that serves as a basis for psychophysical judgement. If this organization of the visual scene could not be ascertained, Hering showed no confidence in comparative colour judgements. Therefore he made thorough descriptions of the way stimulus situations could be set up to ascertain a superficial configuration in which colours are seen as "space-filling qualities". Yet this organization could not itself be made the subject of experimental investigation, rather it was introduced as a prerequisite for psychophysical studies in the area.

In earlier works on binocular vision Hering (1861, 1879) seemed to think that psychophysical judgements required proper organization in the visual field. The distances or directions to be compared should not appear for the observing subject as independently existing objects in space, rather they should appear as parts or features of an integrated structure such as a plane, a sphere or a line.

Our point is that any study in psychophysics rests on the assumption that the visual or auditory environment of the subject is organized in a particular manner. This organization cannot itself be studied psychophysically, and it restricts the type of problems that can be investigated with a psychophysical procedure.

At the same time it should be emphasized that a description of a certain perceptual organization does not include all that we ordinarily refer to in the experiment as "observing conditions". "A superficial organization" in a psychophysical study of colour discrimination may also be said to constitute a condition for observation. As a rule, however, we specify the observing conditions in physicalistic terms. A "superficial organization" in this case does not comprise all of what we may call the observing conditions.

Evidently Hering considered only the superficial organization, not the amount of light reflected or radiated from the surrounding areas, to be a prerequisite for reliable colour judgements. Thus variation of the background intensity did not influence the reliability of such judgements. Background intensity, or the test-field–background intensity relation, could thus be introduced as a parameter in psychophysical studies of achromatic colours. Hence the ground was also laid for studies of visual contrast effects and the lateral inhibition mechanism.

However, a controversy over the reliability and validity of the response data may be raised in the case where the two test-fields in an experiment on colour discrimination are placed in separately illuminated areas. In other words, may illumination intensity, for example, be introduced as an experimental variable or parameter in psychophysics? Psychophysicists do not seem to have taken an explicit position with regard to this question.

One might say that the introduction of an illumination gradient disrupts the perceptual unification of a scene, and hence this gradient will invalidate the comparative judgements of coloured surfaces in the scene. On the other hand, one may, by varying the intensity of illumination, provide an illumination gradient that does not necessarily interfere with the critical unification or organization of the visual scene.

This example shows that it may be difficult to distinguish aspects of the visual scene which form part of a critical organization from other aspects which may be introduced as systematic variables. In other words, it may be difficult to *limit exactly* the scope of psychophysical research.

As a rule, however, psychophysical studies seem to require the type of perceptual organization that ascertains a spatial unification of elements or parts which are present simultaneously in the situation. Also, when stimuli are presented in succession a spatial unification is needed. The specimens to be compared should be thought of as parts of an organizational whole, while at the same time they must be abstracted or differentiated from this whole. In other words, a colour specimen or a coloured test-field should not appear as an independent material object to the perceiver. Notice, in this connection, that Titchner's "stimulus error" was also called "the object error".

On this basis one may question the tenability of a psychophysical approach to the study of object perception. Eventually, it may be important to define the concept of a material object, hence this concept will be thoroughly discussed in Chapter 4. Historically, however, "object" and "organizational whole" have been used as more or less synonymous terms in psychology.

It is our contention that perceptual organizations cannot be explained by reference to psychophysical laws. Rather such organizations form part of the *a priori* preconditions of psychophysics.

When Koffka posed his well-known question of why things appear as they do, he seemed to think that psychology would eventually give the right answer. He even proposed one himself, and stressed that the world we perceive is organized into structured wholes. According to him these wholes could not be reduced to elementary sensations. We have restated this position by saying that perceptual organizations cannot be explained by reference to psychophysical laws. Yet Koffka may not have acknowledged the point made here that perceptual organizations form part of the prerequisites of psychophysical studies. Though he discarded proposed solutions to the problem of the appearance of objects he still seemed to think that this problem could be raised within the sensory/perceptual research tradition of the modern sciences.

In our opinion Koffka could not raise the problem of the appearance of things within this research tradition, and since it was not clear on what other grounds he stated the problem, he can hardly be said to have initiated a fruitful debate regarding man's interaction with the external world.

According to Helmholtz (1896, 1962 Vol. III) discriminatory activities are always based on a premise — made by the perceiver — concerning the kinds of objects and object relationships which are present in the surrounding environment. Such a premise, we may say, constitutes a type of understanding; thus so far we also agree with Helmholtz. On the other hand, however, he did not treat the observer's premises as parts of the preconditions for psychophysical studies. Such premises were said to depend on mental activity that could be inferred by the researcher, given the proper sensory data and a knowledge of the observer's previous experiences. Thus he said that "such objects are always imagined as being present in the field of vision as would have to be there in order to produce the same impression on the nervous mechanism, the eyes being used under ordinary normal conditions" (1962, p.2). Evidently, Helmholtz took for granted that a researcher can understand "the impression on the nervous mechanism" independently of an assumption regarding the perceiver's understanding. In this way the sensation becomes the primary fact from which the researcher thinks he can reason about the perception of the external world.

Moreover, Helmholtz maintained that an observer can only assess his sensations after considerable training and assistance. Ordinarily sensations pass unnoticed, yet they are unconsciously used as signs or cues about external objects. Thus unconscious activity could be likened to the inductive inferences in logic, particularly the inferences which take the form of syllogisms. According to Helmholtz, the perceiver seems to build his judgement regarding a certain attribute or event in the external world on two premises. The first was said to constitute an assumption regarding an object or a constellation of objects, while the second was said to be a sensation of, say, a retinal image or some other stimulus configuration.

The notion of an unconscious inference in perception has had a tremendous impact on psychology. For example, the transactionalists will say that perceptual judgements generally give rise to actions that transform the perceiver's assumptions regarding the external objects. These transformed assumptions form the basis of new inferences, and so on.

The position taken by Helmholtz and the transactionalists has been criticized for its empirical emphasis and for its postulation of unconscious sensations. We shall not be concerned with this criticism, which we consider relatively uninteresting. The point is that perceptual organization has been given an ontological status and treated as a subject of empirical investigations when in fact it has served as a methodological prerequisite of psychophysics. Within the sensory research tradition of the modern sciences, the organization of the surrounding environment into coherent objects and continuous surfaces is tacitly taken for granted and cannot, within the same research "paradigm", be made the subject of systematic investigations.

Any statement of a sensory capacity implies an assumption of a perceptual organization. Thus if we make a conceptual distinction between sensation and perception, we run the risk of introducing an entity which is unrelated to methodology, and which is therefore devoid of empirical meaning.

2.4   The sensory threshold considered as a point of least change of interaction within the modality

We have so far been concerned with the concept of a modality and the basic prerequisites of psychophysical research. In general, psychophysics is said to be concerned with measurements and evaluations of sensory capacities. We shall now deal with certain terms which are used to describe such capacities. First of all we shall call attention to the concept of a sensory threshold.

Quite frequently, the threshold has been described as a point on a physical continuum which separates an energy range with some specified effect from an energy range with no effect on the sensory apparatus. In our opinion such a description is an inadequate one since it does not show that sensory discrimination also involves an active choice on behalf of the organism.

Moreover, a distinction is generally made between the absolute and the differential threshold. It will be shown that this distinction is not a meaningful one. Rather, all thresholds will be considered as incremental or differential ones. We shall ask: differential with respect to what?

Now to consider the notion of a threshold as a point separating two ranges of a stimulus continuum. This notion has been criticized by the advocates of signal detectability theory (Swets, 1964). In general they have maintained that such a point does not exist: the sensory effect of a stimulus is continuous or incremental, while the organism selects a response criterion according to which it decides whether the effect is merely noise or noise plus a specified signal transmitted by the sensory pathways. The advocates of a signal detectability theory have thus made clear that sensory discrimination involves an active choice on behalf of the perceiver.

In our opinion, however, the choice should be related to the subject's use of language. That is to say the subject chooses between two categories or aspects which can be labelled one way or the other. These aspects belong to the same modality, and thus the threshold can also be looked upon as a resolution power of intra-modal aspects. It can be said that the subject chooses between two response alternatives such as "darkness with a light spot/darkness with no light spot" or "in front/behind".

A choice between signal and noise is not related to the subject's use of language in the way that the alternatives can be clearly labelled and communicated about. To call something noise means to say that the something is not subject to communication. Moreover, noise is unspecific with respect to the modality. Signal detectability theory does not distinguish noise in the visual system from noise in the auditory system.

Psychophysics, however, is concerned with the modalities, whereas the signal detectability theory's emphasis on the noise–signal relationship makes its relevance to problems of psychophysics an unclear one.

Nevertheless, the term noise has been used extensively in the research literature. Also the research workers who do not make use of a signal detectability design for their experiments have apparently found this term a useful one. But "noise" is generally translated into a modality specific term, when the study is concerned with the characterization of a particular sensory mechanism.

To illustrate our point let us call attention to an experiment by Barlow and Sparrock on the role of after-images in dark adaptation (1964). They took into consideration the fact that regeneration of rhodopsin does not sufficiently account for the drop of threshold during dark adaptation in vision. The suggestion was made that the increase of sensitivity might be explained by reference to changes in the noise level.

In signal detectability theory, however, signal and noise are not defined with reference to independent and different sets of experimental variations. Signal sensitivity and noise level are both determined in relation to the same "decision axis". Thus it may be difficult to evaluate sensitivity as a function of noise level in a particular sensory system. It is important, therefore, that noise level is considered as an intra-modal aspect and defined with reference to certain conditions of stimulation.

Noise level in vision can be specified as an intra-modal aspect. Hering spoke about *intrinsic grey* and Barlow and Sparrock introduced the term *dark light*. The latter writers suggested that this dark light rises by the bleaching of pigment in the receptors, whereupon it subsides to its final value during regeneration of the pigment. Moreover, the rise of this dark light is noticed by the organism merely as a dim, evanescent positive after-image, and the fading of the after-image secures an automatic brightness control and hence prevents the perceiver from being dazzled by intrinsic light.

The two researchers made use of a technique whereby the brightness of a positive after-image could be matched by a stabilized image in an adjacent retinal area. The threshold of light superimposed on the after-image was shown to be the same as the threshold of light added to the stabilized retinal image of equivalent brightness. Barlow and Sparrock pointed out, therefore, that "the threshold during dark adaptation is the increment threshold against the background of the positive afterimage" (p.1964, p.1314). Noise was thus specified as dark light or brightness of a positive after-image. Without this specification the two researchers could hardly have inquired into mechanisms underlying dark adaptation.

The work has also shown that there is no reason for maintaining a clear distinction between the absolute and the differential threshold, for there is always some background reference against which a stimulus or signal is registered. At the same time the background as well as the signal should be considered as intra-modal events: light is distinguished from darkness, sound from silence, etc. The organism, in a discrimination task, is engaged in a choice between entities, aspects or events which are both subsumed under the same modality. In other words there is always a pair of aspects involved in sensory discrimination, and the threshold defines the acuity with which these aspects are separated. The fact that they belong to a modality also shows that they are interactional aspects. That is to say that sensory stimulation can only be studied by way of a change in the interaction with the environment.

Evidently noise has not been considered as a form of interaction with the environment. Rather the signal detectability theorists seem to have considered noise to be the lack of an interactive relationship with the environment. That is to say that those theorists have placed themselves in a difficult position with regard to the study of sensory mechanisms and functions.

By way of conclusion we would like to say that the concept of a sensory threshold is still a useful one granted that it is used with reference to a least change of interaction with the environment. Moreover all thresholds are by necessity differential ones.

2.5   Can cognitive factors contaminate psychophysical data?

The advocates of signal detectability theory have also criticized traditional psychophysics on the ground that its methods do not prevent a contamination of sensory data with cognitive factors. In particular it has been argued that data of sensory threshold measurements tend to be contaminated by the attitudes and expectations of the subject.

Under the general term cognition, we should like to include attitudes and expectations. Assumptions regarding these factors we consider to be preconditions for the study of a sensory capacity. From this position, therefore, the expression stating that cognitive factors tend to contaminate psychophysical data becomes a meaningless one.

In general we acknowledge the possibility that a set of factors A may be contaminated by another set of factors B, as long as the two are, in principle at least, separable and substantially different events. The advocates of signal detectability theory seem to consider cognition and sensory discrimination to be substantially different events, whereas the separation of their effects on the response data in sensory experiments is a question of methodological and statistical improvement. This position is first of all an ontological one which forms the main premise for a criticism of traditional procedures for the measurement of sensory thresholds.

In stating that assumptions regarding cognitive factors form part of the basic preconditions of psychophysics, however, we have taken a substantially methodological position. Therefore, we cannot reject the criticism of traditional psychophysics as a false one, but we can show that it is not an adequate one: in the "paradigm" of psychophysics there are a number of explicit and implicit rules that state the conditions under which sensory discriminations are valid — and thus the conditions under which sensory capacities can be studied.

Consider, for example, a test of visual acuity in which the subject is told to discriminate the gap of a black C printed on a white background. Explicit rules concerning the administration of such a test require that the subject is properly informed about the task. Furthermore, the examiner presupposes the subject's willingness to co-operate, etc. Without such a presupposition the subject's reports cannot be used to evaluate visual acuity. Or if, for some reason, the subject thinks he is being fooled all the time, his discriminitatory responses cannot be considered as valid ones. Thus cognition will *always* be part of the conditions which validates or invalidates sensory discrimination, it cannot be considered as an extraneous element that sometimes interferes with this discrimination.

A variation in the response data can be attributed to a variation in the subject's self-instruction. The problem is on what ground the experimenter can ascertain a change in the subject's self-instruction. In signal detectability theory such an instruction is tantamount to a response criterion which is used to detect a signal on a background of noise. Traditional psychophysics requires this criterion to remain constant, whereas signal detectability theory stresses its variability. From the position of the latter theory this criterion constitutes, for all practical purposes, the only source of variability in the response data. This way of thinking rests on the supposition that the sensory reception of the signal does not vary noticeably during some specified test session.

The sensory mechanism, it is said, is constantly sensitive for the type of signal studied. Moreover, the sensory effects of noise and noise plus signal are assumed to be of the same kind and thus liable to an ordering along one so-called "decision axis".

In a way, therefore, signal detectability theory reverses the position taken in classical psychophysics: rather than making assumptions about the constancy of cognition, it makes assumptions about the constancy of the sensory apparatus. Sensory properties are to a great extent introduced axiomatically, and great demands are thus made on existent knowledge of the sensory system. This is why signal detectability approaches have been mostly applied in engineering contexts, while in basic research on the senses and in clinical examinations the traditional procedures, or adaptations of such procedures, may still be the most admissible ones.

Our question as to whether cognitive factors can be said to contaminate psychophysical data is answered in the negative. Rather than contaminating discriminatory response data, cognitive factors can only validate or invalidate such data.

2.6 Limits of psychophysics

As pointed out in the first section of this chapter definitions of the modalities in physics have served to delimit the scope of psychophysical research. Thus early physics provided a kind of research "paradigm" for psychophysics. In effect, therefore, this branch of science is clearly limited with respect to the type of problem which can be investigated. In general the research problems which can fruitfully be studied within a certain area depends on the goals and objectives of its respective science.

Psychophysics, in dealing with forms of interaction with the environment, is generally expected to cast light on problems of perception. Certainly this branch of science has also made great contributions towards an understanding of perceptual problems. Yet there exist certain limits with respect to the types of perceptual problem which are eligible for psychophysical investigations. In the remaining part of this chapter we shall be concerned with the main factors which delimit the prospects of psychophysics as a "perceptual" science. As already pointed out, the *a priori* requirement of perceptual organization restricts the type of problems that can be studied by way of psychophysical procedures. Moreover, factors which limit the prospects of this science have to do with (1) the treatment of the "equal" response category, and (2) the forms of behaviour that reveal discriminatory capacities in psychophysical studies.

2.6.1 Treatment of the "equal" response category

Miller (1969) said that failure of discrimination has been made a measure of similarity or subjective equality in psychophysics. The equation between confusion and similarity, he maintained, was introduced by way of definition. It was not a discovery. Also the definition of subjective equality as failure to discriminate was implicit in Fechner's attempt to measure similarity, i.e. the smaller number of just noticeable differences there are between, say two shades of a colour, the closer the shades are to each other.

Now to return for a moment to Blakemore's experiment on the horopter. We mentioned that the position which was judged 50% of the times "to the right" was taken as the position whereby the two targets appeared to lie in the same visual direction. This means that equality of visual direction was defined as a maximum of uncertainty, since in this position the judgement "to the right" was given as frequently as the judgement "to the left". We can also say that equality of visual direction was specified as a maximum of confusion between a left and a right position in relation to the upper target. Thus apparently equality, uncertainty and confusion have been treated as one and the same event.

Sensory discrimination, we have said, involve a choice between two categories or aspects of a modality. Therefore, a forced choice between two response alternatives is commonly used in psychophysical studies of the type we have mentioned here. One may ask, however, whether it will be possible to communicate in greater depth about the environment if more response alternatives are specified in the instruction. In Blakemore's experiment for example, an "equal" category may have been added. This might represent a particular event or characteristic which can be communicated about. More precisely we can say that an "equal" report in this case is applicable with reference to the characteristic of being *in alignment with* the upper target (a vernier alignment), and this characteristic represents an understanding of the stimulus display which clearly differs from each of the other alternatives. Yet the researchers, in experiments of this kind, tend to omit the "equal" category.

In various experiments on sensory discrimination, subjects have insisted on being allowed to say "equal" or to make some equivalent comment. Fechner made use of an "equal" category in addition to a plus and minus category. Examples of the latter were heavier/lighter or left/right. Fechner, however, presumed that "equal" was only used by the subject when doubtful. Therefore, he suggested that the "equals" should be equally divided between plus and minus. The use of a third category was apparently considered to be an awkward procedure that merely served to meet the subject's request.

If the "equals" are not divided between plus and minus, the data can still be used to calculate sensory thresholds. Woodworth and Schlosberg (1965) suggested that a mean point of transition between plus and not-plus (T +) and a mean point of transition between minus and not-minus (T-) should be calculated. The interval between T + and T- is the interval in which neither plus nor minus judgements have a clear majority, and it is therefore called the "interval of uncertainty". The midpoint of this interval is generally defined as the point of subjective equality, and one half of this interval is defined as the differential threshold.

This procedure for the calculation of thresholds shows that "equal" judgements have been considered as expressions of uncertainty. The instability of the T + - T- interval is generally taken to support such a view. Thus it has been shown that subjects who are instructed to give "conservative" plus and minus estimates maximize the number of "equal" judgements, but subjects who are instructed to give "liberal" plus and minus estimates minimize the number of "equal" judgements (Fernberger, 1931). In short, the uncertainty interval is said to be influenced by the attitude of the subject.

Now let us consider an experiment with the Howard–Dolman apparatus. It consists of two vertical black rods which are mounted on blocks and parallel tracks so that each rod can be moved toward or away from the subject. Both rods are seen against a bright and uniform background. One rod is fixed in a position 3 m from the subject, while the other is randomly placed at different distances relative to the fixed rod. By way of instruction the subject is told to judge whether the variable rod appears in front of (-), behind (+), or at the same distance as the standard rod (=). Relative frequencies of each of the three response categories are shown in Fig. 3.

The inset of Fig. 3 shows an alternative way of representing the response distributions. Note that the three categories are not sharply separated along the stimulus continuum.

As long as the "equal" responses are considered to be expressions of uncertainty the = area of Fig. 3 does not represent a *category of judgement* in the same sense as the + and - areas do. The great overlap between the plus and minus judgements might be taken in support of such a view.

By varying the instruction and the spatial framework, however, it may be possible to arrive at a number of other relative response distributions. A few examples of possible s–p plots are shown in Fig. 4.

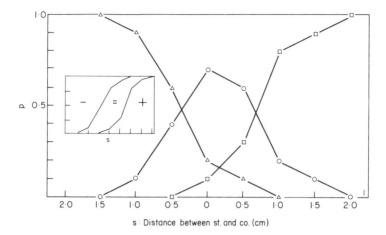

Figure 3 Relative distributions of three response categories in an experiment with the
Howard-Dolman apparatus. ——△——: in front, ——○——: equal distance,
——□—— : behind.

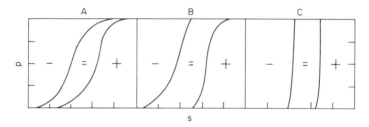

Figure 4 Possible types of distributions of three response categories in a psychophysical
experiment on relative distance estimations.

In Fig. 4c the areas are separated by steeper lines and there is no
overlap between the + and – judgements. Therefore, in this case one
may be tempted to say that the = area depends on the use of a
judgement category. It cannot merely be the result of doubtfulness
with respect to the plus and minus alternatives. Yet it is possible to
think of a conservative attitude of the subject which will bring about
such response distributions regardless of whether the "equal" reports
have a specific environmental referent. Therefore, one cannot decide
afterwards what types of judgement have been made, and thus what
types of interaction were involved in the experiment.

The equation between equality or similarity on the one hand and
confusion or failure to discriminate on the other has been introduced

by way of definition, and there is no way of showing empirically that this definition is a wrong one. This definition also rests on an assumption that certain categories are used by the subject. Uncertainty, and thus failure to discriminate, is always specified in relation to judgemental categories.

One may say that the psychophysicist should be free to make other assumptions with regard to the judgemental categories used by the subject. For example in the Howard–Dolman situation, "same distance" might be said to constitute a judgemental category or an event which is communicated by way of an "equal" response. On this assumption the = area cannot be treated as an area of uncertainty. Therefore a different procedure for the calculation of a threshold must be adopted: there are now two intervals of uncertainty, one between – and = one between = and + . One half of each of these intervals can be taken as a measure of the threshold. Consequently, the measure of sensory acuity depends on assumptions which are made concerning the judgemental categories.

However, since subjective equality is defined as failure to discriminate, it follows that equal responses must be considered as expressions of uncertainty. All the judgemental categories are related ones such as "left/right", etc. There is no way of introducing concrete response categories, i.e. specifiable objects. Although the subject may be permitted to state, as one of his response alternatives, that two points or colours belong to the same physical surface, this response will still have to be treated by the experimenter as an expression of uncertainty. Psychophysical procedures, in a sense, rest on assumptions of object idenficiation, and as a precondition to the procedures such identification cannot be studied psychophysically. One cannot easily overcome this restriction merely by redefining terms such as equality, similarity and identity (cf. our discussion of perceptual identity in the next chapter).

Nevertheless, the psychophysicists themselves have generally presumed that their work will eventually shed some light on the perception of objects. Pioneering researchers such as Helmholtz and Hering have already stressed that the main function of the eye is the perception of objects in space. But they had difficulty trying to show how the visual apparatus mediates the perception of material objects. In their attempts to extend theories of vision to include the organism's interaction with external objects, they tended to introduce unwarranted assumptions. We shall mention one example, namely Hering's treatment of the total horopter:

As pointed out, the concept of the horopter is related to the concept of retinal correspondence (see the "Vieth–Müller circle", p.17). The total horopter constitutes, for a certain position of "the double eye", the locus of all points which are imaged on corresponding points in the two retinas. Hering defined retinal correspondence by way of the *substitution method*, thus if two uniocular images could be substituted for each other without change of apparent direction, these images were said to be "corresponding". In this way, he maintained, identity of visual direction served as a criterion of retinal correspondence. We would like to add at this point, however, that the substitution method involved nothing more than a failure of discrimination.

On the assumption of a certain distribution of directionally sensitive elements along retinal meridians and certain dioptrical characteristics of the eyes, the total horopter could be geometrically defined. The empirical horopter, as defined by the substitution method, deviated from the theoretical horopter. This deviation thus called for a certain correction of the assumed distribution of direction sensitive elements of the retinas.

Neither the theoretical nor the empirical horopter turned out to be a plane containing the point of fixation as suggested originally by Aquilonius (see Boring, 1942). Yet the horopter would, according to Hering, appear for the observer as a fronto-parallel plane (the horopter as "Sehding"). The substitution method, however, was said to rest on the criterion of identity of direction. Nevertheless Hering maintained that object points which are seen in the same visual direction, must also be seen at the same distance to appear *single* in the strictest sense of the word. (Several examples are mentioned in the classical literature which apparently contradicted this rule, but Hering stressed that only objects differing in form and size could be seen at different distances in the "same" visual direction.)

If the substitution method could be said to require the comprehension of a particular distance, this method might also be said to define an object, and furthermore this object would appear to lie in the fronto-parallel plane which contained the point of fixation and which divided the visual space between something in front and something behind. On this basis Hering unwarrantedly introduced an additional characteristic to the total horopter, and to stress that the horopter, with the additional characteristic of distance, was a plane separating objects behind the fixation distance from objects in front of this distance, he frequently made use of the term *Kernfläche*.

The essential point in Hering's theory of retinal correspondence and the horopter is, therefore, his conception of the linkage between binocular direction and distance: when uniocular images are shown, by substitution, to give rise to identical visual directions, these images when fused must also give rise to *one* impression of distance. This assumption also underlies his dictum of the unity of colour and visual direction (see particularly his discussion of binocular colour mixtures in *Lichtsinn*, 1907).

Hering postulated three local signs for every retinal point — one for depth in addition to those for the vertical and horizontal dimensions. That is to say that a certain depth and direction values were attributed to each point. Moreover, the distribution of depth values was systematically related to the distribution of values for the vertical and horizontal dimensions. Corresponding points with respect to visual direction were disparate with respect to depth. Yet such points were always said to have equal depth values, one point, however, negative and the other positive. The fusion of uniocular images located at corresponding points with respect to direction, therefore, gave rise to zero depth value which was always the depth value attributed to the foveas or the fixation point images.

In this way the concept of a *Kernfläche* was well integrated in his theory of binocular vision. The construction of this theory, however, rested on the postulate that singleness of vision implied a particular distance and hence the perception of an object in space. Such a postulate did not necessarily form part of the preconditions underlying the substitution of uniocular images. The observer was assumed to be capable of disregarding distance, rather than apprehending a particular distance, when substituting one image for another. But although the subject in such studies may assume identical distances, he does not have to concentrate on a particular locus in space. Hence the material object was not necessarily a part of the mutual understanding presupposed by the use of the substitution method. Hering's postulate was unrelated to this method.

We may now return to the general definition of subjective equality in psychophysics. As already mentioned the point of subjective equality has usually been defined as the point of maximum uncertainty. It is important to remember, however, that this procedure implies two relational categories, + and − . Therefore, some dispersion measure of the equal responses can be taken as a measure of the threshold.

On these grounds the procedure for measuring sensory thresholds has been simplified by giving the subject only one response alternative, namely the adjustment of a colour, a half-image, or a sound until it appears indistinguishable with — or equal to — a certain standard. Distribution of the subjective settings is taken as an expression of the degree of the subject's uncertainty, and therefore, a measure of its dispersion, for example the s.d. (standard deviation) is frequently used as a measure of the threshold.

If the standard and the comparison cannot be made indistinguishable in all respects, it becomes necessary to explain thoroughly the meaning of the matching task. This can hardly be done without the experimenter referring to a pair of relational categories. When not mentioned in the instructions a pair of such categories will implicitly be assumed by the subject, and these categories need not be the categories presupposed by the experimenter.

A "match" criterion can be said to involve a pair of relational categories and thus a certain form of interaction with the environment. When the subject is told to choose one criterion and to overlook another, the assumption is thereby made that the subject is making a real choice between two forms of interactions in the situation. This raises the question of which events can be controlled independently of each other.

The problem is exemplified by a study which was done by Krekling (1975). In depth-matching with visible diplopic images at different degrees of eccentricity, the subject may either do a vernier alignment or a depth adjustment. A vernier alignment refers to the type of match which can easily be done in Blakemore's experimental situation (see p.18). It involves the relational categories "left/right", while a depth-match involves the categories "in front" and "behind".

Krekling did two experiments. In the first a mirror (50:50 trans-mission) haploscope was used to make double images of test lines R and Co appear in stereoscopic depth (see Fig. 5). The half-images directly above and below the fixation point were fixed in the position shown, while the half-images to the right in the figure could be moved into different positions independently of each other. The disparity of the reference line R, and hence the position of the upper right half-image in the figure, was preset by the experimenter. Applying a method of adjustment the subject set the disparity of the comparison by operating a device carrying one of Co's half-images. His task was to adjust the double images of the comparison and reference line so that they would appear to lie at the same stereoscopic depth for a series of disparity settings of R″ (see legend to Fig. 5).

The situation made possible a stereoscopic depth-match as well as a vernier alignment. The problem is in what sense these matches might be said to differ. They imply different pairs of relational categories, but both types of matches require that the subject adjusts the lateral angle of the adjustable half-image of Co. This raises the question whether a perfect depth-match would also be a perfect vernier alignment. The disparity setting will not reflect the pair of relational categories used by the subject, and hence the two matches cannot be defined by different operational procedures.

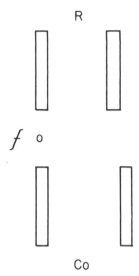

Figure 5   Binocular view of reference (R) and comparison (Co) lines in experiment with visible diplopic images. The lines directly above and below the fixation point (f) were projected to the left eye and fixed in the position shown. The right line of R which could be presented to the right or left of fixation point f to introduce divergent or convergent disparity, was produced by the fusion of two half-images. The right line of Co was likewise produced by the fusion of two half-images. This fusion took place when the disparity of the half-images was increased above a certain limit. The half-images were produced by etching opaque lines on glass plates, which were inserted into the arms of an haploscope. The task of the subject was to adjust the position of the half-image of Co presented to the right eye until the R and Co lines appeared equal in depth (from Krekling, 1975).

To prevent the subject from performing a vernier alignment the subject was trained in the observation of double images and he was given "explicit instructions about the relevant criterion as well as the subjective attribute in question". Apparently, the training procedure was performed to make the subject capable of disregarding an alignment in the lateral direction while emphasis was being laid on an adjustment of the half-images in depth. In other words the visible half-images were supposed to be matched with respect to one attribute while differing with respect to another. One may liken the assumed match with the so-called "heterochromatic matches" in colorimetry where the brightness of colour samples differing in hue are equated by an observer. In colorimetry, however, it has been possible to define the two attributes with reference to different operational procedures, i.e. brightness and hue can to some extent be varied independently of each other, while in the present experiment depth and lateral position could not be varied independently of each other. Therefore, the subject may not have been able to use the pair of relational categories implied by depth (the relevant criterion) while disregarding other relational categories implied by lateral position (the irrelevant criterion). When the subject is trained to overlook lateral position, he may also be less capable of making an accurate depth-match. This is because, we think, lateral position is the main factor which determines the accuracy of a judgement of depth. Therefore, the training procedure will generally mean that depth thresholds are raised, and that depth-matches will be particularly difficult to make for more eccentric positions of the half-images.

Krekling performed a second experiment in which one half-image of both R and Co was occluded. Therefore, the test lines did not appear

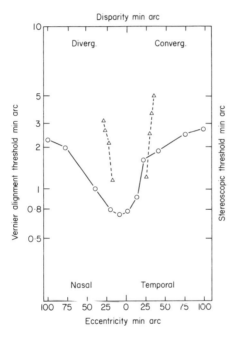

Figure 6 Vernier alignment and stereoscopic thresholds as functions of eccentricity of target and divergent and convergent disparity. Circles represent data for vernier alignments, and triangles represent data for depth adjustments (from Krekling, 1975).

stereoscopically for the observer, and thus only a vernier alignment was possible. Krekling's data are shown in Fig. 6, where vernier alignment thresholds (Experiment 2) and stereoscopic thresholds (Experiment 1) are plotted for different min arc eccentricity/disparity. The scales of the left and right ordinates are identical and the scales of the upper and lower abscissas are identical. Clearly the stereoscopic thresholds are higher than the vernier alignment thresholds. Furthermore, depth-matches could not be done for settings of R above 40 minutes of arc divergent disparity and 35 minutes of arc convergent disparity.

If sameness of distance forms a prerequisite for an accurate vernier alignment, then vernier alignment may also form the most favourable condition for an adjustment of the half-images in depth. The two criteria may have been concatenated in the situation. To call attention to them did not mean that the subject was given a choice between different interactions. In the first experiment the thresholds may thus have been determined for a set of less favourable conditions than in the second experiment, while it is impossible to say whether different sensory functions were involved. The former instruction may have invalidated the response data and hence made the experiment an inconclusive one.

In other cases the subject may have several criteria at his disposal, some of which are unknown to the experimenter. Therefore, a match which is specified by one set of operational procedures, does not necessarily show the perceptual or judgemental activities guiding the responses of the subject.

We intend to return to more specific problems concerning the use of match data. For the present we shall consider the other main factor which limits the scope of psychophysics.

2.6.2 Forms of behaviour involved in studies of sensory capacities

In most studies of sensory capacities the researchers make use of behaviour learned by an organism. As a rule such behaviour also includes the use of language.

The reasons for the use of learned behaviour can be understood in view of the definitions of the modalities in physics and the general cultural knowledge of light, colour and sound. Notions of light and colour certainly depend on abstractions. Therefore, communication about aspects of light, which is an essential part of psychophysical studies of light and colour, require a certain conceptual development and also to some extent verbal skills by the subject. Consider, for example, the skills needed to make a vernier alignment in Krekling's experiment or a comparative judgement of brightness in a visual contrast experiment. We have tried to emphasize, at several points in this chapter, that studies of sensory capacities require that the subject is capable of understanding the environment in certain ways.

On this basis, adult, mature, and linguistically competent persons have generally been used as subjects in psychophysical studies. In the classical era studies were frequently done with a few intelligently sophisticated persons who were, in some way or another, connected with the leading laboratories and institutes of Europe.

This is not to say that psychophysical studies cannot be done with infants or animals. Knowledge of discriminatory behaviour by adults may lead to certain conclusions concerning which activities or interactions may take place in an infant. In other words, psychophysical knowledge which is acquired by the studies of adults can be applied in studies of infants. Thus knowledge of the psychophysics of colour — in particular knowledge of the hue-wavelength relationship — has provided a basis for studies of infants in which optikinetic nystagmus has been used to show that children, a few days old, can discriminate between hues (see Munn, 1965).

We can demonstrate the presence of a certain sensory capacity in an infant or an animal, but we can hardly make certain that the assessment of the capacity in question has been done under the most favourable conditions for the organism. Sensory acuity may thus be underestimated. Also, in studies of adults it may be difficult to ascertain a set of optimum conditions. But due to our restricted possibilities for communication with infants we meet with particular difficulties when attempts are made to provide accurate measures of their sensory capacities.

In short we can say that the basic knowledge of psychophysics is established by studies which have involved the learned behaviour of adult human beings. However, infants as well as adults show spontaneous and unlearned forms of behaviour. They maintain several types of interactions with the environment which differ from the types of interactions presupposed by accepted definitions of the modalities. Turning of the head, smiling, sucking, grasping and crying are examples of forms of behaviour which occur spontaneously in infants or which may be elicited by particular stimuli independently of previous learning. Such forms of behaviour probably also involve orientations or attitudes of great survival value.

Psychophysics, however, hardly provides an adequate reference system for an understanding of the sensory/perceptual regulation of such behaviour. On the other hand, it is possible to conceive of unlearned behavioural interactions with the environment as alternative bases for a classification of the senses into modalities. In this way we might provide a point of departure for the study of the senses which pertains to biology rather than physics.

Psychophysical data are valid only in relation to particular forms of interaction with the environment. Hence we can hardly speak of an absolute resolution power — either spatial or temporal — of a sense. A sensory threshold always implies a change in a form of interaction. Reasoning from other forms of interactions, we may ask if physical events which are ordinarily considered as sub-threshold events for a particular sense, may still be discriminated by an organism. But in such a case, however, we cannot speak of a sensory capacity with reference to the conceptual framework of psychophysics. "Sensory capacity" will then have to be defined in terms of other forms of interaction with the environment.

Since other forms of interaction have not been introduced as systems of references for the senses, our knowledge of sensory functions must still be considered as specific and limited. We may also say that psychophysics has made possible an effective communication about certain forms of interaction with the environment, while other forms of interaction are, for the present, not subject to an equally effective communication.

3

Perceptual identity

The tasks performed by subjects in psychophysical experiments on perception can be described as comparative judgements of environmental events or characteristics. Many of these judgements are judgements about the identity of, for example, the colour of two spots or the relative direction of two line segments in the field of vision, the loudness of two sounds, or the taste quality of two liquids. The experimenter or the subject adjusts a comparison object until it appears the same as a standard or reference object. The adjusted value of the comparison is generally referred to as a "subjective setting" or "match".

In this chapter we shall discuss the concept of perceptual identity and the question of whether we ought to distinguish between different types of identities. There are also a number of subordinate questions that may be dealt with in this connection, and particularly we shall treat with some reservation statements of psychophysical correspondences based on subjective matches rather than judgements of differences. However, these questions will be discussed in Chapter 6.

The meaning of identity has been vigorously discussed throughout the history of philosophy, but since our main interest lies in the analysis of empirical studies of perception, it will not be necessary to raise the whole complex of philosophical problems of identity. The part of this complex that bears upon the way identity judgements can be performed in experimental situations will, of course, be discussed. No distinction will be made between identity and equality, therefore, the terms identical and equal will be used interchangeably in this book.

In the chapter on psychophysics we have already mentioned a few examples of identity judgements in perception. We have particularly called attention to the judgement of a vernier alignment in studies of stereo-acuity: the subject makes a certain response when two bars in the plane visual field appear to be aligned along the same visual direction. A second example is one in which the subject is told to compare the hues of two spots which differ in brightness. He may, for instance, be told to say whether the comparison spot is more green or more blue than the reference spot or whether both have the same blue-green colour. In the latter case the identity judgement includes at least a reference to a certain hue quality, namely the quality of blue-green.

In each of the examples mentioned the statement of identity included a reference to a certain quality or category of the external world. We suppose that this quality forms the subject matter of communication between observer and experimenter. However, we have not yet shown how it is possible for the subject to make such a statement. To show this, it may be instructive, at first, to examine an experimental situation in which an identity statement can be looked upon as a statement of something that cannot be discerned.

As indicated in the preceding chapter "subjective equality" has been defined as lack of discrimination. Thus it has been presupposed in psychophysics that equal reports can only serve to express doubtfulness or an inability to decide between opposed categories of judgement. As an example, consider a subject comparing the colours of two semi-circular fields in a colorimeter. The two fields may be given exactly the same luminance and chromaticity while the wavelength of the right semi-circular field can be made to vary in very small steps. The left semi-circular field is given a constant wavelength and serves as the bearer of the reference colour. In this case the two semi-circular fields may be made indistinguishable in all respects for the subject, i.e. the two fields may disappear and become one homogeneous circular field, having one hue, brightness and saturation.

According to Brindley (1960), this match constitutes a type "A" observation in psychophysics. Observations of this type are made whenever two events or objects are said to be indistinguishable in all respects or just distinguishable in some respect. Observations of type "B" constitute the kind of matches we have already described, and which follow when the subjects abstract from two parts or events a certain quality which they have in common.

To test a physiological hypothesis that is also expressed in psychological terms, i.e. an hypothesis which says something about a mechanism and its sensory function, observations of type A are the most adequate ones according to Brindley. Conservative opinion will hold that this type of observation is the only one which can be legitimately used to shed light on functions of the visual system, whereas the liberal view permits any observations that can be made with a certain degree of consistency and upon which different subjects may agree. According to the liberal view, therefore, observations of types A and B are equally admissible as means of analysing functions of a sensory system.

The reader may ask whether this distinction implies more than one type of identity judgement in experiments on perception. Perhaps we should speak of one type of identity which corresponds to type A observations and one type of identity which corresponds to type B observations.

The point is, however, that a consistent use of "identity" implies at least some reference to a category or quality that can be the subject of communication between the observer and the experimenter, i.e. a criterion of identity. Hence we should take the person using the identity term as our point of departure. In the case of a hue match between semi-fields of equal brightness and saturation, the subject may be told to use the "equal" term when the two fields can no longer be separated. However he cannot necessarily be expected to refer to a perceptual category since such a category must be opposed to a difference between the parts matched.

To make an identity judgement, the subject must give reference to a change or diversity in the situation. Moreover it is supposed that he will be able to make such a reference. The point is that an identity judgement presupposes that the subject making the judgement knows in which way(s) the two referents differ. Once the referents become indiscernible, there is no way of referring to a difference between them unless the identity statement is considered as part of an extended activity in relation to a continuous change in the comparison field.

We have so far analysed the situation from the perspective of the subject. Consider for a moment the same situation from the perspective of the experimenter. He has information about the semi-circular fields which is of theoretical importance, but which is of no relevance to the task to be performed by the subject. The experimenter knows, for example, the wavelength, the luminance and the chromaticity of the reference field, and he knows that the comparison field is composed of three primaries, λ_a, λ_b, and λ_c, the proportions of which can be systematically varied. The subject's statement that the two fields are inseparable now determines a *metameric match*, i.e. the category which includes, by way of definition, a difference of spectral composition between the two semi-fields. However, this category cannot be communicated between the subject and the experimenter, unless the subject can also take the perspective of the experimenter. In this case, therefore, a metameric match cannot serve as a reference category of perceptual identity. Such identity should always be defined from the perspective of the subject.

The requirement that an observer will have to refer to a change or diversity in order to judge two entities as equal, can hardly be reconciled with an analysis that claims that phrases of the form

$$x \; = \; y \tag{1}$$

are intrinsically complete. According to such analysis (1) is complete and unambiguous since its referents are indiscernable. In our scheme the referents will have to be discernible in some respect, otherwise it will not be possible to refer to a change or diversity in the situation. If they are totally indiscernible, like the semi-fields in the colorimeter situation, they can no longer serve as separate referents.

If (1) is to represent the identity judgement made in any of the three situations described earlier in this chapter, allowance should be made of its incompleteness, since, in our opinion, the phrase will only make sense when interpreted according to a pluralistic position (Geach, 1962; Gabbay and Moravcsik, 1973). Ordinarily "equals" is the English word connecting the two entities, and when introduced in (1), the whole phrase when completed should read:

$$x \text{ equals } y \text{ with respect to } Q \tag{2}$$

where Q is the symbol for some quality or category that serves as a criterion of identity. The recognition of this quality, however, requires a certain change. Hence an identity statement cannot be understood without the assumption of a temporal perspective.

A match of semi-circular fields in a colorimeter can be said to satisfy the definition of identity in psychophysics and hence submit to an analysis that claims that phrases of the form (1) are intrinsically complete. In other words, it may be looked upon as a statement of indiscernibility. But once it is said to be a statement of the identities of hues, this statement is also considered as part of an extended activity in time. This activity generally comprise a pair of relational response categories, for example, the categories "more blue than" and "more green than".

In general philosophers will maintain that the identity judgements described here involve only *qualitative identity*, whereas the type of identity mostly discussed in connection with (1) is *numerical identity*. The former may be said to constitute unity (amid diversity), and the latter may be said to constitute permanence (amid change) (Stroll, 1967). Granted that (1) is treated as a statement of numerical identity, "the same as" will be the expression in English which most adequately links the two entities in the phrase. When the expression is substituted for =, the whole phrase should now read

$$x \text{ is the same } C \text{ as y,} \qquad (3)$$

where C is the symbol of some category that serves as a criterion of identity. An example of a statement of numerical identity would be: "this chair is the same piece of furniture as the armchair once built by the carpenter M".

We may ask why philosophers have generally accepted statements of numerical identity as having a different status than statements of qualitative identity. Many statements of the former type (numerical identity) are accepted unquestioningly in everyday life, and so we may ask if they reflect basic knowledge of the world of physical objects which is not necessarily involved in statements of the latter type (qualitative identity). Can we speak of some basic knowledge or assumptions that also serve as the necessary conditions for initiating a discourse on the numerical identity of things which are similar in quality? To answer this problem Enç (1975) analysed an extraordinary situation in which the behaviour of objects may be said to conflict with our physical laws:

> Suppose we have a billiard table with no pockets, and two billiard balls: a white and a red. The white ball has a black dot on it. The player hits the red ball with the cue; the red ball rolls and strikes the white one. At the instant of collision we observe the red ball stationary adjacent to the white ball's original position and *two* white balls rolling away from it. Upon inspection, each of the white balls turns out to have a black dot.
>
> (p.11.)

The event may not only call for a revision of physics, but also of basic assumptions of our conceptual scheme with regard to the external world. Thus we may either have to abandon the belief in a singly connected space-time continuum, or the belief that no two objects can occupy the same place at the same time. Otherwise we shall have to abandon "the condition which all principles of conservation that take these entities into their domain must satisfy: when a is converted into b (where both a and b belong to the set of entities in question), under a conservation principle C, the ϕ which C conserves must be traceable" (Enç, 1975, p.15).

Enç showed that in the cases where one of these assumptions or beliefs were dropped "numerical identity could only be decided by considerations of qualitative similarity, and where qualitative similarity to some desired high degree did obtain, it made no sense to ask whether also numerical identity obtained" (Enç, 1975, pp.15-16). The basic assumptions of our conceptual scheme, therefore, form the necessary conditions for a discourse about the numerical identity of qualitatively similar things.

However, as is rightly pointed out by Enç, these assumptions cannot also form the criteria for deciding whether an object at t_1, which may or may not be qualitatively similar to an object at t_2 is numerically identical with the one at t_2.

In his discussion of the necessary and sufficient criteria for the numerical identity of objects, Enç ran into a number of problems of great interest in the present work. We shall, therefore, pursue for a while some of the other points he made on the issue.

With reference to Frege's classic example of the morning star and the evening star, Enç proposed that there should be a requirement of scientific laws which makes the path of the object traceable, or traceable in principle. But once the object changes, the related requirement of "traceability" of individual parts or the "traceability" of the arrangement of parts comes into consideration. If, however, the requirement is formulated in terms of the continuous "traceability" of all the parts of the entity, it becomes an unsatisfactory one since there is no way of answering the question of how "fine bits of an object count as parts of an object". Similar difficulties, Enç maintained, hold with regard to the preservation of the arrangement of the parts. If we do not require the continuous traceability of all the parts, the question arises as to which parts should be traceable or traceable in principle. This question is related to the question of tolerance against change, i.e. in which ways an object can change and still be considered numerically one and the same. We may also form the latter question as one of continued existence vs disruption or conversion into a numerically different entity.

Enç examined the possible effects of changes inflicted upon (a) a heap of 25 marbles, (b) a fashionable dress, and (c) an electric amplifier. These objects were supposed to be either (1) totally destroyed and reconstructed by qualitatively similar parts; (2) changed by the substitution of all parts except one with qualitatively similar parts; (3) changed by the substitution of one part with one of a similar kind; (4) changed by the substitution of a set of parts with a qualitatively similar set, and by way of the new set the remaining parts are reconnected to form the original pattern; or (5) changed by the complete rearrangement of all the parts.

In his discussion of the possible effects of these changes Enç made an important point: he said that tolerance against change depends on whether the object is ascribed some use, purpose or function. If the change does not interfere with the possibility of the object serving the same function after the change, the numerical identity of the object will not be affected. Yet, despite the preservation of function we may find borderline cases in which numerical identity is hesitatingly ascribed to the object. Thus when an electric amplifier has retained only its chassis, while all other parts are substituted for qualitatively similar components, it is not clear whether we are still in possession of the same amplifier.

Enç, however, warned against what he considered to be an absurd claim of numerical identity, namely that an entity which was at a certain time, while ". . . at a later time it (one and the same entity) was not, and now it (again one and the same entity) is" (1975, p.19). He, therefore, introduced a second requirement which stated that parts must be replaced gradually. This requirement, he said, is a necessary one on two counts: "first the danger of *doppelgänger*, and second, the danger that a material object during its 'life time' can pop in and out of existence several times in succession" (1975, p.22).

Yet it is not clear why the requirement was considered to be a *necessary* one, for he did not show that replacement of all the parts at the same time inevitably produced a "doppelgänger". He only spoke of a danger in this respect, and tolerance against change was also said to be influenced by our willingness to claim numerical identity. In cases of doubt as to whether the object is a "doppelgänger" or numerically the same one as the object observed a previous day, our willingness to claim identity will decide the question.

But willingness to claim identity is rarely generated independently of the functions of the object in an observer–environment interaction. For the most part, therefore, it will be the criteria of use, purpose or function that determine questions of numerical identity. But Enç had a particular reason for laying stress on the criterion of replacement of parts. He made the dubious assumption that there are objects which neither have, nor to which can be ascribed, any function whatsoever for an observer. For such objects to retain identity, they must preserve all their parts. The arrangement of parts is irrelevant since they are in fact "pseudo-objects". (A heap of marbles he considered as a "pseudo-object".) Thus questions of their identity "become parasitic on questions of identity of the parts of the pseudo-object." Preservation of parts of an object having a clear function in our daily life was said to be less important, while preservation of the arrangement of parts which is directly related to its function, will be of prime importance in making decisions on the numerical identity of the object. Having thus (1) opposed the role of function and preservation of parts, and (2) made the criterion of function relative to what sort of an object the object under consideration is, Enç introduced his notion of "objecthood": he said that we decide the numerical identity of an object which has undergone change by taking two factors into account:

> The first is the identity of the material *thing* as an unidentified object; the second is the identity of the *kind of thing* which that thing is. The more we are interested in a thing as a member of a particular kind, the less weight we tend to place on the first factor. And also, if what kind of an object the object under consideration is has no bearing on our interest in the object, then most of the burden of numerical identity is carried by the first factor.   (1975, p.25.)

These statements include a number of ontological assumptions which we can neither confirm nor invalidate by ordinary procedures of analysis. We would like, however, to point to certain problems associated with the position taken by Enç: firstly we may ask what it means to take into account "the identity of the material thing as an unidentified object". Regardless of the ontological status of this postulated factor we shall never know whether it enters into a certain judgement of identity or not. The main difficulty, we think, is this: there is no way of referring to a particular thing without predicating something about the thing. Hence reference will always include, directly or indirectly, an assertion of a kind or a quality (Saugstad, 1977).

It should also be stressed that since function is relative to the question of kind or quality, no object can be without a function. Hence there is no need for a separate criterion of replacement of parts, and the only criterion left will be the purpose, use or function of the object. Due to the connection of function and kind we may say that a similar criterion comes into consideration in questions of qualitative identity.

As shown already, statements of qualitative identity can be given the general form:

$$x \text{ equals } y \text{ with respect to } Q,$$

whereas statements of numerical identity can be given the general form:

$$x \text{ is the same } C \text{ as } y,$$

where Q and C serve as the criteria of identity. Q serves as such a criterion by referring to a category or quality, C by referring to an individual who belongs to a certain category or group. Both types of identity statements involve categories or groups, but the category referred to in statements of numerical identity may be said to submit to a principle of individuation (Woods, 1965) whereas the category referred to in statements of qualitative identity does not. The Q in statements of qualitative identity is generally a property term, a mass term or else it is an expression whose referent category does not submit to a principle of individuation.

However, we need not be concerned with problems of individuation, since these problems may apply more to the thinking than the perceptual activities of an individual.

The point to be made is this: questions of the identity of objects always involve questions of purpose, use or function. These questions, therefore, have bearing on activities relating an organism to the environment. Questions of qualitative identity also have a bearing on such activities. Thus the distinction between qualitative and numerical identity is hardly warranted from the point of view of the psychologist. An analysis of statements of perceptual identity will generally lead into considerations of an organism–environment interaction rather than considerations of a material object.

Identity and non-identity have been considered as discrete categories, while similarity has been used with reference to a continuous arrangement of events. Yet we believe that our point applies equally well to the concept of similarity. Geometrical representations of similarity have been questioned in modern literature, but hardly on the ground that such representations apply to hypothetical objects rather than perceptual activities. Thus the set-theoretical approach advanced by Tversky (1977) as an alternative to a metric analysis of similarity involves an arbitrary system of object classification, while its relevance to activities of perception is an uncertain one.

According to a set-theoretical approach an object can be represented by a collection of qualitative features. Tversky admitted that this collection is "a product of a prior process of extraction and compilation", but he did not inquire into the way features have been extracted, and the way they can be used by an organism interacting with its environment. On the other hand qualitative features of objects such as colour, form, smoothness, etc. can be communicated in everyday language, and they tend to enter into common judgements of the similarity of objects. Therefore, such judgements most probably reflect aspects of the use of language rather than perception.

Tversky's model stating that the similarity of objects can be expressed as a "linear combination of the measures of their common and distinctive features" is based on a "thing" language whose relation to perception is entirely unknown.

In short, the researcher in present-day psychology is not in possession of an independent system for ascertaining the identities or similarities in perception. Such a system when developed should be conceived of as a reference system for the classification of perceptual activities, i.e. a reference system that adds something to ordinary use of language. Moreover, a system of reference must be linked to a research method that serves to define the entities studied.

Apart from the psychological definition of identity as lack of discrimination, psychologists have merely had at their disposal common conceptions of identities between things perceived. Such conceptions of identity have not been formed with reference to particular research methods or procedures, and hence they can hardly be said to involve a defined set of research problems in psychology. In particular, conceptions of object identity have been presented in the literature without the writer ascertaining a procedure for the study of such identity. Consequently, we can hardly tell what the scope and objectives of a study of object identity should be.

4

Concept of a material object

4.1 Can we give criteria for distinguishing between objects and non-objects in the environment?

In ordinary language the term "object" may be used in a number of ways; it may be used about ends, aims, motives or anything which arouses feelings in an observer (see "object" in Webster's Third New International Dictionary). In this book, however, "object" is used in the sense of a material object, i.e. something visible and tangible in the external world.

It is hardly possible to describe the domain of the psychology of perception without mentioning material objects. Thus definitions of perception tend to include some reference to objects, i.e. such definitions generally include expressions like "information about objects and events" or "contact with the environment of external objects". No doubt, we may say that objects are of central concern for the psychology of perception. In the past, research workers such as Katz and Brunswik distinguished between the visual impressions that were linked or attributed to objects and the visual impressions that were related to the interstices, the air or empty space. Katz's distinction between the film colours (Flächenfarben) and the surface colours (Oberflächenfarben) may serve as a well-known example.

We may expect, therefore, that psychology is able to delimit the class of entities called material objects. In everyday life we can usually distinguish between objects and non-objects. But as far as we know, psychological literature still lacks a formal definition which defines the boundaries of this class very clearly.

In philosophy, Broad (1937) suggested a definition according to which objects have (1) *duration*, usually longer than the time they are observed, and (2) *extension* in space. Furthermore, objects (3) exist *independently* of the perceptual and cognitive processes in an organism. They are (4) *public* in the sense that they can be observed by different persons on different occasions. Also, they (5) *interact* with other physical objects, and (6) they have *qualities other than the relational qualities of space and time.*

Evidently, stones, books and cars may be said to have all these characteristics, and we do not hesitate to call these entities material objects. But there are borderline cases which show that the application of Broad's definition is a problematic one. Consider, for example, a mirror image. It certainly has duration and extension, and it may also be said to exist independently of the perceptual and cognitive processes in an organism. Furthermore, it may be observed by different persons on different occasions once the conditions of observation are specified. It may even be said to have qualities different from the relational qualities of space and time. For example, it may be said to have a shiny quality as when the moon is seen reflected from the surface of a lake at night.

The problem is, however, whether the mirror image can be said to interact with other physical objects. In the first instance we may be tempted to answer this question in the negative, but we cannot give reasons for rejecting the possibility of interaction without taking recourse to assumptions and principles which are not stated in Broad's definition. Thus interaction in this connection cannot be interpreted without some further knowledge of objects. The definition as it stands, therefore, is not a thorough one. For a thorough definition we shall have to compress, into a single definitory statement, an enormous amount of knowledge, i.e. assumptions, experiences or principles regarding the external world. Unless we take most of cultural knowledge about objects into consideration, our definition will not be able to define the boundaries of the class clearly. But an attempt to form such a definition, we guess, will probably not be a successful one, and hence we shall still be lacking a formal definition of material objects in psychology. On these grounds we may have to question whether psychology can form principles concerning perception that pertain to objects *per se*, or whether it would be more fruitful for this science to concentrate on objects of particular types, having specific significance in the interactions between the organism and its environment.

4.2   Cultural knowledge of objects, computer analysis of visual scenes and speculations on an "object-forming mechanism" in the nervous system

Although the class of material objects cannot be delimited rigorously, human beings have still accumulated great knowledge about objects. Some of this knowledge applies to all objects, since it forms part of our conceptual scheme of the world. For example, all objects may be said to be extended in space, and at a certain moment in time each object can occupy only one space. Other characteristics may be said to apply to all objects, or to some objects only, depending on cultural standards or use of language.

Naturally, the various cultures of the world also include standards for the sub-classifications of objects. Such classification may differ greatly from one culture to another. Rigid objects, however, may have constituted an important sub-category in most cultures of the world. The development of material culture, we believe, has depended on an early use or concern with rigid objects. It should be stressed, therefore, that human beings are well acquainted with this type of object.

Rigid objects are generally considered incapable of deformation and show, therefore, great stability with respect to size and form. In other words, these objects are devoid of the properties of elasticity and plasticity, but able to undergo rotational and translational motion. According to classical mechanics, a rigid body is one in which each point is always at a fixed distance from every other, i.e. an ideal state of matter which is realized only approximately, but often to a very high degree of precision.

By far the greater part of psychological research on perception has been concerned with activities related to rigid objects in the environment, but some research work has also been concerned with elastic objects (see particularly Johansson, 1964). In this work we shall mainly be concerned with research in connection with rigid objects, and we shall start by taking a critical view of the way research problems have been formulated in this area.

Naturally research problems cannot be formulated independently of cultural knowledge of objects. Hence the researchers have tended to take as their point of departure object characteristics of common acquaintance in everyday life. The research task may easily be conceived of as an epistomological one, in the sense that the researcher tries to account for the origin and the mechanisms mediating this knowledge of objects. In our opinion, problems which are formulated according to such objectives purely for research tend to be unfruitful ones.

An object occupies space, i.e. extended and limited. Yet it is problematic to assume some mechanism in the nervous system that enables the perceiver to isolate an object from its background. Certain basic assumptions must be made; firstly that we can isolate or limit a sub-space, i.e. a place extended in three-dimensional space. Another assumption is that an object occupies or inhabits this sub-space. The "something" which is said to be an object must be qualified in some other way than the sub-space in question. To say that this something is an object implies a unity that is not given by the spatial segregation *per se*. To ascertain that this unity can be responded to, the researcher must give an instruction which requires a linguistic capacity by the subject. Hence there is no method available according to which perceptual isolation of an object can be separated from characteristics of the perceiver's use of language.

Miller and Johnson-Laird (1976) speculated on the functions of so-called "object-forming mechanisms" in a perceiver. They maintained that such mechanisms make possible the integration of "diverse exposures to a thing into a coherent psychological unity", but admitted that this function cannot be sharply distinguished from cognition. Their difficulties with regard to a distinction between perception and cognition might be expected to have definite consequences for the way in which research problems are formulated. Firstly it may be asked whether a description of "object-forming mechanisms" can be anything but a description or specification of knowledge about objects. Miller and Johnson-Laird seemed to assume that, in principle at least, there is a difference between the characterization of mechanisms in the perceiver and the specification of knowledge about objects.

In their opinion an "object-forming mechanism" is a mechanism of the nervous system which is particularly apt to exploit the evidence which is present in lines, edges, vertices, textures and shadows of a visual scene. Such a mechanism, they said, explains how it is possible to see "static, two-dimensional line drawings of blocks as representations of three-dimensional objects". In referring to Minsky and Papert (1972) they pointed out that a set of rules can be formulated that will divide a scene into separate objects, and that will specify certain relations between objects. For example if lines in a two-dimensional scene come together in the form of an arrow, the surfaces inside the arrow can be said to belong to the same object. Also the intersection of lines forming a Y may be said to represent a corner, etc. This type of analysis can be implemented in a computer program in order to simulate object perception by human beings. Computer programs of the type developed by Guzman (1968) are usually considered of great importance in this connection.

Miller and Johnson-Laird pointed out that the perceiver must have a certain conception of what objects look like in order to exploit the evidence given by vertices, edges, corners etc.; hence the difficulty of making a sharp distinction between perception and cognition. They missed, however, a second point of equal importance, namely that the perceiver must also have a conception of what two-dimensional line drawings should look like in order to represent three-dimensional objects.

Waltz (1975) devised a system for analysing line drawings of scenes with a shadow and showed that a computer could decide whether a line was an edge, internal seam, crack, shadow, or an obscuring edge in a way which is analogous to the solution of sets of algebraic equations. Junctions of lines in the two-dimensional drawing corresponded to vertices in the original scene, and like equations in algebra, these vertices served as the constraints for the task of the computer. Line segments were divided into eleven categories and given separate labels depending on their physical origin. The vertices now served to limit the number of possible combinations of labelling at a junction, and the scene analysis thus reduced to a determination of physically realizable configurations at each vertex.

If scene analysis is also to be used as a simulation of the perceptual activities of an organism, the theoretical status of the constraints should be discussed. Like the computer, the human perceiver might be said to be able to decide which are the physically realizable configurations. For example we can easily decide that the two-dimensional configuration of Fig. 7 is a physically impossible one. But the very fact that we have this capacity does not necessarily show that the nervous system has a built-in "object-forming mechanism".

Generally, constraints in the perceiver's interaction with the environment should be related to a knowledge of phylogeny and the evolution of culture. Two-dimensional line drawings are human accomplishments of a relatively late date in phylogeny. Line drawings which are based on the principle of perspective are particularly the accomplishments of modern man (for a history of perspective in art, see White, 1972). In order to draw a scene of the type studied by Waltz, we must be in possession of a specific skill, and for the spectator to interpret the same drawing, some acquaintance with two-dimensional representations of objects will be needed. The person drawing a scene and the person interpreting the two-dimensional drawing must share a set of cultural standards for pictorial representations of objects, and this set of standards will form the basis of the constraints in the system developed by Waltz.

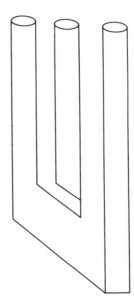

Figure 7   An impossible object.

On this basis, computer analysis of visual scenes can hardly be said to provide evidence for, or to suggest the existence of, a particular mechanism in the nervous system for the separation of an object from its background.

4.3   The object considered as an organized whole

We have pointed out that isolation of an object from its background implies that the object is referred to as a unity or as an organized whole. Similarly a two-dimensional figure, which is perceptually separated from its background, has also been referred to as an organized whole. In this respect objects and figures have theoretically been given equal status by Gestalt psychologists. In present day psychology it may be difficult on theoretical grounds to distinguish between objects and figures. Miller and Johnson-Laird maintained that there are objects which one perceives as two-dimensional. They mentioned Bierwisch's examples "Strasse" and "Fenster" as objects having only two dimensions.

Consideration of an organized whole easily brings about some consideration of parts. Thus we shall necessarily be involved in the problem of the part–whole relationship. We tend to agree with Saugstad (1977, p.69) who maintained that to speak reasonably about a whole, one must also make clear what the parts making up this whole are. Yet it is not clear whether qualities, attributes and properties may be considered as parts of a whole, or whether we can only speak of parts in connection with spatial sub-divisions of a thing. The concept of a part, we believe, is related to the activity of partitioning or separating. Nevertheless, attributes such as colour, size, form, solidity and weight are generally considered as parts of an object. This implies that colour, for example, is in some way separated or removed from the object, and this means that colour involves an abstraction. However, colour is never separated from an object in the same way as a brick is separated from a house. Separation involves different types of activities in the two cases.

Saugstad admitted that in visual appearance the material object may represent some sort of a whole, but at the same time he stressed that "it is difficult to conceive of this whole in a way which does not involve some sort of abstraction" (p.69). We might add that if the object is considered as an abstraction, it becomes nonsensical to speak of its parts. Thus it may be asked if there is some way of conceiving of an organized whole that does not leave us with a part–whole puzzle.

Consider for a moment the possibility that the object *is* an organized whole *and* that it also represents an abstraction. An organized whole may just as well be referred to as a unity, and a unity of course depends on some sort of abstraction. The point is that reference to a unity in perception presupposes recognition of a diversity or variation. In this way the object may be said to ascertain a certain identity in perception, and thus the problems discussed in this section may be said to relate closely to the problems discussed in the preceding chapter. There is no simple way of distinguishing between the concepts of identity, unity and organized whole.

By stressing that the object constitutes a certain unity, we need no longer be concerned with the part–whole puzzle. Rather we shall be concerned with the conditions under which reference can be made to a certain unity in perception. As pointed out, a perceiver may refer to a unity or make a statement of identity on the condition that consideration is taken of a diversity or variation in the situation. Yet this diversity does not count as part of the unity in question.

It is generally assumed that a child learns, for example, the concept of a ball by seeing, touching and manipulating a ball, and by listening to the sound it produces when dropped to the floor. The concept of a ball, therefore, might be considered as a multi-modal concept by the child, i.e. the visual, tactile and auditory attributes are assumed to be parts of the ball concept. In our opinion, however, the activities of seeing, touching, manipulating, and listening provide the necessary conditions for learning the concept of a ball. The sensory events involved in these activities need not necessarily be part of the concept. On the other hand, the activities of seeing, touching, etc. may have some influence on the ball concept attained by the child. The concept and the perceptual activities are not independent of each other.

Ettlinger (1967) however, considered the possibility that object concepts may be uni-modal ones, in the sense that a certain concept of a ball, for example, may be based on the activity of seeing only. He said that classical neurology had already adopted this scheme by accepting the occurrence of modality-specific agnosia. According to reports of such cases patients with visual agnosia may be able to recognize an object by touch but not by vision, indicating loss of the visual but not of the tactile object concept.

At the same time he made the dubious assumption that the object concept can be distinguished from the name of the object. The latter he considered to be a supra-modal symbol for the type of object in question. Thus he postulated a single neural mechanism which is involved in the designation of the object by its name, irrespective of the sensory channel through which it is perceived. It follows that inter-modal effects should be closely related to language in that object recognition would be independent of sensory inflow to the extent that the organism had developed a capacity for labelling.

In support of this Ettlinger (1967) referred to a number of experiments which have shown that cross-modal transfer of a specific discrimination habit is not possible in animals. Only if they are trained to respond to the onset of stimulation in one modality, can transfer of response take place to the onset of stimulation in another modality. On the other hand transfer of a specific discrimination habit has been demonstrated under conditions where verbalization (by human subjects) was possible. Cross-modal matching performance has been demonstrated by non-human subjects, but as argued by Ettlinger, the same kind of behaviour is not being tested in transfer and matching experiments. (For a discussion of the development of cross-modal transfer abilities and intersensory equivalents, see Lian, 1976).

Transfer of principles or learning sets have been demonstrated for animal subjects. However, Ettlinger accepted only cross-modal transfer of a specific discrimination habit as evidence of a supra-modal mechanism for the object concept. The problem is how to account for the specificity of a discrimination, say between a triangle and a disc. If the task is said to be specific with respect to modality, the transfer test becomes an absurd one. Hence the task must be said to be specific in some other way. A possibility is to say that the task is specific with respect to a category or concept independent of modality, but this begs the question of cross-modal transfer. The last possibility, and the one we think Ettlinger had in mind when he was speaking of specificity, is to say that the same particular objects have been used in the training and test sessions. That is the triangle has been considered an individual thing rather than member of a category. The assumption seems to have been that shape may be attributed to a particular thing that mediates transfer and which thereby makes the task of discrimination a specific one.

If this is correct Ettlinger has placed himself in the position taken by Enç which involves the assumption of an unpredicated extra-linguistic entity, i.e. the material thing as an unidentified object. The problem of conceiving of an individual object will be treated in greater detail in the next section. At the moment we shall only point out that it is hardly possible to characterize a discrimination task or habit by referring to a concept of an individual object.

For Ettlinger the main difficulty seemed to have been the interpretation of reports on modality specific agnosia. In our opinion, cases of this type of agnosia should not be considered as evidence of uni-modal object concepts by an individual. The ball concept, for example, depends on the child's ability to take notice of the various properties of the ball, i.e. the visual, the tactile, and the auditory appearances. The appearances themselves do not constitute separate concepts of the object. However, an individual may lose his ability to take notice of the visual appearance of the ball (other capacities of visual interactions may remain intact), and thus he will be unable to recognize an object by vision alone. The ball concept constitutes an understanding by the child that cannot be attributed to a mechanism for the integration of the appearances. Without this understanding there would be no appearance of a ball. Yet the ball concept, we believe, will in some way or another depend on the perceptual activities, for the child can only make an identifying statement concerning the ball by noticing the various aspects of appearance.

4.4 The individual object

Since the researchers in the psychology of perception have been mainly concerned with rigid objects, they have tended to consider *invariance* as an important characteristic of objects. In this sense the object was considered independent of the perceptual activities. Yet it could be "intended" in perception (Brunswik, 1934) or serve as a goal towards which "transformations" takes place (Katz, 1930) or "phenomenal regression" is directed (Thouless, 1931). Thus it seems likely that researchers in this field have conceived of the object as an extra-linguistic entity — an unpredicated individual thing.

Although this conception of an object does not follow from everyday discourse, it may easily be formed by reflecting upon the way we speak of or refer to a single object in an everyday situation. Consider, for example, a stationary cube that we constantly fixate while we walk around it. The cube seems to be in the same position all the time, and it seems to maintain the same form regardless of the perspective from which it is seen. Also the cube seems to maintain the same size and colour independent of viewing distance and illumination. Yet, when we change our own position, and when viewing distance and illumination are changed, certain changes of size, form and colour are also noticed. These changes, however, are recognized as incidental due to the viewing conditions, such as illumination and orientation of the cube relative to ourselves as seeing persons. The observed changes of form, colour and size are said to be changes of the "accidentia" of the object. The cube itself has remained unchanged.

We may ask: what is the cube itself? Or: how can we deal with the individual object? There seems to be no simple way of answering these questions, which have preoccupied philosophers for years. The cube itself should be what Aristotle called *substance*, i.e. the concrete individual thing. "Substance, in the primary and most definite sense of the word, is that which is neither predicable of a subject nor present in a subject; for instance, the individual man or horse" (*Categoriae*, 2a 11). This general conception of substance was specified in different ways. Firstly he contrasted the independent existence of substances with the dependent or parasitic mode of being of qualities and relations. Secondly he asserted that substance is what "while remaining numerically one and the same, it is capable of admitting contrary qualities" (*Categoriae*, 4a 10). Later philosophers have developed from these specifications of substance the theory of a *substratum* underlying the qualities of a thing.

In modern philosophy, no one seems to have seriously defended this theory, although it may be implied by Enç's treatment of objecthood. Also the theory of a sub-stratum has crept into modern theories of reference (see particularly the discussion of reference and meaning in Saugstad, 1977, pp.190–194).

Naturally we cannot communicate about a "something" "which is neither predicable of a subject nor present in a subject". This "something" — the individual object — cannot therefore be given a theoretical status in the psychology of perception.

On this basis a number of propositions in Miller and Johnson-Laird become problematic ones. They maintained, for example, that although objects can be assigned to some class or category, we still "perceive a particular instance of the category . . ." (1976, p.42). In one sense it is of course possible to make reference to an individual object, otherwise enumeration of numbers would be impossible. But it is not possible to separate reference to a certain object from a predication of the same object. Therefore "the individual object" cannot be introduced as a theoretical term independently of category terms in perception. So it must be asked, what is the x in the object predicate Obj $(x, 3d)$ mentioned in Johnson-Laird's book?

Obviously, it is the question of numerical identity which has puzzled Miller and Johnson-Laird, for they present in the same connection the following example:

> An observer stands watching a scene. He sees a man and hears the man call to a friend. At that point the observer turns away momentarily. When he turns back, he sees the man again, and again hears the man call to a friend. The observer believes that he saw the same man both times. The man is perceived as an object persisting through time, but the call is perceived as an event that occurs and is gone   (1976, p.42).

In this quotation "the same man" serves the role of C in a statement of numerical identity (p.50). Although, reference to "the same man" is supposed to be the result of some individuating function, this is also a reference to the category of man. It is the individuating function that constitutes the main difficulty in this connection. Miller and Johnson-Laird included in the their discussion of objects a formal representation of an individuating function, but they did not say what it means to assign such a function to human perception or cognition. Woods (1965) has suggested a possible answer to this question. It follows from his treatment of "the principle of individuation" that we make use of implicit rules of everyday language — essential to the enumeration of numbers — which means that we avoid counting an entity twice in answer to questions of the type "how many x's are there in A?".

It should be stressed, however, that this principle or function does not show that we can make reference to an individual object independent of a predication of the same object.

On these grounds we shall interpret computer routines for object recognition or identification as routines for the identification of characteristics of a class. As a good example we can mention the FREDDIE system developed by Popplestone and others (Wilson, 1973).

4.5   Concluding remarks

We have shown that it is hardly possible to give a rigorous definition of the class of material objects. Still, human beings have accumulated an enormous amount of knowledge about objects. This knowledge must be taken into account by the research worker in the psychology of perception. Furthermore it is not possible to postulate that there is an "object-forming mechanism" in the nervous system independent of a specification of general knowledge of objects in the culture. Also, we have pointed out that the object may be considered a unified whole, and this probably constitutes some kind of understanding in view of which the various appearances of objects should be interpreted. However, it is not possible to make any reference to the individual object independently of a predication of this object.

The present discussion should be seen against an historical background: psychologists, since the era of Katz and Brunswik, have tended to claim that perception of objects is a fascinating field of research which extends beyond the scope of classical psychophysics. Yet the concept of a material object has remained unclear from the start of this era to the present day. It is thus our contention that the research problems have remained equally unclear.

5

What is constant
in the perceptual constancies?

The perceptual constancies include a number of phenomena which have been extensively studied by psychologists. In this book, however, we shall merely be concerned with colour constancy, size constancy, and form constancy. Among other types of constancies worthwhile mentioning is location constancy, which has been studied by Kohler (1964).

What is supposed to remain constant in the various constancies? The literature on constancy has provided no clear answer to this problem. We shall therefore review some classical formulations of the perceptual constancies. The aim of this chapter will be to show that such formulations have no precise meaning due to a confusion of certain problems of psychophysics with certain problems of metaphysics. It will be shown that the latter type of problem has pertained to the identity of the individual object.

We shall mostly be concerned with formulations of colour constancy, but whenever possible we shall compare these formulations with similar formulations of size and form constancy. Thus despite the emphasis on colour constancy we shall try to make clear points of general relevance for the three constancies mentioned.

Colour constancy has traditionally been defined as meaning the tendency of an object colour to remain constant under large variations in the intensity and quality of the illumination. The first systematic treatment of colour constancy was given by Hering (1907, 1964). He measured the variations in the intensity of the light which was reflected from white paper and black letters at different times of the day, and he found these variations to be large in comparison with the negligible changes in perceived colour, for "in the one illumination as well as the other, the letters appeared black and the paper white" (1964, p.15). Furthermore, he asserted that

> the approximate constancy of the colors of seen objects, in spite of large quantitative or qualitative changes of the general illumination of the visual field, is one of the most noteworthy and most important facts in the field of physiological optics. Without this approximate constancy, a piece of chalk on a cloudy day would manifest the same colour as a piece of coal does in a sunny day, and in the course of a single day it would have to assume all possible colors that lie between black and white. Similarly a white flower that is seen under a green arbor roof would show the same color as a green leaf under the open sky, and a ball of yarn, white in daylight, in gas light would have the color of an orange.   (1964, pp.16–17).

These formulations show that different types of problems may have been confused by Hering. On the one hand he was concerned with a problem of psychophysical correspondence, and on the other, he was concerned with a problem which had some bearing on the recognition of objects. We shall first consider the problem of psychophysical correspondence.

Evidently Hering reasoned from an expected correspondence between variations of light energy on the one hand and variations in perceived colour on the other. That is a correspondence which is expected regardless of whether the energy is radiated from a luminous source or reflected from an opaque surface. However, sometimes this correspondence breaks down as large variations in light energy are accompanied only by negligible variations in perceived colour. Thus one may speak of constancy in the sense of a lack of variation of perceived colour, despite large variations in the light energy stimulating the eye.

Similarly apparent size has been said to depend on the size of the retinal image. Wundt (1862), however, described a case in which this expected correspondence breaks down: a subject is looking monocularly at a screen with a circular hole in it. At some distance behind the screen there is a homogeneous white surface, part of which is visible through the hole. A vertical black thread is suspended between the screen and the wall, and from the position of the subject the thread passes through the centre of the circle as exposed by the hole. As the thread is made to move backwards and forwards in a saggital direction, a decrease and increase in the width of its retinal image is taking place. Under these conditions the subject reported seeing the motion of a thread with constant thickness or size. Again we may speak of constancy in the sense of lack of variation in apparent size despite considerable changes in the width of the retinal image.

An object, inclined at different angles relative to the line of sight, appears to have the same form despite great variation in the form of the image projected on the retina. In this case constancy may be said to mean lack of variation in apparent form.

Thus one might say that there is always some attribute which remains constant in the perceptual constancies. But the constancy of a perceptual attribute is not particularly interesting unless it is contrasted with variations in the proximal stimulation that are expected to have an effect on the organism. On this basis it is possible to conceive of the constancies as *examples of insensitivity* with respect to certain types of stimulation. Cornsweet (1970) maintained that whiteness constancy is *loss of information* about variations of light stimulation arising from intensity changes of the general illumination.

Hering (1907) explained in detail why large variations in light energy do not always lead to considerable changes in the attributes of a colour. In particular, he explained why large variations in the intensity of light do not always lead to noticeable changes in the whiteness of a certain area of the visual field.

Firstly, there was a regulation of retinal illumination by way of the pupillary mechanism, and secondly there was a successive adaptation of retinal sensitivity to light stimulation. Thirdly, there was a visual contrast mechanism by which the sensitivity of a retinal area increased or decreased in proportion to the stimulation of surrounding areas.

Cornsweet proceeded, to a great extent, along the same line of thought by assuming that the psysiological properties of the visual system permit a logarithmic transformation of the incident illumination followed by strong lateral inhibition. But as to size and form it has not been possible to demonstrate the same type of mechanism that would make the visual system insensitive to the respective aspects of proximal stimulation. Thus eventually one would have to conceive of the three constancies in terms of different sets of principles.

In any case, an explanation of the constancies considered as insensitivities for certain types of stimulation would have to take into account the proposition that the constancies in question are but approximate ones. That is to say there will be some change in the whiteness of an object when the intensity of the general illumination is varied above some critical value. However, the change falls below the degree of change that can be expected on the basis of the variation in the proximal stimulation. Hence, it would be important to determine, quantitatively, the deviation of a whiteness function from an expected or theoretical function. One might compare the research task with the task performed by Hering and Hillebrand when they assessed the deviation of the longitudinal horopter. Hering and Hillebrand could estimate the response deviation with reference to the theoretical horopter or the Vieth–Müller circle, whereas in constancy research it may be difficult to specify a similar set of reference values. (In Section 6.4.4 objections will be raised against using "the stimulus match" as a reference value for constancy.)

But even when consideration is made of the proposition that the constancies are relative ones, an explanation in terms of insensitivity or loss of information will meet with a number of other difficulties. For example, the lateral inhibitory mechanism of the retina procures, within limits, a constancy of whiteness as long as the intensity ratios of the light intensities reflected from different surfaces of a scene remain the same. In other words, this mechanism may account for a constancy as well as a variation in the colour response depending on whether the whole scene or merely one or more local fields are affected by a change in the intensity of illumination. How is it possible then, that an organism can distinguish differences of light intensities which are dependent on the reflective powers of objects from differences of intensities produced by inequalities of illumination?

Cornsweet admitted that loss of information *per se* cannot be said to have survival value. But if loss of information about changes in the intensity of illumination makes perception more correlated with the properties of objects themselves, it may still be said to aid the survival of the species. However, loss of information about illumination will make the organism unable to distinguish between the types of differences just mentioned. Thus we can hardly see how perception, on Cornsweet's premises, should be more correlated with the properties of objects themselves.

Hering also tried to extend his theory of the visual mechanisms so as to explain aspects of everyday perception. He was, for example, convinced that the contrast mechanisms are responsible for our ideas that objects have fixed colours. But since object perception could not be fully explained by reference to these mechanisms, he took recourse to the "memory colour" which was supposed to be the particular colour "in which we have most consistently seen an external object". The difficulty consists in arguing why constancy should be a sufficient reason for the attribution of a colour to a certain object in the environment. For although we claim that objects generally have fixed colours, it must be admitted that variations in the general illumination of a scene *are* accompanied by great changes in perception.

So also with the alleged phenomena of size and form constancy: the black thread in Wundt's experiment is seen to *move* backwards and forwards, and the object, inclined at different angles to the line of sight, is seen with *different slants* in relation to one's own viewing direction.

An explanation of perceptual constancy in terms of insensitivity or loss of information thus seem to be an unrealistic one. On the assumption of a certain alertness of the organism, we tend to agree with Koffka, who said that any change in proximal stimulation which exceeds a critical value will be accompanied by some change in perception. The difficulty is to tell what type of change will follow. In our opinion the subject can merely see the type of change that can be based on his understanding of the visual scene. That is not to say that the type of change seen is an arbitrary one. Rather the change seen may be an event which upon evolutionary development of behaviour has turned out to be of great significance in the organism's interaction with the environment. Probable examples may be mentioned the change in the illumination of a surface, the motion and the displacement of an object.

What is constant in the perceptual constancies? Although great changes in perception may be said to accompany variations in illumination and viewing distance, some entity is still supposed to remain the invariant one. Hering mentioned several objects, such as a piece of coal, a flower, and a ball of yarn, which retain their colours during variations of the general illumination. We shall disregard, in the following, the possible objections which may be raised against these assertions on phenomenological grounds. Rather we shall ask whether the assertions can be accepted as identifying statements, i.e. as statements which identify the invariant entity in colour constancy. In the first instance one might say that the statements quoted identified colour as the entity. To say, however, that a colour, such as green, is the constant entity is not the same as saying that the colour of a certain object is constant. Evidently Hering did not say that colour *per se* is constant in colour constancy; rather it was the colour of a particular object that was supposed to be the invariant entity.

Hering's statements should primarily be considered ontological ones. He did not show how we are informed about the colour of the object, nor how we can proceed to study colour constancy. The first studies of colour constancy were undertaken by Katz (1911), and Jaensch and Müller (1920). But Hering made one statement concerning the possibility of knowing the colour of an object by inference from characteristics of the light reflected from that object. He said that the organism must know the colour of the object in order to use the reflected light as an index of its illumination, while conversely the organism must know the illumination of the object in order to use the reflected light as an index of its colour. The proposition has become known as his circularity argument concerning the colour-illumination relationship.

Considering that the colour of the object is the invariant element in colour constancy, how do we proceed to identify this element? The reflective power of an object can only serve as an index of the relative location of its colour in a series of colour samples when these are all presented under the same set of viewing conditions. The whole series, however, will be influenced by the viewing conditions, whereas the colour of the object is supposed to be independent of the viewing conditions. Yet we sometimes say that the colour seen is an accidental one and due to the particular viewing conditions under which the object is observed. Evidently the invariant element in constancy must be the real colour of the object, not the accidental one.

Katz maintained that real colour could be defined with reference to normal illumination. He did not see that the latter term is an equally problematic one. Gelb (1929) objected to his conceptions of real colour and normal illumination. However, Katz never came to grips with the critic.

Likewise, real size and real form may have been considered as the invariant entities in size and form constancy. In fact, Thouless (1931) made this point clear by stating that the constancies of size and form do not merely constitute exemptions from a "stimulus dependent vision", but rather "regressions towards the real object".

Now, to reconsider the example of the cube mentioned on page 60. To say that we can know the real colour of an object involves the assumption that we can distinguish this colour from its possible accidentia. In other words the assumption seems to have been that we can deal with the sub-stratum underlying the appearance of a thing. Also to say that we can know the real size and form of an object seems to involve the same assumption.

We may now finally answer the question of what is constant in the perceptual constancies: the identity of the individual object has tacitly been considered as the invariant entity in the constancies. Hering's classical formulations may have implied speculations on the identity of the individual object. Later researchers have been unable to separate these speculations from theories of vision. This is the reason why constancy research may have been led into a blind alley.

We do not accept the assumption that there is a certain object identity which is the constant element in the constancies. At least we do not accept this assumption if object identity is said to mean something extra-linguistic which is separated from the predications of the object. But returning to the examples mentioned by Hering, it may still be admitted that something remains constant which permits one to speak of, for example, the same leaf under different illuminations. However, the constancy is first of all a characteristic of the understanding of the visual scene, and although this understanding may be said to reflect or correspond to constancies in the physical world, it cannot be explained with reference to a physical display considered as a stimulus structure.

6

Colour and illumination

6.1 Plan of the chapter

There are two objectives of this chapter. First, to give a critical examination of well-known research works in the field of colour constancy and illumination perception; Sections 6.2 to 6.4 with 6.5.2 will serve to deal with this objective. Second, to give a thorough analysis of theoretical statements and interpretations of colour constancy and the colour–illumination relationship. In particular Section 6.5.1 will serve this second objective.

The research works to be examined are mainly taken from the classic literature on perception. We shall start with a consideration of the works which deal with colour constancy. Thus Katz's (1930, 1935) experiments on achromatic colour constancy will be given particular consideration. Next we shall examine a simple proviso on the breakdown of constancy which was reported by Gelb (1929), and which we shall refer to as Gelb's "spotlight" experiment. Thirdly, we shall examine some of Hsia's (1943) experiments on whiteness constancy.

There are several reasons why these works have been selected for examination. Firstly, they are generally considered classic in the sense that they have established basic facts of perception. Secondly, they are still being referred to in modern textbooks on perception which tend to ascribe to them central theoretical importance (see for example, Forgus and Melamed, 1976).

A few works bearing on the problem of information about illumination in the perception of achromatic surfaces will also be examined (Krüger, 1924; Beck, 1959, 1961, 1971).

The research works will be considered as psychophysical studies, and they will be examined according to our presentation of the preconditions of psychophysics and our description of the prototype experiment. In particular we shall be concerned with the preconditions which have to do with assumptions of the subject's understanding of the visual scene. Firstly, however, we shall ask what can be identified as the independent variable and whether this variable has been specified in relation to a sensory system? In other words, our examination will start with a consideration of some formal aspects of the experiments. By taking the dependent variable into consideration, we shall also ask whether the results can be expressed in the form of a psychometric function (see p.17), and whether the experiments can be said to cast light on a discriminatory capacity in the organisms studied.

These classic research works are not expected to show the refinement of experimental control which characterizes some modern experiments in psychophysics. Our questions, however, are generally concerned with elementary requirements of experimental research. Only the requirement that the independent variable should be specified in relation to a sensory system tends to involve a more advanced form of experimental control. Thus our primary intention is not to compare the classic works with modern standards of laboratory research, but by relating them to the general framework set forth in Chapter 2, we shall confront the methods used with the research problems formulated and thus re-evaluate the prospects of this research tradition.

The constancy experiments can be said to serve the general purpose of psychophysical research only in so far as they meet the requirements stated in Chapter 2. However, these requirements are concerned with procedures that rest on an assumption of a common understanding of the discriminatory task. This task involves the judgement of objects in a particular visual scene. Thus a certain perception of the scene must be taken for granted in order to ascertain a common understanding of the discriminatory task.

In the following examination we shall ask, what is involved in the experimenter's assumption of a common understanding of the discriminatory task? Does the task which is set for the subject in these experiments, also require a veridical perception of illumination, and hence an ability to comprehend the objects and object characteristics in the scene?

Our examination of the experiments will form a broad basis for a discussion of theoretical statements and interpretations. Taking the experimental data into account, such statements are expected to focus on the nature and function of colour constancy. Theoretical statements are naturally not expected to focus on the preconditions for experimental procedures. These preconditions, which include assumptions about the subject's understanding of the visual scene, cannot be said to form a theoretical issue. In addition to the main statements and suppositions made by Katz and Hsia, we shall also analyse statements and theoretical positions taken up by writers such as Koffka (1935) and Cornsweet (1970).

Opinions expressed and research strategies proposed by other writers will also be assessed. However, this chapter will not serve as a review of the literature on colour and illumination, but aims at a re-evaluation of a research tradition. To a certain extent our selection of studies to be examined is an arbitrary one; the points we make will apply to most studies in the area. We have chosen some of the best known works — the classics — to question whether it is possible to define any basic facts of constancy.

6.2   Katz's experiments on achromatic colour constancy

6.2.1   The cast-shadow experiment: presentation of procedures and results

Our examination of the experiments requires that we go into some details of the experimental set-up, the procedures and some of the results. However, Katz's experiments have many characteristics in common. Therefore we shall start by giving a particularly detailed presentation and analysis of the "cast-shadow" experiment which has also been considered as Katz's main experiment. Our treatment of some of the remaining experiments can therefore be made shorter.

Katz's work on colour constancy and related phenomena was first published in 1911 and then republished with a few additions in 1930. The following presentation is based on the latter edition. An English version of his work on colour constancy was published in 1935. However, this version is somewhat abbreviated, and we advise the critical reader of this examination to consult the German original of Katz's work.

The main restrictions and difficulties indicated in the following examination will apply to most studies of colour constancy. This examination, therefore, is also meant to be a general discussion of research problems in the area.

The cast-shadow experiment was set-up using rotating colour wheels — which we shall call colour mixers — white and black cardboard, and a pair of wooden screens. Figure 8 illustrates the set-up with the distribution of light and shadow in the experiment room.

Two colour mixers were standing in front of a homogeneous grey background. B_2 and B_1 were colour discs which had black and white sectors. The room was illuminated by natural daylight from the

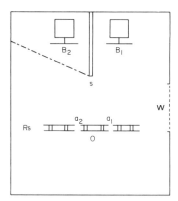

Figure 8 Arrangement of screens and colour discs in the cast shadow experiment. B_2 and and B_1 are colour discs with white and black sectors. Screen S casts a shadow on B_2. Rs: reduction screen. a_2 and a_1 are apertures for reduced view of the colour discs. Adapted from Katz, 1930.

window W. A screen, S, was placed between the discs in order to cast a shadow on the disc B_2. The intensity of the illumination of B_2 was thereby reduced in relation to the intensity of the illumination of B_1. The depth of the shadow, or in other words, the intensity of the illumination of B_2, was varied in four steps using screens which had different translucencies. The screens were made of (1) black cardboard, (2) folded tissue paper, (3) single-ply tissue paper, and (4) oiled tissue paper.

The subject was seated in front of the discs at a place indicated by O in the figure. A reduction screen, Rs, stood between the discs and the subject. This screen was made of two opaque cardboard plates slightly separated by small wooden blocks. In this screen there were two circular apertures a_1 and a_2. Each of the apertures served to restrict the field of view to a small area of the disc. The experiment consisted of two parts, one with and one without the use of the reduction screen. We shall refer to them respectively as Part I and Part II of the experiment.

In both parts of the experiment B_2 served as the standard disc. This was white with no sector of black paper. It was thus said to have a brightness value of 360° white. B_1 served as the variable disc. It consisted of a white and a black sector. The brightness value of this disc was varied in ascending and descending series, i.e. the relative size of the white sector was gradually increased or decreased in alternating series of variation. Occasionally a variation in this disc was effected depending on the method of production. The illumination of the standard remained constant during one trial, or in other words, the standard remained in a shadow of constant depth while the setting of the variable disc was adjusted.

In Part I of the experiment the reduction screen was used to restrict the field of view of the subject. The intensity of the light which passed through a_2 was constant, while the intensity of the light which passed through a_1 could be altered by varying the value, and hence the reflectance of B_1. Katz did not state clearly to the reader what particular instruction he had given the subject in this part of the experiment. On the one hand the subject may have been told to match the brightness ("Helligkeit") of the aperture colours. On the other hand the subject may have been told to match all possible attributes of the colours, i.e. to undertake a complete colour equation. The value of B_1 which was calculated as the point of subjective equality, was briefly referred to as the *value I* of the experiment.

The colours which were seen in the apertures of the reduction screen seemed to "fill" these apertures, and partly therefore they were called "film colours". They did not seem to belong to the surface of a particular object. Katz claimed that it was a relatively easy task for the subject to compare the colours in the apertures of the screen.

In Part II of the experiment the reduction screen was removed. The subject could now freely observe the discs, the background, and the screen which separated the discs. Katz said that the subject was able to survey completely the conditions of illumination. According to the subject's statement the discs, which had been matched in Part I, now appeared to be different with regard to colour. B_2 was said to be "too white" (*zu weissleich*) or "much too white".

In Part II the task to be performed by the subject was to equate the discs with respect to grey quality. Note that "grey quality" and "Helligkeit" were used in the same way by Katz, namely with reference to the series of greys ranging from black to white. Both terms have traditionally been translated as "brightness" in the English literature, and hence we also use brightness in this section with reference to the black–white series. In Section 6.4, however, we shall see that Hsia used "whiteness" with reference to this series, and that he apparently used "brightness" as the subjective correlate of physical intensity. See also Koffka's distinction between brightness and whiteness on p.103). In the instruction Katz stressed that only the quality of the disc should be considered. All other attributes should be overlooked or ignored by the subject. In his report of the experiment Katz did not specify the response categories used by the subject. Statements such as "too white" and "less white than" may have formed the response categories, but the subject may also have been told to make judgements in terms of "darker" (*dunkler*) and "brighter" (*heller*).

In this part of the experiment the value of B_1 which was calculated as the point of subjective equality was briefly referred to as the *value II* of the experiment.

In addition to the possible response categories which were used, the subject also gave a number of other statements about the colours of the discs. Partly on the basis of statements from the subject, and partly on the basis of his own observations, Katz gave a detailed description of the colour appearances of the discs. In all experimental conditions of Part II the standard, which was placed in a shadow, was said to have a certain quality of grey with a slight tint of red. The colour was not an "intense" one; it "intruded" on consciousness to a very small extent. Furthermore, the colour of the standard disc was seen through an over-layer of shadow. The colour of the variable disc, B_1, was also seen to have a certain quality of grey, but unlike the colour of B_2, it had no red tint.

It turned out to be a difficult task for the subject to equate the discs in respect of quality. Because of the red tint of the standard the quality of the discs could not be equated to the full satisfaction of the subject. However, Katz told the subject to match the standard which was red in appearance with a certain grey of the variable disc. He argued that there was always a grey quality which was darker, and a grey which was brighter, than the red-appearing standard, and hence there was some intermediate point between the two grey qualities which would serve as a subjective match. As a consequence there always remained at least a chromatic difference between the two discs. According to Katz other differences were equally unavoidable. Thus he said that the standard appeared less "pronounced" ("ausgeprägt") than the variable disc. This difference implied that the discs could not be equally well located along a series of black–grey–white colours. The subject, he said, could only compare the two colours by way of a "hard-to-make" abstraction, i.e. the difference of "pronouncedness" had to be overlooked by the subject in order to equate the quality of the discs. Katz also said that the subject had to take into account the difference of illumination in order to match the quality of the standard.

Katz discussed at length the results of one of his subjects (R). These results are presented in Table 1.

Katz also performed the experiment with a second subject (U). The same screens were used, except the one which consisted of single-ply tissue paper. However, we shall disregard the results from U, since Katz based his conclusions mainly on the results which he obtained from R. The table shows that in Part I of the experiment the subject always matched the standard with a very low value of B_1. Katz concluded from these matches that the colours in the reduction screen — "the film colours" — were to a great extent dependent on the intensities of the reflected light.

Table 1

Screen	Value I	Value II
Black cardboard	4·2°W	116·0°W
Folded tissue paper	65·9°W	178·6°W
Single-ply tissue paper	80·1°W	180·0°W
Oiled tissue paper	202·4°W	246·0°W

From Katz (1930).

In Part II the standard was always matched with a comparatively higher value of B_1. This showed, according to Katz, that the surface colours of the discs were relatively independent of the intensities of the reflected light. He asserted that if the shadowing of B_2 had been completely taken into account, all of the settings in this part of the experiment would have been 360° white. In other words, all settings would have shown a complete constancy of the colour of B_2. To measure the degree of constancy of the colour, Katz employed a so-called brightness quotient = B_1/B_2 at the point of subjective equality. Constancy of the colour was said to increase as this quotient approximated unity. The settings of R in Part II at the four illumination levels gave the following brightness quotients (B-quotients, given from lowest to highest illumination intensity): 0·33, 0·50, 0·50, 0·69. On the basis of these results Katz concluded: *the qualitative modification of the white disc lying in a shadow becomes greater as the shadow is intensified* (1930, p.198).

As mentioned previously the colour of B_2 appeared too white when the reduction screen was removed. A change in colour had taken place, namely the change which is associated with the transition from "film colour" to surface colour. Katz referred to this change as a *transformation* of the colour, and in this particular instance "transformation" was said to involve a "brightening of the colour" (Aufhellung"). As a measure of "brightening" Katz used the quotient between Values I and II, the Q-quotient. The settings of B_1 in the four experimental conditions gave the following Q-quotients (given from the lowest to the highest illumination level): 11·8, 2·6, 2·2, and 1·2. These quotients showed, according to Katz, that *the deeper the shadow is, the greater is the relative brightening of a white surface seen in it* (1930, p.199).

6.2.2 Analysis of the cast-shadow experiment

Can we say that Katz's cast-shadow experiment was run according to the procedures of the prototype experiment which we described in

Section 2.2? If so, then it will be possible to represent the response data in the form of a psychometric function (see p.17). Moreover, from such a function we can derive statements about a discriminatory capacity.

The brightness value of B_1, the variable disc, may be said to constitute an independent variable, and number of times the subject reported this disc to be whiter than the standard can be considered as the dependent variable. On this basis it would be possible to draw psychometric functions from the response data, i.e. one function in connection with Part I of the experiment and one function in connection with Part II.

In passing it should be stressed that other requirements of a prototype experiment were not fulfilled. Thus the brightness value of B_1 was not specified in relation to response characteristics of the visual system, and the response categories were not clearly spelt out by Katz.

Evidently, the purpose of a prototype experiment in psychophysics and the purpose of Katz's constancy experiment were different ones. As pointed out, Katz proceeded to study the qualitative modification of an achromatic surface colour receiving an "abnormal" intensity of illumination. Hence the intensity of the illumination of the standard disc was considered as the independent variable. Notice that number of times the subject reported "more white than standard" could not be related to illumination intensity in the form of a psychometric function.

The purpose of Katz's experiment could only be fulfilled when a direct measure of qualitative modification was provided. He made the dubious assumption that the degree of modification could be read directly from the setting of B_1 (the subjective match), and without discussing problems of subjective quantification he thus employed the B-quotient as an inverse measure of such modification. In other words, the higher this quotient the less modification of the surface colour had taken place. A quotient of 1 meant absolute constancy of the surface colour. In this connection, therefore, constancy was looked upon as complementary to change along a certain colour dimension.

Qualitative modification was supposed to take place along the series of black–white colours. However, modification cannot be defined merely by referring to a certain grey in this series, namely the grey adjusted on B_1. Modification must involve some type of activity and thus a whole set of discriminatory responses. In other words, a definition of qualitative modification must include a reference to this activity, as well as to the viewing conditions under which the activity takes place. One may say, therefore, that essentially the definition should take the form of a psychophysical experiment.

Rather than basing his statements on a discrimination function Katz made direct use of the subjective match. This fact is the problematic point in Katz's work, for how can the match be said to represent some sort of modification? Not even the variability in the subjective settings were used in this connection, thus apparently the point of subjective equality was considered as the bearer of information about qualitative modification. However, we can conceive of this point either as representing a report about a category or relationship in the visual scene, but hardly as representing a report about a certain degree of qualitative modification of a surface colour.

Katz admitted that a subjective setting of B_1 in Part II was a difficult task for the subject. It was apparently considered a task requiring a complex activity which may have involved cognition as well as sensory discrimination. When Katz referred to a B-quotient as representing some degree of constancy, or inversely, some degree of modification, he assumed that a certain type of activity had taken place: the subject notices certain clues to the illumination of the surface, and in judging its colour he takes the level of illumination into account. This activity can be a more or less successful one. When the B-quotient approximated unity, Katz assumed that the illumination was fully taken into account and a complete transformation of the colour had taken place (absolute constancy of the colour). Thus according to Katz, theoretical statements of constancy are statements about a postulated activity underlying the subjective equation of the two discs. Therefore, it is not possible, on theoretical grounds, to distinguish terms such as "constancy", "transformation", and "taking account of the illumination".

In Part I of the experiment the subjective equation was not supposed to rest on the same type of activity. Rather, the aperture colours were said to depend entirely on the sensory effects of the light stimuli.

In our opinion Katz's speculations on the activity underlying the subjective equation in Part II are concerned with the minimal conditions for psychophysical studies of perception. As pointed out, these conditions constitute a certain understanding of the visual scene. Katz made the subject's understanding of the visual scene a theoretical issue, and thus prevented himself from establishing an empirical basis of constancy. As we shall see later research workers have made the same error over and over again.

The understanding of the visual scene which forms the prerequisite for the present study applies in particular to the differences between the two surfaces. Unless these differences are, in all essential ways, known by the subject, the experiment must be considered to be inconclusive. If we are questioning the subject's understanding of the difference in illumination between the two discs, we are in fact questioning the minimal conditions for performing the experiment. According to these conditions the subject's understanding of the illumination of the scene is a prerequisite for the matching procedure. This understanding, therefore, cannot be studied empirically by using the B-quotient as an index of the extent to which the illumination has been taken into consideration by the subject.

We do not claim, of course, that the *difference* in illumination has passed unnoticed by the subject. For any pencil of rays converging in the eye a human subject can generally tell whether and how the light has become modulated by the physical environment. In other words, he can tell whether the light is reflected from an opaque surface, transmitted through a translucent medium, or radiated from a self-luminous source. Only in some rare cases would he be mistaken about the modulation of light reaching his eyes. This ability, however, should be considered in relation to the subject's general acquaintance with the external environment. By virtue of this general acquaintance the subject can also be said to know to some extent the nature of objects which are presented visually for him without being able to identify more specifically the types they belong to. He can, for example, make the assumption that visually presented objects are rigid and stationary ones, having invariable edges and non-fluorescent surfaces. On this basis he tends to see differences in the sharpness of contours and the visibility of textures as differences in illumination.

Problems concerning information about illumination will be more thoroughly discussed in Section 6.5. For the present the supposition can be made that the differences of illumination, which were present in the cast-shadow set-up have been perceived by the subject. To study the perceived colour of the standard, however, the experimenter had to make a further assumption. To match the colour of an object in a particular illumination a certain thinking activity on behalf of the subject person to be postulated.

This means that the subject had to make clear for himself what the brightness of the standard would be if this disc had been illuminated with the same light intensity as the variable disc. Katz expressed this point by saying that the "anormally" illuminated colour was to be "transformed" into a "normally" illuminated one, i.e. in the illumination of the variable disc.

As we have seen, Value I served as a reference value for estimating the degree of "transformation". Yet the transition from Part I to Part II, which obviously involved a change in the situation, may have been accompanied by a new understanding of the visual scene. Hence the subject could hardly have noticed a category common to both parts of the experiment. But in order that a certain colour be "transformed" from one level of illumination to another, Katz postulated one colour as an invariant which was identified by the subject in Part II of the experiment. That colour was the colour of the standard disc, for to identify the colour as an invariant meant to identify it as the colour of an object.

Since the two colours could not be located along the same black-white series, no relative colour judgement could be performed. Rather it seemed likely that the colour of the standard had to be identified in some absolute sense. Although Katz characterized the procedure as a relative colour judgement, he also made remarks showing that an absolute identification of the standard had taken place (see Section 6.2.5). But an absolute identification could not be based on an isolated aspect of the viewing situation. Katz could not lay the burden of proof on characteristics of the reflected light, since, as Hering had pointed out, the subject must know the colour of the object in order to use the reflected light as an index of its illumination, while conversely he must know the illumination in order to use the reflected light as an index of its colour. Contrary to what Katz seemed to believe, Hering did not mean that a human observer is incapable of discriminating differences in illumination. Nor did he mean that it was impossible to discriminate differences in illumination from differences with respect to surface colour. His point was a logical one concerning the absolute identification of the illumination or the colour of an object.

Almost any aspect of the visual scene may influence the local colour, thus if this colour is to be identified in some absolute sense, all aspects will have to be taken into consideration. This holds true whether it is the colour or the illumination of a surface that is to be identified. The point is that we are considering a surface which belongs to an object of (presumably) invariant attributes, and when we say that the subject is expected to identify the colour in some absolute sense, we mean that he is expected to identify the colour of a particular object. But to know the colour of the object, the subject also has to know the exact position of the object, and hence the expectation applies not only to the identification of a colour, but to the identification of a unique object.

This identification is implied by the presupposition that the subject can take account of the "normal" illumination of the standard. This involves the assumption of a certain understanding underlying the subjective setting of B_1, and as such it can be said to belong to the minimal conditions for doing research on perception. Also, this identification is supposed to be founded upon the constancy of a surface colour, and as such it has been treated as a theoretical issue by Katz.

A "unique" object can be interpreted either as a rare object, or as an object which is to be identified with itself in opposition to its possible accidentia. Katz apparently treated the standard as "unique" in the latter sense of the word. But as argued in Section 4.4, the researcher cannot deal with the individual object as an unpredicated individual thing. Therefore the presupposition that the subject is able to identify a unique object is an erroneous one.

6.2.3 The illumination perspective experiment

Katz conducted a number of other experiments in order to study constancy of surface colours. We shall now examine the so-called "illumination perspective" experiment. Consider the following set-up and the main results reported by Katz:

Coloured rotating wheels carrying variable discs were set up in a room with two windows (see Fig. 9). A and B are the coloured discs. The subject, O, sat near the window F_2 which was partly covered by a roller-blind. (The other window F_1 was covered completely.)

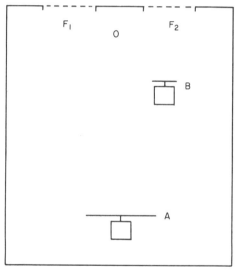

Figure 9 Positions of colour discs in the illumination perspective experiment (from Katz, 1930).

The variable disc B was placed near the window (distance 1·5 m), and its illumination therefore, was said to be approximately "normal". The standard disc A was placed at a distance of 5 m from the window. Furthermore, the backgrounds of the discs were made equal with respect to light intensity, and the two discs submitted to equal visual angles at O.

The subject was told to equate the two discs with respect to grey quality. Disc B was varied in ascending and descending series in order to determine a point of subjective equality with the standard. In this experiment, too, the setting of the variable disc was used to calculate a B-quotient.

We shall consider some of the results of this experiment. Katz found that the B-quotients were generally high when a white or light-grey standard was used, while these quotients tended to decrease for standards having darker shades of grey. Figure 10 illustrates the relationship between the B-quotients and the values of the standard disc.

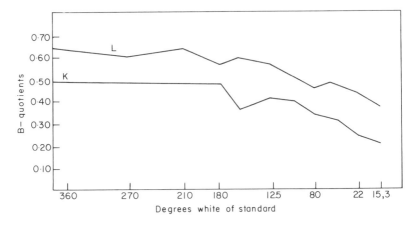

Figure 10   Brightness quotients as a function of relative reflectance (brightness value) of the standard (from Katz, 1930].

On the basis of this relationship Katz concluded:

When the intensity of the illumination is steadily decreased, the colours which retain their qualitative character most stably are white and the colours near it; the influence upon the qualities of the colours becomes stronger the farther we pass from white and its neighbouring colours.

(1935, p.98)

In this experiment, too, the intensity of the illumination was considered to be the independent variable. Yet no systematic variation of the illumination of the standard disc was undertaken, and it would not be correct to say that "the illumination is steadily decreased". As long as the two discs remained in the fixed positions each of them received a constant amount of light energy. Consequently the subject's responses could not be related to the intensity of illumination in the form of a psychometric function.

Like the cast-shadow design, this design also made possible a study of the relationship between the B-quotients and the illumination of the standard. Such a study required that the distance between the standard disc and the partly covered window be systematically varied. But still, the relationship could not have been characterized as a psychometric one.

However, Katz seemed to be more interested in the B-quotients as measures of constancy than in a possible discriminatory capacity of brightness. Evidently the main problem of the experiment was not the relationship between the responses of the subject and a variable of stimulation, rather is was the success of a certain postulated activity leading to the subjective setting of the variable disc. In the present setting the discs differed, not only with respect to illumination, but also with respect to distance from the observer. Thus the brightness of the standard could not be perfectly matched with a certain value of the near disc. The subject, who nevertheless accepted a certain shade of grey as the nearest possible match, was supposed to have identified the colour of the standard in some absolute sense. Position as well as illumination would have to be taken into account, which meant that the subject had to identify a unique object.

6.2.4   The episcotister experiment

In this experiment Katz used an episcotister to vary the amount of light which reached the eye of the subject from the surface of a certain object. He did not physically change the illumination of the surface, but by way of the episcotister he created an impression of a dim illumination or veil covering the surface of the object. Figure 11 illustrates the design of the experiment. A screen S is placed at a distance of 90cm from the window F_2. In the screen there are two circular apertures, a_1 and a_2, each with a diameter of 0·7 cm. The apertures are placed 3 cm apart. Colour wheels with discs B_1 and B_2 are set up 1·4 m from the screen. Both discs have a diameter of 11 cm. B_1 rotates with another larger disc D_1, which serves as background of variable brightness. The background of B_2 is a screen S_2 of a neutral grey colour.

Close behind the screen S is an episcotister of variable opening. The interstice between the screen and the episcotister has a width of 0·5 cm. Thus when the subject is looking through a_2 little or no light falls on the episcotister from the windows. Furthermore, the episcotister is painted black. Therefore Katz claimed that practically no light

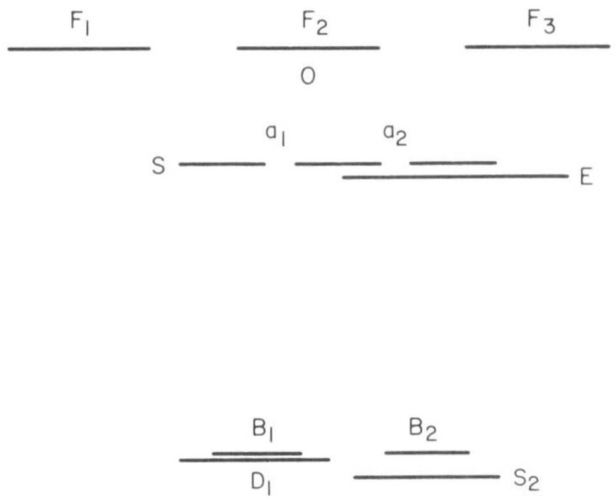

$$F_1 \qquad F_2 \qquad F_3$$
$$O$$

$$S \quad\overline{\quad\quad}\; \overline{a_1}\;\; \overline{a_2}\; \overline{\quad\quad}\quad E$$

$$\overline{\quad\;\; B_1 \quad\quad B_2 \quad\;\;}$$
$$D_1 \qquad\qquad S_2$$

Figure 11   Equipment for the episcotister experiment (from Katz, 1935). For explanation, see text.

was reflected from the surface of the episcotister into the eye of the subject.
In Katz's own words the design made possible:

> . . . certain experiments in which the opening of the episcotister was varied. B_2 was a disc of $360°$ W. When the observer looked through a_2, he saw B_2 with its surrounds clearly. Now the problem was this: with a given opening of the episcotister (e.g. $3°$), the observer was to set up a colour of the same quality on the disc B_1 which was seen through a_1. B_1 was varied in accordance with the method of limits.   (1935, p.105)

Table 2 shows the colour matches (in degrees of white) and the B-quotients corresponding to the different episcotister openings (E) for one subject person (Mü).

Table 2

Setting	B-quotient	Setting	B-quotient
E 270°C	$299\cdot9/360 = 0\cdot83$	E 60°C	$122\cdot0/360 = 0\cdot33$
E 180°	$249\cdot3/360 = 0\cdot69$	E 30°	$107\cdot3/360 = 0\cdot29$
E 90°	$139\cdot7/360 = 0\cdot38$	E 3°	$68\cdot0/360 = 0\cdot18$

From Katz (1930).

The table shows that the settings of B_1 and the B-quotients varied as a function of the episcotister opening. Apart from the first settings with episcotister openings of $270°$ and $180°$, the results gave very low

B-quotients. Apparently constancy of the surface colour was procured to a small extent in this situation.

In his discussion of the experiment, however, Katz asserted that two different measures of constancy could be used. As in the cast-shadow experiment, he could either use the B-quotient or the Q-quotient. (In this connection he did not calculate the latter from a reduction screen setting, since he could determine, on the assumption of Talbot's Law, the value of a "stimulus match" or a setting to photometric equality.) A series of Q-quotients was calculated for the settings of the same subject and with the following episcotister openings is shown in Table 3.

Table 3

Setting	Q-quotient		
E 90°	121·0/90	=	1.34
E 30°	102·4/30	=	3.41
E 10°	91·6/10	=	9.16
E 3°	85·7/3	=	28.6

From Katz (1930).

According to the series of B-quotients shown in Table 2 constancy increased with an increase in the episcotister opening. But according to the Q-quotients shown in Table 3 constancy decreased with an increase in the episcotister opening. Apparently the use of the two measures led to exactly opposite conclusions.

One might say that by way of the Q-quotient the colour response was related to a "stimulus dependent vision". The higher this quotient, the more the response could be said to deviate from an expected psychophysical correspondence. Thouless and Brunswik have taken this point into consideration and suggested that the response should be related to a "stimulus match" as well as to an "object match" (i.e. the reflectance or linear size of the standard). A ratio which takes both relations into account would serve as the best measure of constancy (see Section 6.4.5).

When the response is related to a "stimulus match", the researcher seems to be concerned with the psychophysical aspect of constancy, i.e. constancy considered as a deviation from an expected psychophysical correspondence. When the response is related to an "object match", the researcher seems to be concerned with the metaphysical aspect of constancy, i.e. constancy considered as the identity of an individual object. Evidently the two aspects of constancy have been confused in Katz's discussion of the episcotister experiment.

It should be stressed, however, that the B-quotient as well as the

Q-quotient relate the response to a constant. These measures, therefore, do not give information about functional relations characterizing the achromatic colour vision of the subject.

Katz, nonetheless, assumed that an adjustment of B_1 gave information about an identification of the object as well as a dependency of the response upon the light energy reflected from the surface. However, "information" in this connection could be nothing but Katz's own speculations of which activity had made the adjustment of B_1 possible.

In his speculations he was concerned with the subject's ability to take illumination into account. The situation apparently required that the subject could separate the veil from the colour of the surface, i.e. a requirement which implied that the subject could identify the standard as a unique object. The same presupposition was evidently underlying all of Katz's constancy experiments.

6.2.5 Katz's presupposition on the relation of object and grey quality

Katz distinguished between relative and absolute colour judgements, and as mentioned in Section 6.2.2, he claimed to have used a procedure of relative colour judgements in his experiments. An absolute colour judgement, he said, takes place when we say of a certain object that is it white or red, whereas a relative colour judgement takes place when we say that a certain object A is brighter than another object B. The difference, he suggested, should be considered merely as a difference in procedure. It should not be taken too literally "since analysis shows that no absolute judgement, taken quite strictly, rests solely upon itself, and that no relative judgement is possible without some reference to absolute judgements" (Katz, 1935, p.76).

He may have been right in saying that no judgement "rests solely upon itself", for as pointed out by Lenneberg (1975) linguistic categories are relationships, and thus categories such as "white" and "red" must be defined contextually. Every time we refer to a colour by its name, we imply some relationship to other colours. However, communication may be effective without this relationship being specified by the speaker. At the same time it should be stressed that the contextual relationship defining 'white' may vary a great deal.

On the other hand, when we judge one colour as brighter than another, we have included in the statement a reference to a *specific* series of colours. Similarly, when we say of two colours that they are equal with respect to brightness, we also make reference to a specific series of colours. The category brightness is still a relationship, but more specific than a category such as white.

Judgements of difference or equality require that the series or dimension in question is represented in the situation, i.e. where the two colours are to be located in the series. If the two colours cannot be located, no judgement of difference with respect to the series can take place, still each of the colours can be referred to by the use of particular colour names.

In Katz's experiments the subject was told to make judgements with respect to the black-white series of colours (grey quality). Yet the two colours could not be equally well located in this series. He said that the two colours could not be related by referring to a certain colour difference. Therefore, we do not agree with Katz that the situation made possible a procedure of relative colour judgement. However, he did not always give consistent comments on the matter. In fact he also assumed that a different type of judgement took place in the experiments:

> Bei unseren Versuchen lag nun mehr ein Verhalten der Vp. nahe, wie wir es sonst im Leben beobachten. Sieht die Vp. auf Kreisel A eine bestimmte Farbe, der sie eine Farbe auf Kreisel B qualitativ gleichmachen soll, so bemüht sie sich, wie auch ihren Angaben über den Vergleichsvorgang folgt, häufig zunächst die entfernere Farbe (meist wörtlich) zu charakterisieren. Zu diesem Verhalten sieht sich die Vp. durch die besonderen Versuchsumstände gedrängt. Die Verschiedenheit der Beleuchtungs verhältnisse für die Kreisel A und B zwingt sie in besonderen Masse, auf die *Qualität* der Farben zu achten, während bei Farben, die sich unter gleichen Beleuchtungsbedingungen befinden, das Urteil mehr auf den Qualitäts*unterschied*, nicht auf die Qualitäten selbst geht. So sagt sich die Vp. etwa: ich sehe die Farbe von Scheibe A weiss, grau usw. und wird die Farbe von Scheibe B solange variieren lassen, bis sie auf sie dieselbe Bezeichnung anwenden kann.
>
> (1930, pp.146–147)

The quoted passage shows clearly certain assumptions regarding the actual procedure followed by the subject. Firstly the subject was supposed to proceed by a verbal characterization of the colour of the standard disc. For example, by saying to himself "I see the colour white". In this sense, therefore, he might be said to have performed an absolute colour judgement. At the same time the viewing conditions made impossible a direct comparison of the two colours with respect to a continuous series of colours, i.e. the subject was prevented from making a judgement of difference. In other words, the subject could not have followed a procedure of relative colour judgements.

When saying, however, that the subject was expected to identify the colour in some absolute sense, we did not merely mean that he was supposed to characterize the colour by its name. The assumptions regarding the procedure followed by the subject have gone much further. One may ask why the experimenter was not satisfied with a verbal statement of the colour of the shaded disc. After all the subject was prevented from making a relative colour judgement, and yet the setting of the variable disc was considered an essential step in the experiments.

The point is, however, that a verbal statement including the name of a colour is made to refer to a category, whereas Katz was interested in the identification of a particular object. Hence the setting of the variable disc was assumed to give information about an object, not of a colour relationship.

Although this point was not literally expressed by Katz, it was tacitly assumed by saying that the subject could not attend to a colour difference, only to the grey qualities themselves. Since it was impossible for the subject to notice the specified difference in colour, constancy could not be opposed to variation. Thus one may ask what was supposed to remain constant in colour constancy? Evidently it was the identity of a particular object. The grey quality was supposed to belong to an object, i.e. to be something inherent in the object. Grey quality was, so to speak, considered as being inextricably bound to the surface of the object.

6.3   Gelb's spotlight experiment

6.3.1   Theoretical background

By 1911 Katz had already published most of his experiments. Thus Gelb could give a comprehensive review and discussion of these works in a monograph on colour constancy in 1929.

According to Gelb, Katz should be credited for having designed a number of experiments, collected a number of relevant data, and impressively described the form of appearances of colours. However, Gelb held some strong views against Katz's theoretical interpretation of constancy. His own experiments served, partly as means of criticizing Katz, partly as support for a reformulation of the problem of colour constancy. Before presenting his so-called "spotlight" experiment we shall, therefore, give a brief introduction to the theoretical position taken by Gelb.

He started by pointing out that theoretical controversies about colour constancy were also controversies about fundamental problems and principles in the psychology of perception. They were, so to speak, controversies about the nature–nurture problem of perception, i.e. controversies in which it was commonly taken for granted that one could distinguish between two types of events or processes in perception: on the one hand, there were the elementary or primitive events such as the discrimination of colour, sound, taste, etc. These were said to depend for the most part, on physiological factors operating in the peripheral nervous system. On the other hand there were the complex and "higher" events such as the perception and recognition of objects. These were said to depend on psychological factors operating through the action of the brain or the central nervous system. The distinction went side-by-side with the distinction between sensation and perception.

As pointed out by Gelb, the problem of colour constancy had been treated by previous researchers in the light of this distinction. Even Hering, who did not generally distinguish sensation from perception, treated the factors of contrast and successive adaptation apart from the psychological factors attributed to the action of the central nervous system. Although constancy was considered as a special case of contrast and adaptation, the way we perceive the colours of objects in everyday life could not be fully reduced to the action of such factors. Due account should also be taken of psychological factors. Thus it was, in the view of Hering, pertinent to speak of the "memory colour" of the object.

Helmholtz held a more "cognitive" view of constancy and since the days of Helmholtz and Hering, controversies have been going on as to whether constancy should be explained by reference to peripheral and physiological factors on the one hand or to psychological factors on the other. Gelb, however, considered this distinction to be an unfruitful point of departure for studies of colour constancy. He particularly warned against introducing speculations about "higher" events in perception in order to account for a lack of correspondence between stimulus and colour response. Katz's concept of "transformation" rested on speculations of this kind (see especially Gelb's *Ein "paradoxer" Versuch*, pp.652–656).

Gelb proceeded by calling attention to a visual scene in which the colour of a certain object may be perceived in one of two ways. It may either be perceived as white in dim illumination, or without changing the optical conditions, it may be perceived as black in an intense illumination. According to Gelb there is no way of showing that the one impression is more primitive or elementary than the other. In the same way, he argued, that the aperture colours in Katz's experiments cannot be said to depend on more primitive factors than the colour of the discs in the open view situations. Similarly he argued that one cannot decide which of the two appearances, the spot or the shadow, in Hering's spot-shadow example is the most primitive or elementary one.

According to Gelb the perception of well-defined surface colours involves a structural organization ("Strukturform") of the visual world which permits one to attend separately to the colour or the intensity of illumination on the one hand and the colour which is being illuminated on the other. The perception of aperture colours involves another structural organization, neither of which was given genetic priority, but following Gelb's holistic position, both may be said to represent different organism–environment relationships.

> Nicht auf reizbedingten und unverarbeiteten "primären Empfindungen" und Emfindungskomplexen, gleichsam als auf einem ursprünglichen Rohstoffe, baut sich auf Grund von "akzessorischen" höheren (zentralen, psychologischen) Vorgängen unsere Sehwelt auf, sondern von Haus aus steht die Ausbildung unseres Sensoriums unter solchen Bedingungen, dass wir je nach der äusseren Reizkonstellation und inneren Einstellung eine in dieser oder jener Weise, bald reicher bald ärmer gegliederte und gestaltete Welt von "Dingen" vorfinden. Mit dieser Gliederung und Gestaltung stehen solche Momente wie "Sichtbarkeit einer bestimmten Beleuchtung", "Gegebensein straffer Farboberflächen" und "reicher Sehfeldgliederung" — also Momente, die für das Auftreten der beschriebenen "Farbkonstanz" — phänomene in prägnanter Form, wie wir gesehen haben, unbedingte Voraussetzung bilden — in einem Wesenszusammenhang.   (Gelb, 1929, p.673)

The problem of colour constancy was thus reformulated as the problem concerning the conditions under which a clear separation of illumination and illuminated colour takes place. To show how some of these conditions, i.e. the external stimulus conditions ("Reizkonstellation"), may be specified by the researcher, he performed the experiment described below.

6.3.2   The experiment

In a weakly illuminated dark-room, a velvet-black disc is fixed to a colour wheel and rotated at high speed to remove the visible microstructure of its surface. The strong light from an arc lamp is projected upon the disc in such a way that the external border of rays coincides with the circumference of the disc. No light strikes any surface of the surround.

Under these conditions the disc looks white in the same weak illumination as the rest of the room. The light cone from the lamp is visible, and it too is seen as white in the weak illumination of the room. Although the observer is aware of the actual light conditions, he cannot even by a concentrated effort make himself see the disc as black in the intense illumination of the lamp.

Then the experimenter holds a strip of white paper close to and in front of the rotating disc. Two surfaces of different reflectance are now seen within the light cone from the arc lamp. Under these conditions the disc looks black in the intense and separate illumination of the lamp. A unification of illumination has taken place for the surfaces which are seen within the cone, and at the same time the illumination of the paper strip and the disc can be clearly separated from the illumination of the rest of the room.

When the strip of paper is removed, the disc looks white as before. The change of impression was a very compelling one.

Gelb concluded that at least two surfaces of different reflectances must be simultaneously present in the field of view in order that a perceptual separation of illumination from something illuminated can take place.

6.3.3 Critical comments

In our opinion there was no ground for making such a conclusion. The various surfaces of the weakly illuminated room must also be taken into consideration. Thus two or more surfaces with different reflectances were constantly present in the situation. The experimental control needed in this case was a type of Ganzfeld arrangement, for unless one cannot do without two reflectances, it is not possible to conclude that the presence of two form a minimal condition for the perceptual separation of illumination and illuminated colour. In any case, Gelb could not say that differently *reflecting* surfaces constituted the critical factor. The surfaces of objects transmitting light differently might equally well permit a perceptual separation of illumination from something illuminated.

Since two or more surfaces with different reflectances were always present in the situation, the observer could at any time give a report about the illumination as well as the colour of the disc. Although the content of his report varied according to external circumstances, for the perceptual separation of illumination and colour — *sui generis* — did not depend on the presence of the strip of white paper in the light cone. Such a separation was reported in both steps of the experiment.

On the other hand the presence of the strip of white paper clearly influenced the unification of the perceived illumination. In the beginning the observer may be said to have organized the areas of the scene into one field of unified illumination. According to Gelb, presentation of the strip of paper in the light cone caused a reorganization of the visual scene in such a way that a unification was replaced by a diversification of illumination. Also according to Gelb, concealment of the penumbra in the spot-shadow demonstration caused an opposite reorganization, and removal of the reduction screen in Katz's experiments caused a similar reorganization of the visual scene.

The point was an important one. However, it is in need of further explanation. Firstly, the reorganization of the visual scene did not create a separation of illumination and illuminated colour. It took place *on the occasion of the presentation of the strip*, and it can merely be said to have effected the *appurtenance* of one field to another (Koffka, 1935). Secondly, it is not clear how the reorganization of the scene procured constancy, unless constancy is said to mean the report of one colour, say black, that is supposed to be an inherent characteristic of the material object. But the result of the experiment emphasized the necessity of defining colours in context.

In our opinion the reorganization changed the basis for making statements about identities in the visual scene. As pointed out in Chapter 3, the subject must be able to refer to a difference or diversification in the situation in order to judge two things; fields or surfaces as identical in some respect. The strip of paper added one difference to the visual scene, and thus occasioned another judgement of identically illuminated surfaces. From the point of view of the experimenter the differences can be specified as intensity gradients. A unification of illumination implies a unification of the intensity gradients in the way that some or all of them are included in the same black-white series. Koffka argued that in the beginning of the experiment the disc was at the top of the only intensity gradient present, i.e. the gradient of the room and the disc intensity, and it should therefore look white. But after the introduction of the strip it was also at the bottom of a new gradient, namely the gradient of the disc and strip intensity, and it should therefore look black. Evidently, a reinterpretation of the disc colour had taken place. However, this reinterpretation was dependent on the fact that the strip, rather than the room, was located in the same black-white series as the disc, and had nothing to do with the intensity gradients *per se*. Fundamentally, therefore, it was the observer's understanding of the scene which made aspects of the light energy distribution critical ones. The change in reaction could not be explained by reference to aspects of the experiment.

As pointed out, introduction of the strip of paper caused a reorganization of the visual scene, and this reorganization changed the basis of the understanding of the task. Since the field was no longer seen as uniformly illuminated, the conditions under which coloured surfaces could be compared were also changed. The strip of white paper in the spotlight involved a basic condition for colour judgements, rather than an experimental variable to which the judgemental reports could be related.

It is noteworthy that Cornsweet (1970, pp.368–369, 373), discussing a similar example of an object being separately illuminated by a hidden projector, almost entirely overlooked the transition from unification to a diversification of the illumination of the scene. Rather he laid emphasis on the change in brightness when a piece of white paper was placed in front of the separately illuminated object. Cornsweet's explanation in terms of lateral inhibitory mechanisms in the retina might be a reasonable one as long as consideration is only taken of a change in brightness, but it is not at all clear that a diversification of illumination could be explained by reference to the same mechanisms. In any case the suggested explanation requires that presentation of the piece of paper is not followed by a change in the understanding of the visual scene.

In the introduction to this chapter Gelb's experiment was, in accordance with the views expressed by later research workers (see for example Woodworth and Schlosberg, 1965, pp.441–442; Cornsweet, 1970) termed a proviso for the breakdown of colour constancy. Woodworth and Schlosberg said that the physical setting had made possible a concealment of the illumination. Our examination has shown that this interpretation of the design is a problematic one, and it is hard to say in what sense the experiment has demonstrated a breakdown of constancy. Yet the spotlight experiment is an interesting one. By way of this experiment, and in other ways, Gelb has called attention to important ways of understanding a scene involving the visual perception of colours.

6.4   Hsia's whiteness constancy experiments

6.4.1   Introductory remarks

Gelb's monograph, however thought-provoking, did not noticeably influence the types of experiment which were performed by later researchers on colour constancy. As a rule the classic designs of Katz were used, but technically the experiments became more refined, and photometric measurements of the test objects were made. We ask whether such changes can meet some of the objections we have made against Katz's studies? For this purpose we shall present two of Hsia's experiments which may now be considered as classics. However, Hsia was one of the first researchers to make use of Brunswik's constancy ratio in connection with photometric measurements of the grey test surfaces.

Hsia formulated his research problem in terms of a *stimulus match* and a *whiteness match*. The former was defined by photometric equality and the latter by an equality of reflectance between the surfaces compared. According to Hsia, a subject trying to match the whiteness of two objects in different illuminations

> . . . is pretty sure to compromise between a stimulus or brightness match and a whiteness or albedo match. Suppose his match lies halfway between these two extremes when the difference in illumination is small, will it move toward the brightness match or toward the whiteness match when the illumination difference is increased. He is trying for a whiteness match and the illumination is a disturbing factor. Our hypothesis, nevertheless, is that the greater the difference in illumination, the more his match will lie toward the side of a whiteness match and away from the side of a brightness match.   (1943, p.23)

In passing, it should be noted that the stimulus and whiteness matches are, more or less, arbitrary characterizations of the colour responses. The essential point is that these characterizations are supposed to cast light on the main problem studied by Hsia, namely the relation of whiteness to differences in the intensity of illumination. Whiteness was used with reference to the black–white series of colours.

6.4.2   Designs, procedures, and results

Hsia made use of a light box which was divided into two chambers by a thin partition. The chambers were open in front and at the back so that the subject could look directly through them against a distinct vertical background. Above each chamber an electric bulb was installed on a lamp board which was concealed from the view of the subject. The lamp boards were suspended with sash cords which extended to the top of the box and over to the outside through a series of pulleys. In this way each of the lamp boards could be pulled up and down to make possible a systematic variation of the intensity of the illumination in the respective chambers.

The open chambers of the box provided the observation fields in the experiments. In each field an iron rod extended from the upper frame

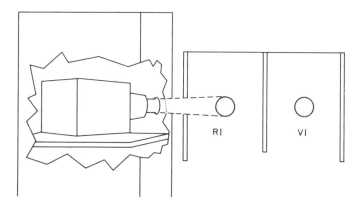

Figure 12   Details from a whiteness constancy set up. RI: reference illumination; VI: variable
illumination. Adapted from Hsia, 1943.

back to the chamber toward the subject, and at the tip of each rod was
fixed an aluminium disc of 3 in. in diameter. The discs had grey paper
coverings from the Hering series of greys. The technical arrangement
of the situation is shown in Fig. 12. Both discs appeared against the
drapery of black cloth hanging 67 in. behind the light box. As to the
procedure and further specification of the experiment, we shall quote
from Hsia's report:

> Now suppose the two fields are differently illuminated, the left being
> dimmer than the right, and suppose we put on the stand of each field a
> grey disc, both discs being of the same shade or albedo, the one in the
> left of the dimmer field will look darker and probably blacker. An
> additional spot of light thrown on this darker disc can raise its apparent
> whiteness to equal that of the right disc. If the total amount of physical
> brightness on the left disc, resulting from field illumination plus the
> spot light, should be equal to the physical brightness on the right disc
> under its illumination, we have a stimulus equality. Under the
> principle of colour constancy, however, the total light on the disc in the
> dimmer field is almost always made lower than that of the lighter field
> to reach the whiteness equality for the observing individual. How much
> is this difference? How will the relative difference change when the
> illuminations of the two fields are made more and more unequal? These
> questions, and especially the second one, are the main points for the
> present investigation.   (1943, p.24)

The additional spotlight was projected from a lantern installed in a
wooden housing (see Fig. 12), and the intensity this light was regulated
by a diaphragm screwed onto the lantern in front of the lenses. Care

was taken to ensure that the diaphragm changed the intensity only, not the spectral composition of the spotlight. By way of a wire or pulley system the subject could operate the diaphragm controller. He was instructed to vary the intensity of the left disc until it matched the whiteness of the right disc.

The illuminations were measured in foot-candles*, and the intensity of the reflection of the grey surfaces was measured in apparent foot-candles with a MacBeth illumino-meter.

Hsia reported four experiments which differed with respect to the intensity relation between the two observation fields. We shall consider Hsia's experiments I and III. In these experiments the illumination of the left field will be referred to as the reference illumination.

Experiment I

The intensity of the illumination of the right chamber was varied in 8 steps, namely 3·4, 4·6, 6·2, 8·3, 11·1, 15·2, 21·5, and 29·8 foot-candles as shown in column 2 of the first portion of Table 4. Column 3 shows the intensity of the reference illumination which remained constant at 0·75 foot-candles throughout the experiment. Grey no. 14, albedo 0·120 was used as standard disc. Column 5 shows the intensities of this grey at the different levels of illumination. These intensities constituted the "stimulus values" (S) of the grey. Column 6 shows the intensity of the same grey in the reference illumination. This intensity (A) corresponded to a whiteness match. The actual matches (R) of the subjects are shown in the lower portions of Table 4.

Hsia was primarily interested in the relationship between whiteness constancy and illumination. To measure constancy he used the Brunswik and Thouless ratios. According to the former, the whiteness constancy is given by:

$$\text{Brunswik ratio} = \frac{R - S}{A - S.}$$

The values of S, A, and R are all listed in Table 4. Thouless suggested a logarithmic transformation of this formula. Hsia calculated the Brunswik and Thouless ratios for the 8 subjects who participated in the experiment.

In Fig. 13 the median of these ratios is shown as a function of the difference in illumination between the left and right fields. Clearly, the Brunswik ratios increase with an increase in the difference of illumination, but there is little, if any, increase in the Thouless ratios.

---

*1 foot-candle = 1 lumen/ft.². 1 lux = 1 lumen/m².

Table 4 Illumination values, and S, A, and R values of Experiment I (Grey 14 as standard, albedo = 0·120)

	Illumination (foot-candles)			Intensity of grey (apparent foot-candles)	
Step	Right field (R)	Left field (L)	R – L	S	A
1	3·4	0·75	2·65	0·41	0·09
2	4·6	0·75	3·85	0·55	0·09
3	6·2	0·75	5·45	0·74	0·09
4	8·3	0·75	7·55	1·00	0·09
5	11·1	0·75	10·35	1·33	0·09
6	15·2	0·75	14·45	1·82	0·09
7	21·5	0·75	20·75	2·58	0·09
8	29·8	0·75	29·05	3·58	0·09

R values (observer's matches in foot-candles)

	Observers			
Step	EJ	HC	NS	HH
1	0·30	0·27	0·38	0·27
2	0·38	0·35	0·56	0·32
3	0·49	0·42	0·74	0·43
4	0·60	0·51	0·88	0·52
5	0·72	0·60	1·10	0·60
6	0·84	0·79	1·57	0·76
7	1·27	0·85	2·07	0·92
8	1·65	0·99	2·92	1·25

	Observers			
Step	BF	AS	JM	EG
1	0·21	0·17	0·30	0·23
2	0·28	0·20	0·47	0·29
3	0·27	0·25	0·63	0·34
4	0·37	0·25	0·73	0·44
5	0·47	0·34	1·05	0·46
6	0·83	0·37	1·35	0·65
7	1·05	0·51	1·92	0·82
8	1·16	0·72	2·48	1·00

	Observers			
Step	SS	AZ	JJ	SF
1	0·30	0·23	0·31	0·33
2	0·36	0·31	0·35	0·56
3	0·41	0·25	0·46	0·56
4	0·59	0·44	0·57	0·77
5	0·75	0·31	0·73	0·90
6	0·96	0·55	0·95	0·82
7	1·36	0·78	1·23	1·67
8	2·00	0·81	1·48	1·93

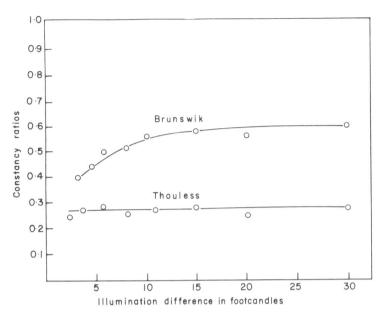

Figure 13 Medians of Brunswik and Thouless ratios as functions of illumination intensity differences (from Hsia, 1943).

Hsia concluded that apparent whiteness is a function of illumination and that there is a slight tendency for whiteness constancy to increase as the difference in illumination increases.

Experiment III
The reference illumination equalled 15 foot-candles throughout the experiment while the illumination of the right field was varied in 9 steps from 3·5 to 27·0 foot-candles. Also in this experiment grey no. 14 was used as standard. Table 5 shows the illumination intensities in the two fields, the intensities of the grey in these illuminations (S and A), and the actual matches (R) of the subjects. In the middle step the two fields are equally illuminated and therefore S = A.

Figure 14 shows how the whiteness matches of the 5 subjects participating in the experiment varied as a function of the illumination. Figure 15 shows that the Brunswik ratios first decrease and then increase as a function of illumination depending on whether the reference illumination is the higher or lower one. In both cases the ratios increase as a function of an increase of the illumination difference.

Table 5   Illumination values, S, A and R values, and Brunswik ratios of Experiment III

	Illumination (foot-candles)			Intensity of grey (apparent foot-candles)	
Step	Right field (R)	Left field (L)	R – L	S	A
1	3·5	15·0	−11·5	0·41	1·80
2	6·0	15·0	− 9·0	0·72	1·80
3	9·0	15·0	− 6·0	0·08	1·80
4	12·0	15·0	− 3·0	1·44	1·80
5	15·0	15·0	0·0	1·80	1·80
6	18·0	15·0	3·0	2·16	1·80
7	21·0	15·0	6·0	2·52	1·80
8	24·0	15·0	9·0	2·88	1·80
9	27·0	15·0	12·0	3·24	1·80

R values (observers' matches in foot-candles)

	Observers				
Step	EJ	HC	NS	AS	HH
1	—	—	—	0·98	—
2	1·22	1·17	0·94	1·17	0·98
3	1·30	1·31	1·38	1·37	1·30
4	1·58	1·44	1·44	1·45	1·35
5	1·78	1·63	1·84	1·71	1·61
6	2·09	1·84	2·11	1·82	1·85
7	2·46	2·34	2·43	2·17	2·12
8	2·64	2·43	2·80	2·30	2·23
9	2·95	2·56	—	2·37	2·40

Brunswik ratios

	Observers					
Step	EJ	HC	NS	AS	HH	Median
1	—	—	—	0·410	—	0·410
2	0·370	0·417	0·204	0·417	0·241	0·370
3	0·306	0·319	0·417	0·403	0·306	0·319
4	0·389	0·000	0·000	0·028	−0·250	0·000
5	−0·090	−0·170	0·040	−0·090	−0·190	−0·090
6	0·195	0·889	0·139	0·944	0·861	0·861
7	0·083	0·250	0·125	0·486	0·556	0·250
8	0·222	0·417	0·075	0·537	0·602	0·417
9	0·201	0·472	—	0·604	0·584	0·533

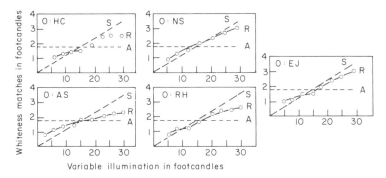

Figure 14   Whiteness matches as a function of illumination for 5 subjects participating in Hsia's experiment (from Hsia, 1943).

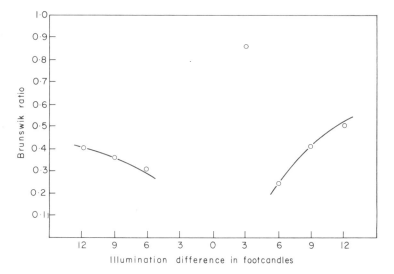

Figure 15   Brunswik ratios as a function of illumination difference. For the left curve the reference illumination is higher than the variable illumination. For the second curve the reference illumination is lower (from Hsia, 1943).

6.4.3   Analysis of the experiments

Hsia explicitly stated that "the illumination in which this grey paper stands is our independent variable, and the observer's match in the constant reference illumination is our dependent variable". In other words the right field intensity has been considered as the independent variable and the setting of the left field intensity (intensity of field illumination plus spotlight) as the dependent variable.

It should be stressed, however, that the independent variable was not defined with reference to characteristics or parts of the visual system, such as the state of adaptation or retinal area stimulated. Nor did it seem likely that the subject could maintain a certain understanding of the visual scene as a kind of cognitive reference for the intensity variation of the right field illumination. Granted that the subject had been told that a certain grey quality always served as a standard, it would have been possible to assume a whiteness invariant as the type of understanding underlying judgements of the right field disc. However, by introducing the assumption of such an understanding on behalf of the subjects, the experimenter would have questioned the very issue of whiteness constancy.

Without defining his independent variable with relation to the organisms studied, Hsia could not proceed to study a psychophysical problem. He could merely show a set of concommitant variations in the sense that the settings of the reference illumination could be monotonically related to the intensity of the right field illumination (see particularly Fig. 15). However, these variations were not psychometric ones. Thus it is hard to say whether and how they shed light on the organism's interaction with his environment.

Evidently Hsia's problem of whiteness constancy was not a clear one. Firstly he seemed to think that this constancy implied a constancy of the colour response for variations in the intensity of illumination. In other words, the subjective match would, according to a "principle of whiteness constancy", remain relatively independent of the difference in illumination between the two fields. At the same time Hsia claimed to have studied whiteness constancy *as a function of difference* in illumination. But if constancy, in this case, was supposed to include by definition a whiteness–illumination relationship, the problem became a meaningless one.

What appeared to be a more or less arbitrary characterization of the subjective match, was in fact also considered as a characterization of a psychophysical relationship. Hsia said, for example, that "we thus determine the relation between the illumination thrown on a grey and the apparent whiteness for the grey as indicated by the physical brightness of the observer's match". Whiteness was said to depend on illumination intensity to the extent that the adjusted intensity of the left field physically matched the intensity of the right field. However, the difference R – S may be said to depend on a constant in the experimental situation. This difference *per se* can neither directly nor indirectly be said to carry information about a psychophysical relationship. Similarly it should be stressed that the difference A – R may also depend on a constant in the experimental situation. This leads to certain problems concerning the interpretation of the Brunswik ratio which will be discussed in the following section.

Like Katz, Hsia may also have speculated about the thinking activity of the subject that made possible a certain adjustment of the illumination intensity in the reference field. On the one side the subject could not equate the whiteness of the discs unless he could take account of the illumination difference. He could thus give a perfect whiteness match by setting the additional spotlight intensity at zero. But on the other hand he could not take into account the illumination difference without knowing the whiteness or the albedo of the discs. Although the task was explained to the subject "with some demonstrations and practise", he was not told that the discs had equal albedoes. Considering that no factors of peripheral sensory processing would completely eliminate the effect of an illumination difference, one may ask how it was possible to explain a whiteness match. Evidently such an explanation would have to take recourse to unknown capacities or activities which leads to a recognition of the colour of the object. It seems likely that Hsia, too, has tacitly made the presupposition that the subject was capable of identifying the disc as a particular object, and that the subject, on the basis of this identification, could take full account of the illumination.

Hsia argued against a contrast interpretation of his results. Evidently, the matches were not looked upon as the results of an elimination of the illumination difference. Rather he referred to Brunswik who, in a personal communication with Hsia, had indicated that "the transformation work" is performed with great effort due to psychological tensions at great differences of illumination. It is not clear what this "work" was supposed to be, but it must allegedly have been directed towards the identification of a particular object.

6.4.4 Critical comments on the interpretation of the Brunswik ratio

According to the research problem formulated by Hsia the match response was to be compared with a stimulus match on the one hand and a whiteness or albedo match on the other. If the response match is nearly equal to a whiteness match the subject is said to have taken the albedo of the disc into consideration, but if the response equals, or nearly equals, the stimulus match, he is said to have taken the intensity of the reflected light into consideration. The Brunswik ratio, being a measure of whiteness constancy, shows the extent to which either alternative has been realized by the subject. In other words, by relating quantitatively the match value to a pair of constants in the situation, the experimenter assumed that one can characterize the perceptual activity leading to a particular colour match.

Nothing would be more erroneous, since the type of activity studied should, in all essential ways, be determined by way of the instruction. If the instruction is not clear as to what type of activity is expected of the subject, the experimenter cannot use the setting of the variable illumination as a *post hoc* indication of the procedure followed by the subject.

Yet it may be possible to identify the critical conditions for the type of activity studied. That is to say one can relate the subject's responses to a specified variable of stimulation according to ordinary psychophysical procedures. The Brunswik ratio, however, does not show how the response can be related, in a systematic manner, to a variable of stimulation. This ratio rests on the erroneous presupposition that functional relationships can be inferred from constant errors such as S – R and A – R.

6.5 Illumination and the dimensions of achromatic surface colours

6.5.1 Interrelationship of problems regarding illumination and the dimensions of achromatic colours

Katz and Hsia both believed that constancy depends on an ability to take into consideration the illumination of a surface. Therefore, to identify the colour of an object, the subject must first identify its illumination, and researchers have asked how it is possible to identify the illumination of an object. Which are the stimulus correlates for the perception of illumination?

Katz suggested that changes in the intensity of an illumination of a surface produced changes in the *insistence* of its colour, and that an organism can infer the illumination of a scene from the "total insistence" of the visual field. At the same time insistence was considered to be a dimension of achromatic surface colour. The other dimensions were, according to Katz, *quality* and *pronouncedness*.

Koffka distinguished between the *brightness* and *whiteness* of a surface. The former term referred to the variations of a colour from very dim to dazzlingly bright, whereas the latter referred to the black–white series of colours. Beck (1974) made a similar distinction, but in accordance with a convention adopted by the Optical Society of America (Committee on Colorimetry), he used the term lightness instead of whiteness. Both considered brightness to be a dimension of achromatic colours in the film or illuminant mode as well as in the surface mode, whereas whiteness was said to occur in the surface mode only.

Furthermore, Koffka and Beck seemed to think that discrimination of brightness may also involve discrimination of illumination — at least when brightness is represented in the surface mode. Beck proceeded to study the perception of illumination (1959, 1961) and brightness (1974) by somewhat different sets of experimental designs. Yet problems pertaining to the discrimination of illumination and problems pertaining to the dimensions of achromatic surface colours are closely related. The question is whether the circular relationship which, according to Hering, exists between object colour and illumination also exists between brightness and whiteness.

Lie (1977) maintained that Hering's circularity argument can be used only to the extent that we stick to "the traditional one-dimensional conception of achromatic colours." He said that within a luminosity range which can be produced by differences in the reflecting properties of surfaces alone, the organism needs certain "cues" to illumination in order to decide whether the observed difference is one of object colour or one of illumination intensity. Without such "cues" it may be difficult to discriminate between a test field of low reflecting power in high illumination and a field of high reflecting power in low illumination. Such a discrimination Lie referred to as a colour/shadow discrimination.

Lie found that the difference between an enclosed field F_2 and a surrounding field F_1 is constantly judged as one of brightness or illumination intensity when the luminosity of F_2 is increased above a critical level relative to the luminosity of F_1. When the luminosity of F_2 was reduced below the luminosity of F_1 no level was found of which the difference was constantly judged as one of illumination intensity. Therefore, the colour/shadow discrimination could not be "satisfactory specified in terms of luminance relations of adjacent areas."

In Lie's first experiment different amounts of contrast effects were produced depending on whether the luminance of the enclosed area was decreased or increased relative to the surrounding area. Lie argued that when the luminosity of the enclosed field F_2 is reduced below the luminosity of the surrounding field F_1, the whiteness of the former field is reduced both as a function of reduced luminance and as a function of induced contrast. As shown in a previous experiment by Lie (1971), however, the brightness of F_2 will be reduced as a function of reduced luminance, "but at the same time the brightness induction from F_1 increases with decreasing luminance of F_2, and this latter effect may be strong enough to partly compensate for the reduction in brightness associated with decreasing luminance of F_2" (1977, p.253). On the other hand both whiteness and brightness of F_2 is increased when the luminance of this field is increased above the luminance of the surrounding field. In view of these perceptual variations Lie suggested that colour/shadow discrimination is a function of *brightness relations* of adjacent subareas of the visual scene.

According to Hering's paradox "we must know the object colour in order to utilize the reflected light as an index of illumination, while we must know the illumination in order to use the reflected light as an index of object colour". Lie maintained that this paradox can be resolved once the bi-dimensionality of the achromatic colours is taken into account. Thus by taking into consideration the brightness relations of adjacent sub-areas one may provide an explanation of why colour/shadow discriminations are made consistently by an organism.

In our opinion, however, this paradox cannot be resolved, since there will always be a brightness–whiteness relationship in a colour/shadow discrimination.

Lie pointed out that a test of the hypothesis relating colour/shadow discrimination to brightness relationships of adjacent sub-areas, required a set of conditions in which the brightness of one area (F_1 in Fig. 16) could be varied independently of its luminance and whiteness.

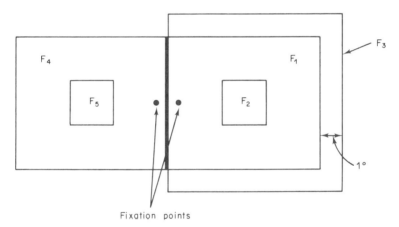

Fixation points

Figure 16   Fields which are illuminated independently of each other. F_1 and F_3 are presented to the right eye and F_4 to the left (from Lie, 1977). For explanation, see text.

Before we consider the set of conditions needed to meet with this requirement, we shall ask whether Hering's paradox, formulated with reference to the distinction between object colour and illumination, may also be said to apply to the distinction between brightness and whiteness. It may be argued that no change in the light reflected from a scene can induce a change of brightness in one of its sub-areas unless the whiteness of that area is already known by the perceiver, and conversely no change in the reflected light can bring about a change of whiteness unless brightness is known by the perceiver. This means to say that the discriminatory judgement is based on a certain understanding of the visual scene: the subject is supposed to perceive the whiteness of a surface in order to discriminate changes in its brightness, and conversely he is supposed to perceive brightness to discriminate changes of whiteness.

As shown in Fig. 16, F_1 is surrounded by a third area F_3. When the luminance of F_3 is increased to some level above that of F_1, the brightness of F_1 will increase rapidly. At the same time the whiteness of F_1 will change towards black. The question is whether this change towards black is a prerequisite for an increase of brightness (cf. Koffka's brightness–whiteness invariant), and whether, therefore, it can be said that brightness has been varied independent of whiteness.

The increase in the brightness of F_1 was tested by presenting haploscopically F_1 and F_3 to the right eye and F_4 to the left eye. The luminance of F_1 was kept constant at 0·5 ft-L and the luminance of F_4 was varied to match the two fields with respect to brightness. Brightness setting were made with four luminance values of F_3. In this way Lie determined the luminance values of F_3 and F_4 by which F_4 and F_1 appeared equal in brightness, but different with respect to luminance and whiteness.

Lie now introduced a pair of enclosed fields F_5 and F_2 to test directly the hypothesis stating that colour/shadow discrimination is a function of brightness relationships of adjacent areas. When the two enclosed fields were set at equal luminances (above the surrounding fields) they appeared equal in brightness. Therefore he maintained that the brightness of an enclosed area is independent of the surrounding field luminances below the luminance of the enclosed area.

By increasing the luminance of F_4 and F_2 above the luminances of their respective surroundings colour/shadow discrimination thresholds ($T_{c/s}$) could be determined separately for the two fields. It was shown that these thresholds varied as a function of F_3 luminance and hence of the brightness relationships between enclosed and enclosing areas of the two monocular fields. On the other hand these thresholds were relatively independent of the luminance relationships of these areas.

However, Lie may have forgotten to mention in his conclusion that $T_{c/s}$ also varied as a function of the whiteness relations of adjacent areas. The luminance of F_3 also influenced the whiteness of F_2. Thus although F_4 and F_1 appeared equal in brightness but different with respect to luminance and whiteness for *each luminance value of F_3 tested*, their whiteness nonetheless changed as a function of the F_3 luminance. Actually the F_3 luminance influenced the whiteness–brightness relationship of F_2. Hence it is possible to argue that $T_{c/s}$

depended on the whiteness-brightness relationships of the surrounding fields. But it is hard to say how the whiteness-brightness relationships on the one hand differ from the colour/shadow or colour/illumination relationships on the other. Lie's explanation of the colour/shadow discrimination may, therefore, be a circular one. He did not resolve Hering's paradox; rather his studies may have shown a different way of expressing this paradox.

It appears that brightness and whiteness have generally been defined relative to each other in such a way as to imply the perceiving of an object. Thus if brightness is said to be attributed to a particular surface or object, there is no way of varying this aspect independently of the other, and vice versa. This point has not yet been acknowledged, and therefore, the research in the area has tended to reach an impasse.

Researchers have, for the most part, failed to look upon their subject matter as constituting of different types of organism-environment interactions. The perceiving of illumination, for example, should not be treated as a kind of impression which is formed in the subject. Rather it should be looked upon as a type of activity which requires a certain knowledge or understanding of the visual scene. Thus in line with the prerequisites of psychophysical studies mentioned in Chapter 2, the experimenter must assume the presence of a certain type of knowledge in order to perform a study of illumination perception. He can hardly inquire into the source of this knowledge, at least not using the same type of study. Similarly dimensions of achromatic surface colours should be defined with reference to types of activities requiring a certain knowledge about the external world, and in dealing with illumination perception and dimensions of achromatic colours we shall probably be concerned with related types of activities.

6.5.2 Studies of the perceiving of illumination

We do not pretend to give a review of studies on illumination perception, rather we shall consider a few studies to illustrate the difficulties involved in a traditional approach to this problem area.

The first study which will be discussed is one reported by Krüger. He wanted to compare the discrimination of illumination with the discrimination of whiteness (grey qualities). In the following, however, we shall mainly be concerned with the procedures he used to study the discrimination of illumination intensities of a visual scene:

A subject is seated at one end of a room which is illuminated by natural light coming through a window. Two black episcotisters, 25cm apart, are placed close to and in front of the subject. When these episcotisters are rotating at a sufficiently high velocity the subject is told to look through one of them at a time. He will notice that the illumination of the room is lowered to some extent. The point is that whether the subject is looking through the one or the other episcotister he can observe the same array of objects.

The one episcotister has a constant sector opening of 180°, and the room illumination as seen through this episcotister serves as the standard or reference illumination. The size of the sector opening of the other episcotister is varied by the experimenter. The task given to the subject is to judge whether the room illumination as seen through the variable episcotister is more or less intense than the reference illumination.

In another series of experiments two achromatic colour discs were set up side-by-side in the same illumination. The subject was instructed to compare the grey qualities of the discs in order that the experimenter could determine the differential sensitivity for grey surface colours. The standard disc consisted of 180° white and 180° black.

Krüger reported the differential thresholds of grey quality (M) and of illumination (E) for the five subjects (O's) shown in Table 6. M was expressed in terms of degrees of whiteness on the comparison disc and E was expressed in terms of angular size of the episcotister opening.

Table 6

O	M	E
Ka	5·9	15·9
Ke	4·6	22·5
Ra	6·4	21·2
Er	4·1	8·9
Bo	2·2	9·8

The independent variables in Krüger's experiments were not defined with reference to the visual system, and since the differential thresholds were determined by different sets of operations, they were not directly comparable. On the other hand one may say that the independent variables were introduced in relation to the subjects' understanding of a constant characteristic of the situation: the colour discs were placed in the same illumination, and the same coloured objects were seen through the episcotisters. In other words, we may presume that the subject apprehended a *sameness* or *unity* for the views or discs to be compared. Since, however, the subject saw a whole scenery of coloured objects through each of the episcotisters, this unity may have been hard to recognize. But in principle, we believe, the situation gave an opportunity for the subject to base his comparative judgements on an understanding of sameness in colour, a point that would have been important to stress in the instructions.

In general the comparison of two fields with respect to illumination becomes a difficult one unless the two are seen to be equally coloured. That is not to say that a comparative judgement of illumination is impossible, such a judgement can of course still be made. But if it is doubted that a sameness of colour has been apprehended by the subject, the response data cannot be interpreted in terms of sensory capacity.

Beck (1959) did some experiments in which the subject was told to equate the intensity of the illumination of two surfaces. The task called for a judgement of apparent identity in illumination, and it should, therefore, be considered in view of our discussion in Chapter 3. He made use of transparencies with either speckled, spotted or striped surfaces. These were placed over sheets of ground glass at the rear end of two viewing boxes. Each box contained a photo-flood lamp centred right behind the ground glass to make possible an illumination of the transparency from behind.

The transparencies had dense and clear portions allowing for the particular pattern of their surfaces. Whiteness of the surfaces depended on transmittance of the different portions. In Experiment I the clear portions of the standard and comparison surfaces had a transmittance of 92%, whereas the transmittance of the dense portions differed for the two surfaces. It was 35% for the standard and 1·6% for the comparison. The area of both surfaces was approximately 50% clear and 50% dense.

Since the standard and comparison surfaces always differed with respect to average transmittance, they would also differ with respect to whiteness. The subject was told the difference between the whiteness and the illumination of a surface. Furthermore, he was informed that the illumination and the whiteness of the standard would remain constant. He was then instructed to "adjust the illumination on the comparison surface until it appeared equal to that of the standard".

Beck was interested in the "stimulus correlates" for the judged illumination of a surface. He said that these correlates may be either (a) the higher intensity coming from a surface; (b) the lower intensity; (c) the average intensity; or (d) a weighted average of the higher and lower intensities. In the experiment Beck tested two hypotheses: (H_1) the judged illumination of the surface will be determined by the higher of the two intensities which were coming from the dense and clear portions; (H_2) the judged illumination of the surface will be determined by the average intensity of the light coming from that surface.

The illumination match did not serve as the type of dependent variable that permits one to set up a psychometric function. Therefore the data from this experiment could hardly be interpreted in terms of sensory capacity. First of all, however, the problem was not a clear one. If the "stimulus correlate" was supposed to mean the stimulus variable to which the illumination responses could be reasonably related, the design and procedure of the experiment must be considered totally inadequate for the testing of the hypothesis. Firstly, the higher, lower and average intensities were not varied independently of each other. Secondly, the match value did not account for a particular relationship between the responses and the illumination variables. Any match may theoretically agree with a number of functions relating a certain illumination response to a certain variable of illumination intensity.

Granted that the subject was properly informed about the difference in whiteness between the two surfaces, the task may be said to have been a meaningful one. This difference may then have served as a basis for a statement of identity in illumination (i.e. an illumination match). The subject, however, was told the difference between the whiteness and the illumination of a surface. But this difference is an abstract one, and could not be communicated to the subject merely by referring to a particular surface. Hence it would not be clear on what grounds the subject might be said to "know" the difference of whiteness between the standard and comparison surfaces.

Any match, be it an equating of the higher, the average or the lower intensities, was therefore an equivocal one with respect to the problem raised by Beck. The subject, we presume, selected an illumination intensity in accordance with some difference in whiteness, and since the experimenter could not make any warranted assumptions as to which difference formed the basis of a match, the results became inconclusive ones. By manipulating the conditions under which the whiteness of the surfaces were perceived, it would be possible to make the subject match any of the intensity measures mentioned by Beck.

Although there was no way of telling which whiteness difference formed the basis of a match, the subject was nevertheless expected to take the whiteness of the surfaces into account. Apparently, therefore, Beck made the presupposition that the subjects could know the surfaces in some absolute sense, i.e. independently of the particular viewing conditions under which they were presented. In other words, the subjects were expected to identify the transparencies as unique and unpredicated objects.

Later Beck (1961) performed some experiments in order to show whether "judgements of lightness and illumination are coupled psychologically". That is, the subjects were told to make both types of judgements in the same experimental setting. But as the one must necessarily form the basis of the other, Beck questioned, in the formulation of his research problem, the minimal conditions for studying either.

Still later (1971), Beck made an experiment in which subjects were told to compare the whiteness of two targets which had identical luminance and which appeared against a black background. One of the targets cast a shadow on the background. This target, therefore, seemed to be illuminated by a spotlight, and accordingly it was also judged to be less white than the other target. The shadow, which was considered to be a "cue" for the illumination of the target, was itself part of an understanding of the illumination conditions. This understanding naturally formed the basis for a comparative judgement of the colours. But since the very concept of surface colours implies such an understanding, we cannot add to everyday knowledge by saying that apparent illumination influences apparent whiteness. Such a statement would, of course, be a truism, as knowledge of the illumination of a surface always constitutes one of the minimal conditions for studying its whiteness. Thus saying that highlights and shiny parts constitute cues for the perception of illumination are only different ways of referring to an understanding of the illumination conditions under which the surfaces are seen.

6.5.3 Dimensions of achromatic surface colours

Discrimination of brightness implies the constancy of another perceptual attribute or category, for example whiteness or hue. Even in heterochromatic photometry we must assume that the observer can make use of a constant attribute, for example saturation, that serves as a basis for discriminations of brightness.

Failing to see this point Beck (1974) set up an experiment in which the subjects were told to make comparative judgements of brightness for two targets presented in the same illumination, while either the albedo of the target or the albedo of the background was varied. Target albedo and background albedo variations may have provided a different basis for the comparative judgements of the subject. Therefore the discriminatory capacities in the two situations were not directly comparable.

In general the discrimination of brightness can be measured psycho-physically. This discrimination, therefore, is a matter of sensory capacity. However, the perceptual distinction between brightness and whiteness cannot be measured psychophysically. In other words, this distinction is a matter of perceptual sophistication and learning rather than sensory capacity. Discrimination of colours which fall in uninterrupted continua is always a matter of sensory capacity, whereas the awareness of such continua or the distinction of one continuum from another depends on a cognitive structuring of the world of colours.

The terms "dimension", "attribute" and "category" tend to be used interchangeably by the researchers. We can give no particular reason why these terms should be used differently in relation to colours. In studies of discriminatory capacities, however, we tend to use "dimension" rather than "attribute" or "category" which are the preferred terms only in connection with qualitative distinctions.

The psychophysics of brightness and whiteness is concerned with capacities of achromatic colour vision. To assess the capacity of brightness discrimination, we have to vary the luminance of a local area inspected by the subject. This relationship seems to have been an implicit one in Bouma's treatment of brightness (Bouma, 1971). Since Hering it has been argued that whiteness depends on luminance relationships between adjacent areas of the visual field (see also Lie, 1969).

In addition to the dimension of brightness and whiteness, we may also mention the dimension of pronouncedness (see p.75). However, it has no meaning to ask for the exact number of dimensions, since this number will vary with learning as well as the interests and motives of the perceiver. An artist who deals with pictorial representation may develop a high degree of sophistication concerning achromatic as well as chromatic colours. He may, therefore, claim more dimensions of achromatic surface colours than a layman having no particular interest in work with colours.

6.6 Concluding remarks

Problems of the relationship between surface colour and illumination may be said to have been raised by pioneering research workers such as Hering and Katz. These two research workers also concerned themselves with the spatial appearances of colours. Yet they formulated their research problems differently, and their experiments may be said to have had different objectives.

While Katz considered the spatial appearances of colours to be a main subject of research, Hering seemed to think that a description of these appearances served to specify the limits of the psychophysics of colour. Thus he claimed that colours considered as "space filling qualities" could be studied psychophysically, not the colours of specific external objects.

Katz, who argued for an extension of the psychophysics of colour, made a point of the spatial appearances of colours. In particular he called attention to the so-called "aperture" or "film colours" on the one side and the "surface colours" on the other. The description of these appearances included, among other things, the conditions under which a perceptual separation of illumination and coloured surface can take place. At the same time it should be stressed that colour constancy and the perception of illumination were considered as aspects of the same perceptual accomplishment. To study the psychophysics of the surface colours, Katz had to assume this accomplishment on behalf of the subject. He thus tended to beg the question of constancy.

Later research workers have run into the same difficulties. Thus the attempt to extend the psychophysics of colour, in the way pronounced by Katz, has failed.

7

Space and object: examination of Poincaré's theory of a displacement group

James (1890) distinguished thematically between the perception of space and the perception of objects. This distinction has been made less clear in modern research works on perception (though the works of Ingle, Schneider, Trewarthen and Held, 1967, can be mentioned as examples to the contrary). Modern writers tend to acknowledge that problems of the perception of space and problems of the perception of objects are interrelated in a complex way.

Nevertheless, in studies on the perception of objects research workers have generally assumed, implicitly or explicitly, certain characteristics of the spatial framework, while conversely studies on the perception of space have rested on assumptions regarding the properties of objects. Such studies usually meet with a number of difficulties since the underlying assumptions are not always warranted ones. Saugstad (1977) pointed out that

> . . . perceiving of the material object presupposes that: space around man is in some way structured, while conversely, the perceiving of direction distance, and extension presupposes the existence of material objects. In other words it may not be possible to distinguish between the perceiving of space and the perceiving of the material objects.   (p.70)

In our opinion these arguments are above all relevant to methodological problems in the psychology of perception, while it is hard to say whether they also invalidate epistomological statements on the priority of material objects. The research worker can probably study space perception only in the form of interactions involving objects.

Piaget (1972) called attention to the prevalent view among atomic physicists that an object exists as an object only to the extent that it can be localized. Similarly, he assured that a child has no idea of an object before he can localize it and take account of successive displacements.

The problem is whether localization can be studied without assuming that the child already has some knowledge of objects. Certainly localization requires a spatial framework, and one may ask whether it is possible to show that such a framework can exist prior to and independent of some knowledge of objects.

According to Piaget the ability to take account of successive displacements depended on a perceptual distinction between changes of state and changes of position. This distinction Poincaré (1952) took as his point of departure when he advanced the notion of a displacement group. Piaget considered this group to form the origin not only of the object concept but also of the development of sensory-motor space. Therefore, we shall now turn more specifically to Poincaré's own formulation of the distinction between changes of state and changes of position and his explanation of how the organism is enabled to make this distinction.

He said that none of our sensations can, by themselves, provide us with an idea of space. We can only understand this idea by studying the laws according to which the sensations succeed one another in time. Sensations are subject to change, and these changes we attribute to either of two types of changes in the objective world: "Sometimes we say that objects . . . have changed their state, sometimes that they have changed their position, that they have only been displaced" (see Poincaré, 1952, p.58). Elastic objects may undergo changes of state, as for instance, a balloon which is being inflated by air. Rigid objects on the other hand can merely change position. Now the problem for Poincaré was this: "Whether an object changes its state or only its position, this is always translated for us in the same manner, *by a modification in an aggregate of impressions*. How then have we been enabled to distinguish them?" (p.58).

He assumed that a "modification in an aggregate of impressions" may sometimes be corrected by voluntary movements of the eye or the body as a whole, sometimes it cannot be so corrected. If there were only changes in position, we can restore the original "aggregate of impressions" by confronting us with "the movable object in the same *relative* situation. We thus correct the modification which was produced and we reestablish the initial state by an inverse modification" (p.58).

It is not clear what Poincaré meant by an "aggregate of impressions". He may possibly have meant a pattern of light on the retina or a visual response elicited by a pattern of light. The reason why voluntary movements were considered important was this: a cyclical event in the environment, such as an object which is growing and shrinking regularly, may itself restore the same pattern of light on the retina of a motionless observer. Therefore, discrimination between state and position cannot merely be based on the restoration of an "aggregate of impressions". It must also be based on a set of non-visual events/ responses which accompany the active movements of an organism. Thus he said that we may pass from an "aggregate of impressions" A, to another "aggregate of impressions" B, in two different ways:

> First involuntarily and without experiencing muscular sensations — which happens when it is the object that is displaced; secondly, voluntarily, and with muscular sensation — which happens when the object is motionless, but when we displace ourselves in such a way that the object has relative motion with respect to us.
>
> (Poincaré, 1952, p.59)

Now consider further Poincaré's assertion that we can compensate for changes in an "aggregate of impressions" by voluntary movements of the eye or the body, i.e. by way of such movements we can restore an original "aggregate of impressions". It may be asked under what conditions will a precise compensation for changes in an "aggregate of impressions" take place, or what are the principles according to which we can decide that an original "aggregate of impressions" has been restored. Poincaré stated that a person who is already familiar with geometry will reason in this way:

> If there is to be compensation, the different parts of the external object on the one hand, and the different organs of our senses on the other must be in the same relative position after the double change. And for that to be the case, the different parts of the external body on the one hand, and the different organs of our senses on the other, must have the same relative position to each other after the double change; and so with the different parts of our body with respect to each other. In other words, the external object in the first change must be displaced as an invariable solid would be displaced, and it must also be so with the whole of our body in the second change which is to correct the first. Under these conditions compensation may occur.   (1952, p.60)

Evidently, the conditions for compensation were derived from the geometry of solids. But compensation was also supposed to take place by an organism which was not familiar with geometry. He said that "experiment shows us that it (compensation) sometimes does take place, and we start from this experimental fact in order to distinguish changes of state from changes of position" (p.60). It may be asked how "experiment" can show us that compensation does sometimes take place. In other words, how is the organism able to decide whether an original "aggregate of impressions" has been restored? Evidently Poincaré assumed that an "aggregate of impressions" existing at t_1 and an "aggregate of impressions" existing at t_2 are conceived of by the organism as one and the same aggregate. But this assumption calls for a criterion of identity. There was, however, no way of introducing such a criterion without assuming that the organism attributes its impressions to one and the same object, and consequently there was no ground for claiming the genetic priority of a displacement group in perception over the concept of a material object understood by an observer.

Yet we think it may be interesting to study the perceptual distinction between changes of state and changes of position, and we shall see later how this study can be made a meaningful one without the researcher having recourse to an assumption about an observer's perception of a material object. First we shall consider a discussion of Poincaré's problem which has appeared in more recent works on perception.

Von Fieandt and Gibson (1959) maintained that "the puzzle of Poincaré" may be resolved once it is shown that the eye is sensitive to two kinds of continuous transformation of the optic array: one kind has to do with the appearance of rigid objects in rotation, and the other has to do with the "rubbery" transformations of the appearance of objects changing form. It should be stressed that this assertion involved a denial of Poincaré's premise, namely that changes of position and changes of state are "translated for us in the same manner, by a modification in an aggregate of impressions". The latter phrase, we have seen, may be said to mean the modification of a pattern of light on the retina. Thus only by showing that the two types of stimuli are optically the same, i.e. non-specific with respect to an object's displacement or deformation in three-dimensional space, will the researcher have a point of departure for discussing Poincaré's problem. Since optical transformations which are non-specific in this respect do exist, and since an organism can most probably, respond to them in a specific way, Poincaré's problem cannot be resolved by saying that there are two types of stimuli for the two types of responses. Neither can one assert that specificity lies *within* the stimulus pattern.

Johansson (1964), however, called attention to a critical point in Poincaré's treatment of the problem. He said that the suggested solution implies that a motionless observer cannot differentiate the two groups of changes. We do not fully agree with Johansson on this point.

Certainly, the principle says that active movements are necessary for the acquisition of an ability to distinguish the two groups of changes, but it does not say that a mature organism having attained this ability will be unable to differentiate the two types of changes when motionless. Thus two transformation patterns, which are non-specific with respect to object displacements and/or deformations in three-dimensional space, but which differ with respect to their displacement vectors in a so-called "picture plane", can give rise to different perceptual responses. For example, one transformation pattern may be reported as an object moving in depth and the other as an object moving in depth and changing form. In fact, this was the main outcome of Johansson's experiments where non-sinusoidal changes in a solid angle of light was generated in a cathode ray tube and observed monocularly by a stationary subject.

Since the transformation patterns used in these experiments were non-specific with respect to object displacements and/or deformations. Johansson thought there must be "principles inherent in the perceptual process which bring about specificity". By applying vector analysis and a rule of least change on the stimulus data, he rendered an accurate description of perceptual specificity. But since the principle of perceptual three-dimensionality thus established was attributed to some unknown perceptual process, it could hardly serve as an explanation of the specificity of perceptual response.

A response specificity in the situation studied by Johansson does not run contrary to the principle of Poincaré. Rather it may be consistent with this principle. However, no treatment of the stimulus data can provide an explanation of the observed response specificity. Such an explanation must be looked for in the conditions under which an acquisition of the discriminatory ability has taken place.

The acquisition of an ability to discriminate changes of state from changes of position, we believe, is essential for all interactions with the environment. Furthermore, we agree with Poincaré that only an organism who is capable of active locomotion can acquire this ability. The question is why locomotion is necessary for an acquisition of the discriminatory ability. For some changes in the environment, such as a prey running away or a predator approaching, gross locomotory movements of the organism will serve to restore certain possibilities of behaviour. While other changes such as the deformations of an animal made in defence against the attack of a predator, cannot be corrected or counteracted by a set of locomotory movements on behalf of the predator.

In this way we can specify the conditions for compensation in terms of behaviour rather than in terms of impressions, and we need not have recourse to a concept of material objects. Gross locomotory movements, it can be said, serve in some cases to restore certain possibilities of behaviour. Thus they provide the basis on which a discrimination between two types of changes can be made.

To say that a transformation pattern of the optic array carries information about the perceptual world, has no clear meaning unless we add that the pattern carries information *by virtue of developmental conditions and structural characteristics of the organism*. However, a reference to developmental conditions may erroneously be considered as the taking of an empirical position. But such a reference does not necessarily entail empiricism any more than nativism.

Von Fieandt and Gibson argued against Poincaré's principle since it involved an explanation in terms of learning. In general, however, they may have considered perception to be a function of stimulation, and they suggested a solution to Poincaré's problem in accordance with this position. Their discussion was not clear since in no way can we contrast a stimulus-dependent vision with one depending on learning. A stimulus dimension exist for the organism only in so far as it forms part of the natural conditions under which an evolution of behaviour has taken place; or else we tend to agree with Lashley and Wade (1946) who said that such a dimension has behavioural relevance only when it is established by differential training. These problems will be further discussed in connection with a discussion of the stimulus concept in the works of J. J. Gibson and G. Johansson.

Also, according to the position taken here, the organism can have no concept of object which is not already part of the conditions governing the spatial behaviour. As research workers we cannot answer questions concerning the priority of objects vs the priority of space in perception. Therefore, Piaget's statement that the perception of objects depends on an ability to take account of successive displacements is, depending on how it is interpreted, either wrong or a truism. In any case this statement is empty of empirical meaning.

8

Size and distance

8.1 Helmholtz on the study of visual size: specifications of ocular activity and assumptions about understanding

As has been pointed out in several places in this book, perception is considered as a type of activity by which the organism may be said to interact with the environment. The perception of size and distance are thus considered as types of activities. Studies of size and distance, therefore, require specifications of these activities. Such studies require that one makes explicit assumptions regarding the way in which the organism perceives the visual scene.

Helmholtz (1962) described a procedure for the study of visual size. In this procedure he made explicit (1) the optimal external conditions for this study; and (2) assumptions regarding how the scene is supposed to be perceived by the subject under these conditions. Furthermore he specified (3) the type of activities involved in the perceiving of size, and he referred to (4) the law by which these activities are related to characteristics of the eye.

(1) and (2) were specified in a description of *the field of vision (Gesichtsfeld)*. (3) was specified as the gross exploratory movements of the eye, and (4) was said to be Listing's Law which describes these movements as the rotations of *the visual globe* in relation to *the field of fixation*.

Consider first the field of vision. This term refers mainly to a mode of appearance of the visual scene according to which:

> . . . distance cannot be discerned; the consequence being that objects cease to look like bodies of three dimensions in space and appear as if they were distributed over a surface. This apparent superficial

configuration of the objects of vision is called the *field of vision (Gesichtsfeld).*   (p.158)

However, the organization, or mode of appearance of the scene may not have been uniquely specified by speaking of a surface. Therefore he added:

> I must beg the reader to notice that I was careful not to say that the objects appear to us to be distributed *in or on a surface,* but only *as if they were in a surface,* in a superficial configuration, that is, in a configuration which is different with respect to two dimensions.
>
> (p.158)

This description was of a *mode of appearance* on behalf of the subject. It was not a description of a stimulus situation as specified by the experimenter's operations. Yet it was possible — and necessary — to identify the optimal conditions under which this appearance could be realized. These were the conditions under which "distance cannot be discerned". Helmholtz suggested that the heavenly sphere of visible stars, or a scene imitating this sphere, may serve as an appropriate setting for the study of apparent visual size.

Helmholtz supposed that man has learned to discriminate visual size in a similar setting. If this is correct visual size must be said to rest on a high degree of abstraction. He maintained that the organism, by letting its eyes wander over the field, could learn about the original arrangement of points in the field of vision. This learning, takes place "without any measurements of dimensions at first". Such measurements, which in Helmholtz' treatise involved the *direct perception* of size, would develop on the basis of certain characteristics of the movements of the eye.

In order to specify accurately these movements he introduced the terms "field of fixation" and "visual globe". The former was said to be the field traversed by the gaze of a mobile eye, and geometrically it was defined as a sphere of infinite radius with its centre in the centre of the eye. The "visual globe" was regarded as "the retina itself with all its images and special characteristics projected outside" (p.164). Hence this latter sphere was said to move with the eye and to displace itself relative to the "field of fixation". Helmholtz assumed that the organism could perceive directly the length of lines "in" the "field of fixation" which can be accurately displaced along one line at the "visual globe". In other words, perception of size or length is possible to the extent that the images of the various parts of the line fall one after the other along the same line on the retina. He reported some experiments which showed that the lines whose lengths could be most accurately compared by a subject were the lines "so situated that their images can be produced one after the other on the same part of the retina". Thus he seemed to have compared the retina with a compass or a rule of measurement.

Helmholtz knew that a compass or rule can be turned deliberately in all directions, while the retina, without movements of the head and body, cannot be turned in all directions. He was convinced that the eyeball could move with only two degrees of freedom, which implied certain restrictions in the way the "visual globe" and the "field of fixation" could be displaced relative to each other. More precisely, Helmholtz ascertained the validity of Listing's Law which states that a change of fixation takes place as if the eye rotates around an axis which is perpendicular to the plane through the point of rotation and the primary and secondary points of fixation. It follows that rotations around the visual axis are impossible, and thus the number of lines which can be imaged in succession on the same retinal meridian is severely limited.

In this connection we need not say which these lines are, nor do we need to discuss the empirical basis of the Helmholtzian system. Such a discussion would also require an evaluation of Listing's Law which might be the subject matter of a different work. However, we would like to stress that Helmholtz, in the way he took into consideration the kinematics of the eye, may be said to have related the length of a line in the field of fixation with validity to the meridians of the visual globe. In other words he showed how the stimulus variable could be accurately described in terms of characteristics of the eye.

Helmholtz admitted that the organism could also compare the lengths of lines or areas that cannot be imaged in succession on the same retinal elements merely by a movement of the eye. Such lines can be compared with the aid of other bodily movements. Helmholtz maintained that the adult individual can compare a pair of lines merely by imagining what movements must be made in order to bring the whole body and the eye into such positions that both lines can be imaged in succession on the same retinal meridian. Surely, in this way a subject cannot compare the length of lines accurately, but in principle, he said, size comparisons are still possible. Such comparisons, however, are not based on characteristics of the field of vision.

8.2 Conditions for an effective communication about the size of objects

The researcher can assess the accuracy of size perception on the assumption that he can communicate with the subject about size. The two must apply similar procedures in determining whether a line A is longer or shorter than a line B, otherwise communication will not be effective. In general the researcher decides whether two lines are equal or different with respect to length by observing them side-by-side at the same distance. The subject, however, cannot follow exactly the same procedure, but he is expected to disregard distance and to observe the lines in the same spatial framework. This is probably the reason why Helmholtz stressed the characteristics of the field of vision, and the reason why he required that size be studied in a situation where "distance cannot be discerned" and where points appear in "the same superficial configuration."

Of course, the researcher cannot guarantee that points will appear in a particular configuration, but effective communication rests on the assumption that points or objects appear for the subject in the same spatial framework. In Helmholtz's case the researcher and the subject were one and the same person. He would, therefore, have to communicate with himself about size by taking steps to ensure that the spatial framework permitted the same abstraction whether he compared the length of lines in the capacity of an experimenter or in the capacity of a subject.

Now consider a visual scene consisting of two objects which may or may not be located at different viewing distances. In this situation, we must assume an exact perception of the relative distances in order to tell how the spatial framework appears for the subject. Consider further, that we can make no assumption as to how the relative distances are perceived. Yet we can tell the subject to make a comparative statement of the objects with respect to size, and granted that he shares our understanding of the category size, he will in some way or another try to bring the objects into the same spatial framework. If he is not permitted to move, he will probably take recourse to some thinking activity by which he tries to establish an equality of spatial framework for the two objects. Since, however, the experimenter has not been able to assume an understanding of the spatial framework in the first instance, he can by no means confirm this activity. In other words, the experimenter cannot communicate to his subject about the size of objects in the field of view, and consequently he cannot decide whether a comparative judgement of size is an accurate one.

We shall now proceed to analyse some well-known experiments on the perception of size. One main task will be to decide whether the experimenter has provided a setting in which it is possible to communicate effectively about the size of certain objects.

8.3 Martius' size constancy experiment

In a size constancy experiment the subject is told to compare the length or the linear size of two objects which are placed at different viewing distances. Such a situation, we think, is not well suited to effective communication about size. Its shortcoming in this respect we shall make clear by an analysis of Martius' pioneering experiment (1889).

He made use of the following setting: two wooden rods were placed in front of the subject. The standard rod was first placed at a viewing distance of 50cm, and later at a viewing distance of only 20cm. However we shall consider only the first case. Three series of trials were undertaken. In the first series the standard had a length of 20cm, in the second a length of 50cm, and in the third a length of 100cm. Martius maintained that the visual context influenced the apparent length of the rods. Therefore, each rod was suspended by a thin thread in front of a uniformly coloured background. The rods were inspected monocularly.

For each length of the standard rod a series of comparison rods was provided. These rods differed by steps of 1cm, except for the rods which were prepared for the 20cm standard and which differed by steps of ½cm. The three series of trials were all performed twice: once with the comparison rod at a viewing distance of 300cm and once with this rod at a distance of 575cm.

The subject could transfer his fixation from the standard to the comparison rod by moving his eye horizontally to one side ("blosse Seitenwendung"). Although the background screens were located physically at different distances, they were separated only by a common border in the visual plane.

The comparison rods were presented for the subject in ascending and descending order. According to the instructions the subject should not attend to the "real" size of the rods. He should rather attend to their apparent size. First he was shown a comparison rod which was clearly longer or clearly shorter than the standard. The task of the subject was to state whether the rods appeared "equal" with respect to size or whether the comparison appeared "longer" or "shorter" than the standard. Martius soon discovered that the word "equal" was never applied to any one rod. This category was applied to a certain range of lengths. To limit this range the subject was permitted to say "a little shorter" and "a little longer". In cases of great uncertainty the subject was permitted to say "equal in the upward direction" ("gleich nach oben") or "equal in the downward direction" ("gleich nach unten"). The subject was aware of the direction of change.

In the beginning of an ascending or descending series the subject said he was quite sure about the size difference between the rods.

Gradually he became more uncertain and within a small range of series the clear impression of a size difference was said to be absent. Martius asserted that equality is nothing but the absence of difference, thus the length of the rod which most frequently was reported as "equal" was, according to this definition, taken as the length of subjective equality.

Two subjects (M.M. and G.M.) were used. These subjects matched the rods in six situations which differed in respect to length of standard and viewing distance to the farthest rod. Table 7 gives the "points of subjective equality" which were calculated from the reports of the subject.

Table 7   "Points of subjective equality" calculated from subjects' reports

Distance to farthest rod (cm)	Subject	Standard rod length (cm)		
		20	50	100
575	MM	21·67	57·62	106·62
	GM	21·92	59·00	110·00
300	MM	20·62	53·87	107·75
	GM	21·62	56·62	109·25

From Martius (1889).

The "points of subjective equality" do not differ much from the objective lengths of the standard rod. Martius also remarked that the adjusted length of the comparison rod increases little as the absolute distance to this rod increases. The difference between the adjusted length of the comparison rod and the objective length of the standard rod increases as the absolute length of the standard increases.

In this experiment the distance to the farthest rod may have been considered as the independent variable, and the subjective settings of this rod as the dependent variable. These variables could not be related in the form of a psychometric function, nor did the settings seem to depend much on the distance from the farthest rod.

The frequency of a "longer" or "shorter" report may also have served as the dependent variable, and this variable may have been related to the length of the comparison rod. But although Martius claimed to have controlled the position and movement of the subject's eye, it is not clear how the size variable could have been specified in terms of retinal projection. Like other researchers on perceptual constancy, however, Martius was not concerned with the measurement of sensory capacity. Rather he was concerned with the events or activities which were responsible for each of the size matches.

The problem to be discussed here is essentially the same as the one discussed in connection with Katz's and Hsia's experiments on whiteness constancy and Beck's experiments on illumination perception, namely, the problem of whether and in what respect the researcher can study the activities leading to a particular match.

In principle the researcher may relate a certain variability in the subjective settings to a variability in the external conditions. However, he can hardly account for the absolute value of a size match. This value will, to a large extent, depend on the subject's understanding. As we have already pointed out, the experimenter cannot investigate this understanding. However, he can specify his assumptions about it. Evidently it was difficult to instruct the subjects in an unambiguous way. Both subjects complained of difficulty in deciding when an equality of size was to be reported. Naturally, therefore, Martius refrained from specifying any assumptions about the subjects' understanding. However, he seemed to think that he could obtain independent evidence of this understanding by way of the single match value; a way of reasoning which we have found to be a most erroneous one.

This is not to say that instructions stressing either the "real" or the apparent size of the object are indifferent ones with respect to the subject's matching activities. Rather it makes a great difference to stress the apparent instead of the "real" size of the object — a point which apparently has been acknowledged by Martius. But regardless of the form of the instruction the experimenter is still bound to make mere assumptions concerning the subject's understanding. Thus Holaday (1933) and Gilinsky (1955), who set out to explore the effect of different instructions on the subjective matches have not contributed very much to theoretical innovations in the area.

Martius said that equality of size is nothing but a lack of difference. In our opinion, therefore, he implicitly and undeliberately maintained that for a certain range in the ascending and descending series it was impossible to communicate about relations of size. We think this assertion was a correct one. It was unlikely that the subject could observe two rods in the same spatial framework, and hence accurate decisions about relations of size would not be possible. In the beginning or end of a comparison series a certain communication about size would be possible, although this would not be an accurate one. The rods may now be said to have differed in a number of ways, and thus the subject may have been more apt to use a response category indicating difference. But in the critical range of the series very few differences were discernible due to a lack of unity in the spatial framework. In this range, therefore, communication may have broken down, and the calculated match value may just as well be considered as the value of maximum uncertainty.

In this way, constancy of size represents nothing but the breakdown of communication about size, rather than the maintenance of the identity of a certain object. But speculation has still leant towards the maintainance of such an identity. Thus Martius told the subject to consider the size of the rod from a position where it could be reached by one hand. This consideration would imply a registration of the distance to move into that position. In other words the subjects were indirectly told to take viewing distance into consideration. Another way of saying this would be that the subject had to take into consideration his own body position relative to the wooden rod. Naturally this could not be done by way of some abstraction. Thus Martius was able to conceive of the whole viewing situation as one, or that he was able to deal with the rod as separate and unique. These speculations are not only unfruitful, but are also erroneous ones since they cannot be defended on logical grounds. There is no way of referring to the unique rod independently of its appearance in the viewing context.

8.4   The "law of size constancy" and the "size constancy design".

The classic literature includes, in addition to Martius' work, a vast number of studies which are generally considered to be studies of size constancy. We may, for example, mention the studies of Grabke (1924), Katona (1925), Beyrl (1926), Cutler (1931), Holaday (1933) and Akishige (1937). However, it was Brunswik (1933) who formally introduced the term "size constancy" and later Boring (1940) and Holway and Boring (1941) who gave formal status to the "law of size constancy". We shall quote from the last work in order to present the precise formulation of this law:

> Accommodated objects which subtend equal visual angles are equal in apparent size. That is the law of visual angle. If the angle θs, subtended by a standard stimulus, is equal to the angle θc, subtended by a comparison stimulus, then

$$\tan \theta c \;=\; \tan \theta s \qquad\qquad (A)$$

> and

$$S_c \;=\; (D_c/D_s\, S_s) \qquad\qquad (B)$$

> where S_c is the linear size of the comparison object; S_s, the linear size of the standard; D_c, the distance from O to S_c; and D_s, the distance from O to the standard S_s. The standard size of the comparison stimulus (= apparent size of the standard) is equal to the size of the standard stimulus multiplied by the ratio of their respective distances.

The law of size constancy, on the other hand, states simply

$$S_c = S_s \qquad\qquad (C)$$

where S_c and S_s have the same meaning as in Eqn (B). Equation (C) expresses exactly the idea communicated to many investigators by the term *size constancy*. The size of the comparison stimulus is equal to the size of the standard irrespective of their distances from O.   (pp.22-23)

Although the writers used the phrase "irrespective of their distances from O", they seem to have disregarded the special case where $D_c = D_s$. They may have tacitly assumed that the "law of size constancy" applies only to objects which are placed at different viewing distances. In other words, complete size constancy will not only require that $S_c = S_s$, but also that $D_c/D_s = 1$. This requirement is evident also from the general design of size constancy experiments. In such experiments two objects, S_s and S_c, are placed at different viewing distances as shown by Fig. 17. Which of these objects is the nearest one may differ

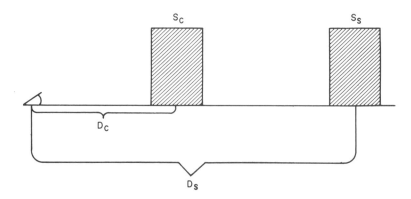

Figure 17   Relative distances (D) of objects in a size constancy experiment. S_c: comparison object; S_s: standard object.

from one experiment to another. The instructions may also differ a little, but in general the subject is told to compare the sizes of the two objects. Furthermore, the subject is told to remain in the same place, but he may assume a number of body positions when he makes his comparative judgements. He is also permitted to move his head and eyes freely. The size match may or may not be repeated with other viewing distances D_s and D_c, yet a single size match is considered to be sufficient for an assessment of the degree of size constancy.

Evidently, the size constancy design was in all essential ways the same as the design introduced by Martius. Therefore, the objections raised against Martius' experiment can generally also be raised against later studies, and "the law of size constancy" cannot be ascribed any theoretical importance. It seems likely that the researchers have consistently been concerned with a type of setting in which it may be difficult or impossible to communicate effectively about size. This type of setting follows from the requirement that $D_c/D_s \neq 1$. Therefore, we think that this research tradition has long ago ended in a blind alley.

8.5   Communication about size for psychophysical and non-psychophysical purposes

Psychophysical studies depend on certain required conditions for an effective communication about size. The effectiveness will be evaluated in view of psychophysical requirements, and the conditions are those which favour a certain understanding of the spatial framework. The conditions which favour a unification of the spatial framework are especially critical ones. The subject, we think, should be enabled to make an abstraction of size in such a way that he can communicate with the experimenter about slight differences in the lengths or extensions of visual targets. Thus communication in a psychophysical experiment always includes a number of *accurate decisions about the relative size* of objects in the field of view.

Under other conditions, i.e. conditions which do not favour a unification of the spatial framework, we can still communicate about the size of objects. If, however, these conditions do not permit communication about slight differences nor a specification of size with respect to the visual apparatus, they do not fulfil the basic prerequisites for a psychophysical study of visual size.

We can make statements about the relative size of familiar and everyday objects. Thus an object which is identified as a playing card will most certainly be judged as larger than an object which is identified as a stamp, regardless of whether both appear in the same spatial framework or not. If the spatial frameworks differ considerably, familiarity, particularly with respect to the function of objects, will be the critical condition for a communication about relative size. But again it should be stressed that fulfilment of this condition does not guarantee the type of communication which is essential in psycho-physical experiments.

Leibowitz and Harvey (1967) pointed out that in previous experiments of size constancy test objects such as rods, boxes, and cubes were used. In fact, such objects may exhibit a wide range of dimensions. Thus Leibowitz and Harvey questioned whether they were "representative of perception outside the laboratory", and they maintained that in everyday life one "views familiar objects which, from past experience are known to have either a definite size or a restricted range of possible sizes" (p.378).

Leibowitz and Harvey performed an experiment of size constancy in a setting which resembled an everyday viewing situation as far as possible. The prevailing conditions did not favour a unification of the spatial framework. Thus, in our opinion, communication in this situation could not well serve the purpose of a psychophysical experiment. It appears from their own description of the viewing situation, that familiarity with the test objects was the only basis for a communication about relative size:

> The test objects were human beings who stood in the middle of a mall on the university campus at distances of 340, 680, 1·020, 1·360 or 1·680ft from S. The mall is flanked on either side by rows of trees, paths, fences and buildings. At all times, there were a large number of people moving about in all directions on the mall. The subjects stood on the steps of the library facing the mall and viewed the comparison stimulus, a wooden rod (surveyer's levelling rod) 2 in wide, which protruded vertically from behind a wall 51ft from S and 90° to his left. The base of the visible portion of the rod was level with S's feet.   (p.379)

The matches were obtained by three different instructions: (1) The subjects were told to "judge which *appeared* larger, the human test object or the comparison rod". (2) The subjects were instructed "to match the physical height of the test objects, irrespective of distance". (3) The subjects were instructed to match in terms of visual angle".

The instructions differed with respect to their emphasis on familiarity with the test object. The first instruction implicitly told the subject to rely to a large extent on his familiarity with the particular class of test objects. The other instructions implicitly told the subject to rely less on this familiarity and more on some other knowledge or ability. It is not surprising, therefore, that the match values depended on these instructions.

Since the experimental setting did not satisfy critical conditions for the psychophysical study of visual size, one may ask whether the problem required use of standard and comparison objects in accordance with an ordinary psychophysical procedure. If the levelling rod had been left out, the subjects would have had to make explicit reference to either the metric system or a system of angular measurement in the eye in order to estimate the sizes of the test objects. Hence the performance of the subject would depend on abilities which are not ordinarily required in psychophysical judgements.

Brunswik (1944) studied the perception of 180 objects in a natural environment with no attempt to follow an ordinary psychophysical procedure. A number of subjects were told to estimate, in metric terms, the size of objects which happened to be placed in the immediate surroundings. Constancy was measured by correlating estimated size and objective size of the objects. A mean correlation coefficient of 0·994 was reported.

Since Brunswik's subjects could rely freely on their familiarity with the test objects, the result need not be a surprising one. The study, however, did not shed any light on the function of the visual system.

Brunswik believed that apparent size is a function of a number of "cues" such as parallax, convergence, linear perspective, etc. However, this belief must have been based on independent evidence, since neither parallax, nor convergence, nor any of the other "cues" were systematically varied in the study.

The ability to estimate the size of objects correctly was characterized by Brunswik as a "natural focussing of the perceptual system upon the distal stimulus variables". This representation was an awkward way of saying that the subjects made adequate use of their familiarity with the objects and the metric system. Yet the study did not serve as a test of some visual capacity, and therefore one could hardly conclude from Brunswik's data that the subjects had "gained command of a particular set of mediational cues and sensory instruments". A correct estimate of size need not imply a good achievement of visual cues; it need not imply anything about the function of the visual system. This point has already been made clear by Bolles and Bailey (1957):

> We would hold that much of the information used in judging the size of a familiar object comes from S's past experience with the object. We suggest that poor achievement of the visual cues to size is a reflection of the fact that S has relatively little need of such cues. The human adult has many habits of language and action which enable him to function more economically on the basis of the identification of the object rather than on the basis of the cues to size. The information from the visual cues in any particular situation may be redundant. In other words, he is not dependent upon immediate information *from* his environment but need only have information *about* his environment.   (p.222)

Bolles and Bailey reported a study where 5 male psychology students made two sets of size judgements. The objects whose sizes were judged were "pencils, light fixtures, furniture, books, articles of clothing, automobiles, lawn mowers, garden shed, print etc." In the first set of judgements the subject closed his eyes, and was told "the genus and species of the object in question". Then he was told to estimate the size, for instance, the diameter of the object. Afterwards, the subject was told to open his eyes and make a second estimate of the size of the object. Visual and non-visual estimates were correlated with measured size. The correlation quotients shown in Table 8 were reported.

Table 8 Correlation quotients

Judgement	Subjects					Mean
	1	2	3	4	5	
Visual	0·995	0·993	0·993	0·995	0·993	0·994
Non-visual	0·992	0·981	0·988	0·993	0·985	0·988

From Bolles and Bailey (1957).

As shown in Table 8 the subjects were able to attain essentially the same degree of size constancy with or without visual information. In 53% of the cases the subjects were unable to improve their estimates when they were allowed to look at the objects. Thus in very few cases did the subject get additional information by observing the object visually.

In this experiment the subject received adequate verbal information about the object. Probably the subject may have had some specific realization of the type of objects, and indirectly, he may even have got some knowledge about size. According to Bolles and Bailey ". . . this assertion is not unreasonable in that size is one of the basic criteria of classification of things in our world, one of the ways in which we know things. The word *cigarette* connotes (among other things) the size of cigarettes. Thus if a thing is a foot long, it can't be a cigarette, and conversely. If a person is able to identify an object according to some classification, he has delimited its size" (p.225).

Evidently, size constancy may also be said to mean a definition of communication about size in the type of situation mentioned by Leibowitz and Harvey, and by Bolles and Bailey. In other words, constancy is procured to the extent that communication about size is an adequate and effective one. On these grounds sensory mechanisms are out of the question, and we have taken a big step away from the possible issue of insensitivity to certain forms of stimulation.

Yet researchers tend to look upon size constancy as a visual phenomenon. The use of the term has not been made clear. Thus we can say that the communication about constancy which has taken place among researchers in psychology has not been effective; problems of psychophysics and possible problems of communication and thinking have not been kept apart in the literature of psychophysics.

8.6 The size–distance invariance hypothesis

Most researchers who have been concerned with problems of space in perception have assumed a valid relationship between apparent size, apparent distance and visual angle. It was, however, Kilpatrick and Ittelson (1953) who first set out to specify this relationship.

In trigonometry the relationship between the size, S, and distance, D, of an object subtending an angle α at an observation point O can be expressed as

$$\tan \alpha \ = \ \frac{S \cos \delta}{D - S \sin \delta} \tag{1}$$

where d is the angular deviation from the vertical, or more simply the inclination of S (Fig. 18). Given that the angle at O is sufficiently

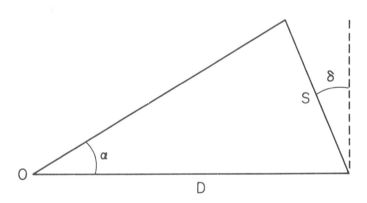

Figure 18 Geometrical representation of an object S, and distance D from an observation point O. d: angular deviation of object from the vertical.

small, $\tan \alpha \ = \ \alpha$, and if $\delta \ = \ 0$ (Fig. 18), Eqn (1) reduces to

$$\alpha \ = \ \frac{S}{D} \tag{2}$$

From this equation the following statements are implied:

(a) When the angle is given, size and distance vary proportionally.
(b) When angle and distance are given, size is uniquely defined.

(c) When angle and size are given, distance is uniquely defined.
(d) When size is given, angle and distance vary inversely.
(e) When distance is given, angle and size vary proportionally.
(Kilpatrick and Ittelson, op cit. pp.223-224)

One may question whether the same rules also apply to apparent size and distance. Thus Kilpatrick and Ittelson maintained that "in some cases equation (2) seems quite accurately to describe the relationship between apparent size, apparent distance and visual angle". Granted that all implications of the equation involve perceptual events, these implications may be summarized in the following statement:

A retinal projection or visual angle of given size determines a unique ratio of apparent size to apparent distance.
(Kilpatrick and Ittelson, op. cit., p.224)

This statement has generally been taken as the formulation of the size-distance invariance hypothesis. It should be stressed, however, that Kilpatrick and Ittelson reasoned from a rigid object geometry, and that they therefore assumed a tangential function relating visual angle to the ratio of apparent size to apparent distance. Yet their statement, quoted above, is compatible with a number of functions relating visual angle to a size-distance ratio, and hence researchers have disagreed on which data will support and which will contradict the hypothesis.

According to Epstein and Landauer (1969) the invariance hypothesis requires that one of the two properties, size or distance, be judged as constant if the other is judged to vary in relation to visual angle. In their experiments magnitude estimations of size and distance under conditions of reduced viewing did not conform to this requirement. Their subjects judged an electroluminescent disc of constant physical size to vary in both size and distance when presented at different physical distances. Moreover discs of different physical sizes were judged as different in both size and distance when presented at the same distance as the standard (115cm). In other words, both properties seemed to depend on visual angle.

Figure 19 shows the mean estimates of size and distance as a function of visual angle in Epstein and Landauer's two experiments (see also legend of the figure).

Gogel (1971), however, maintained a more general form of the hypothesis according to which the ratio of apparent size (S') to apparent distance (D') is a monotonic increasing function of the visual angle. Thus

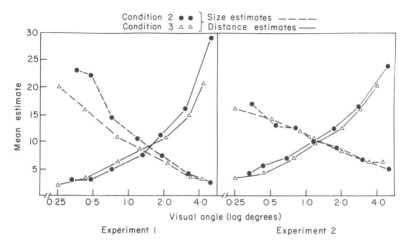

Figure 19   Mean estimates of size and distance in Epstein and Landauer's experiment 1 and 2. In experiment 1 half of the subjects supplied all the size estimates before any distance estimates were solicited. The remaining half gave distance estimates first. In experiment 2 the subject estimated both the size and distance of the comparison object before he proceeded to another object. Condition 2: physical size of comparison object constant while viewing distance varied. Condition 3: distance of comparison object constant while physical size varied (from Epstein Landauer, 1969).

$$S'/D' \; = \; k\alpha \qquad (3)$$

where k is a subject constant. When a variable disc (e) and a standard disc (f) are presented simultaneously, as in the study by Epstein and Landauer, it follows that

$$\frac{S'e/S'f}{D'e/D'f} \; = \; \frac{\alpha e}{\alpha f} \qquad (4)$$

This equation can be applied to Epstein and Landauer's data, since in their experiment the size and distance of the standard was designated 10 and the subject was told to assign numbers to the variable relative to the standard. Thus $S'e/S'f$ and $D'e/D'f$ could be obtained by dividing mean size and distance estimates by 10. It was then shown that

$$\frac{S'e/S'f}{D'e/D'f} \; = \; \left(\frac{\alpha e}{\alpha f}\right)^{n} \qquad (5)$$

In agreement with this equation the general form of the invariance hypothesis was written

$$S'D' \;=\; k\alpha^n \tag{6}$$

If no restriction is stated with respect to the value of the exponent n, most data which have been collected in the area will tend to conform to the hypothesis. Counter-examples will be rare. Gogel just pointed out a mathematical fact that Epstein and Landauer's data *were* consistent with this form of the hypothesis.

Apparently the disagreement between Epstein and Landauer on the one hand and Gogel on the other, was one of form. Hence we may ask what is the most correct or adequate formulation of the size–distance invariance hypothesis. Once agreement is reached on a particular form, it should also be possible to tell which data are consistent with and which data are at variance with the hypothesis. Actually one can specify very few data at variance with the statement of the hypothesis suggested by Kilpatrick and Ittelson (p.134). More data can be specified at variance with the hypothesis when written in the form of Eqn (6). Still more contradictory data can be specified if the hypothesis is said to require that only one of the two properties (S' or D') can vary at a time when visual angle varies.

In short, the need for a formal qualification of the original statement suggested by Kilpatrick and Ittelson is quite clear. But in which direction this qualification should be made is not clear.

The various formulations of the invariance hypothesis assert that apparent size and apparent distance are related. Thus retinal size cannot determine apparent size independent of apparent distance and vice versa. In saying that a visual angle determines a unique ratio of apparent size to apparent distance, one is in fact stressing this point. The perception of size means the perception of size at a distance. Yet we may ask what it means to say that apparent size and apparent distance are related.

Epstein and Landauer concluded on the basis of their data (shown in Fig. 19), that apparent size and apparent distance did not depend on each other under conditions of reduced viewing. These properties were not directly related. In no "case does one judgement depend on the other judgement. The size and distance judgements are independent products of two ways of processing relative visual angle, . . ." (p.272) In Gogel's view, however, Eqn (6) is an adequate statement of a valid relationship between apparent size, apparent distance and visual angle, and since Epstein and Landauer's data conformed to this equation, the two researchers could not be said to have provided "support for the conclusion that a retinal size can determine a perceived size independent of perceived distance" (p.93).

Since the data presentation was a clear and unequivocal one, and since no objections were raised against the procedures, one may ask how it was possible to disagree over the question of whether the two types of estimates were related.

As pointed out earlier, Epstein and Landauer presumed that apparent size and apparent distance are related only if the one property is judged to vary while the other is judged as constant. A correct perception of a rigid object changing distance and a correct perception of an object changing size while it remains at a constant distance will give rise to such judgements. Most probably, therefore, such judgements are considered as duly related because they are consistent with the knowledge of a particular object, or put in other words, judgements of size and distance are related if they can be said to apply to one and the same object. The invariance hypothesis is a simple statement of which judgements are consistent with the knowledge of one object undergoing a certain change or displacement in the field of view.

Since Epstein and Landauer purported to consider only certain types of object events, they have tacitly assumed a specific form of the invariance hypothesis. They have taken for granted that there are only the two possibilities, an object of constant size changing distance and an object at a constant distance changing size, the ratio of apparent size to apparent distance should be related to visual angle by a tangential function. On the assumption that all estimates apply to one and the same physical object, a different function can be described if that object is an elastic one changing size at the same time as its distance is changed.

In our opinion Gogel did not make clear the nature of the invariance hypothesis. This hypothesis does not merely state that the ratio of apparent size to apparent distance is duly related to variations in visual angle. Rather this ratio is related to visual angle in a way which is consistent with the changes and displacements of a particular object in the field of view. Therefore one has to agree on the object events before one can decide whether a certain set of data supports or contradicts the invariance hypothesis. A formal specification of this hypothesis makes sense only in relation to the assumption of the changes and displacements of a particular object.

Epstein and Landauer assumed certain types of object changes and displacements, hence the invariance hypothesis would have to be formulated in accordance with these changes and events. A more general form of the invariance hypothesis, for example Eqn (6) above, would not adequately represent the research problem raised by Epstein and Landauer. Gogel's discussion of their data was irrelevant.

We still maintain, however, that the statement suggested by Kilpatrick and Ittelson needs a formal qualification. This statement is too general. At the same time it should be stressed that there is no single qualification of this statement which is the correct one. Consequently, we should not speak of *the* invariance hypothesis, but depending on the type of object and taking object events into account one can speak of *several forms* of the invariance hypothesis.

One can, of course, pose the question, implicitly raised by Epstein and Landauer, of whether it is possible for an observer to estimate the changes in a solid angle of light from an electroluminescent disc in accordance with certain types of changes and displacements of a specifiable object. One is, in fact, then asking whether an observer can be correctly informed about a certain object in a certain set of viewing conditions. Epstein and Landauer answered this question in the negative.

We shall therefore consider some methodological aspects of their experiments. In both experiments visual angle was changed in discrete steps. Furthermore, the subject was told to compare two discs with respect to size and distance. In Experiment 1 all judgements of either size or distance were completed before any judgement of the other properties was made. In Experiment 2 each variable was judged with respect to both size and distance before another disc was presented for the subject. That is to say the two judgements were made as nearly simultaneously as possible. Yet these judgements were still made separately even in Experiment 2, and the object referred to in one judgement did not need to be the object referred to in the other. The procedure did not guarantee a "size at a distance" judgement. Therefore, Epstein and Landauer's conclusion may have a restricted relevance.

Let us consider the possible outcome of an experiment in which the visual angle is varied continuously rather than in steps. Instead of giving quantitative estimates, the subject may now be told to give qualitative statements of size and distance changes. Thus he may be told to judge whether the disc is (1) approaching and becoming bigger; (2) receding and becoming bigger; (3) approaching and becoming smaller; (4) receding and becoming smaller; (5) increasing in size while remaining at the same distance; (6) decreasing in size while remaining at the same distance; (7) approaching while maintaining a constant size, or (8) receding while maintaining a constant size. The question is which of these response alternatives will be chosen in connection with an increase of visual angle, and which alternatives will be chosen in connection with a decrease of the visual angle.

According to Epstein and Landauer we should still get a size-distance paradox, i.e. alternative (1) should be chosen in connection with an increase of visual angle, while alternative (4) should be chosen in connection with a decrease of visual angle (cf. Fig. 19).

We believe, however, that response alternatives (7) and (8) are the most likely ones to be chosen (see, for example, Johansson, 1964, transformation pattern I). Symmetrical and continuous changes of a solid angle of light will not give rise to a size–distance paradox.

Any judgement of change requires a constant frame of reference. In normal conditions of viewing other objects or surfaces may serve as a frame of reference. Under reduced conditions of viewing, and particularly if only one electroluminescent disc is present in the field of vision, changes can be clearly comprehended only if they are seen as transformations of an invariant — the latter may be serving as a kind of reference. Rigidity or constancy of size may provide for a kind of framework that makes a clear understanding of displacement in depth possible. Other changes can be registered only if other invariants are introduced to the situation.

In general, therefore, statements on the relationship between visual angle, apparent size and apparent distance should include a specification of the viewing conditions such as the type of change in the solid angle of light stimulating the eye (continuous vs step-wise change). At the same time it should be emphasized that such statements only serve to define the set of response data that are valid ones given a certain instruction. Other data which are at variance with a postulated relationship between visual angle, apparent size and apparent distance should be discarded by the researcher. Such a relationship is implied by the task to be performed by the subject; it cannot therefore be said to constitute an empirical problem in the psychology of perception.

8.7 The invariance hypothesis, "size constancy" and Emmert's Law

Several researchers have asked whether "size constancy" can be deduced from the invariance hypothesis. We have argued that an invariance hypothesis is a shorthand statement of which judgements are consistent with an object undergoing certain changes and displacements in the environment. Since an invariance hypothesis thus presupposes a particular object, it also presupposes — in a sense — "constancy".

It has been customary, however, to explain "size constancy" by assuming a function which is a direct implication of a certain form of the invariance hypothesis: If the organism is correctly informed about distance, "constancy" will follow if it also can be shown that apparent size is a joint function of visual angle and apparent distance.

Kilpatrick and Ittelson's statement of the invariance hypothesis can be written

$$\alpha = \frac{S'}{D'}$$

Then we have

$$S' = \alpha D'$$

which is commonly used as an "explanation" of "size constancy". If apparent distance D' is substituted by physical distance D we can write

$$S' = \alpha D$$

This equation states "the principles of size constancy", since it shows that visual angle varies with distance when apparent size S' is constant (Boring, 1940).

In the literature we often find that Emmert's Law (1881) is related to "size constancy" and the invariance hypothesis. Certainly Emmert's Law is a special case of invariance, but it may be questioned whether it is just a corollary of the invariance hypothesis or not.

Let us examine what Emmert said and did. It was Professor Zehender, the editor of the *Klinische Monatsblätter für Augenheilkunde*, who asked Emmert why the size of the entoptic after-image is different in size from the size of the object which generated the after-image. Zehender pointed out that a distance could be found at which the entoptic after-image is the same size as the object. He indicated that ocular accommodation might produce "an idea of distance" which determined the size of the after-image. Zehender thus formulated the problem which led to the now well-known work by Emmert. In this work the following experiment is described.

Screens were placed at different distances, i.e. 0·5, 1, 2 and 4m from the eyes. Black squares were attached to the screen. Emmert fixated one of these squares, and after a period of time looked at another more distant screen on which he noticed the after-image of the square. Thus he could "place" the after-image beside another square of known physical size. In this way he could compare the size of the former with the size of the latter.

According to Emmert the experiment showed that the linear size of the after-image increased proportionally with distance and that the area of the square increased with the square of the distance. Figure 20 shows the geometry of physical optics underlying Emmert's law. We have reproduced the figure from Boring's work and we have used his terms, since these appeared in the discussion of Emmert's Law following Boring's well-known notes compiled in 1940.

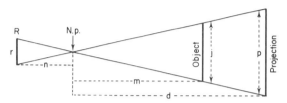

Figure 20 Geometrical relationships expressed by Emmert's law. N.p.: nodal point; r: linear size of retinal image; n: distance from nodal point to retina, R; j: linear size of object at distance, m, from the eye; p: linear size of projected after-image at distance, d, (from Boring, 1940).

According to the geometrical relationships which are illustrated on the figure, we may write

$$j \; : \; p \; = \; m \; : \; d$$

which says that,

$$p \; = \; \frac{j \times d}{m}$$

With respect to the area of the after-image, the formula should be written

$$p \; = \; \left(\frac{j \times d}{m}\right)^2$$

Emmert now turned to Zehender's problem and asked if the invariance could be explained by an "idea of distance". Remember that the latter was assumed to depend on the accommodation of the lens. Emmert, therefore, paralysed ocular accommodation with hyoscine, and he found that the size of the after-image still increased with distance of the projection ground. Then he refuted the hypothesis of Zehender and concluded that "the size changes of the projected image are not psychical but a merely physical phenomenon" (p.450).

It must be emphasized that the equation $p = (j \times d)/m$ is similar to Euclid's principle, since Euclid in his optics established the same geometrical relation between visual angle, object size and distance

(Hirschberg, 1898). Emmert showed (1), that this principle can be applied to the size of the after-image, and (2) that the size of the after-image is a "purely physical phenomenon".

Boring assumed that Emmert had been concerned with the apparent size of the after-image. Therefore, he said that p (Fig. 21) could be substituted for $s =$ the apparent size of p. In this way Boring (1940) ventured to show that Emmert's Law implied "size constancy".

However, the substitution of p by s turned out to be highly debatable. Young (1950) argued that we could only speak about the apparent size of an object, not of an after-image. He wrote:

> We have an apparent size of an object in space which gives rise to a retinal image and an apparent size. In the case of the projected after-image there is no object in space to give rise to a retinal image and, therefore, in the common meaning of the term apparent size of the projected after-image. To say that we could, would be to say that the after-image projected on the screen 3m away is an object which gives rise to a second retinal image and an apparent size.
>
> (Young, 1950, p.278)

It follows that the size of an after-image should not be treated as a psychological concept. Thus, according to Young, Emmert's Law had bearing only on non-psychological, geometrical–optical relationships. Boring, he said, had presented a wrong interpretation of this law.

Young did not seem to win the argument, since among other researchers it was still considered pertinent to speak about the apparent or perceived size of an after-image. Edwards (1950) stressed that an after-image has both a physical and an apparent size, and that these should be kept clearly apart by the research worker. He suggested that apparent size be defined in the following way:

> It (apparent size) is best defined in terms of comparative judgements by an 0, in which he compares one object with another located anywhere in the visual field. A special case of this comparative judgement is that in which the two objects are set side by side at the distance, provided 0 continues to compare visual extensions and does not resort to the observation of coincidences between the boundaries of the object.
>
> (p.607)

As to the definition of objective or physical size, he wrote:

> The second notion of size is based on the operation of observing two or more lines on one subject as corresponding with certain lines on another

object which is next to or on top of the first. In the special case in which the first object is the object to be measured the second object is a measuring instrument, and the two are exactly or approximately in the same plane. This is the conventional operation that measures and that therefore defines physical size.   (pp.607–608)

According to these definitions Edwards suggested two methods for measuring the size of the after-image: (a) the indirect method by employing a comparison object which has a different position in the visual field than the after-image; (b) direct method which requires that the after-image is superimposed on other objects in the plane of projection. The indirect method was supposed to measure apparent size, whereas the direct method was supposed to measure physical size.

The two methods described above have been used by Hastorf and Kennedy (1957) and Crookes (1959). The former writers concluded that the controversy concerning the relationship of Emmert's Law to "size constancy" is primarily a matter of measurement. Crookes emphasized, as did Edwards, that different kinds of size were measured with the two methods.

In a study by Weintraub and Gardner (1970) the direct method was refined and developed into what they called a "null-match" procedure: the subject may, for instance, bracket the right and left edges of the after-image by adjusting two pin-point spotlights, or he may adjust the distance of an identically shaped card until its outlines just surround the after-image. In both cases the subject is in a position to report about the coincidences of certain lines or boundaries in order to determine what is an equivalent physical size. For each subject Weintraub and Gardner's Experiment I. "The plot of adju physical distance (D) as a function of equivalent physical size $(S$ closely approximated a straight line." Thus the proportic involved by Emmert's Law was fully confirmed by a "null-n procedure. The point is that this proportionality is likely to be whenever the same procedure is used, for the "null-match" per in this experiment was not dependent on the perceived distanc plane of projection.

To emphasize this point, Weintraub and Gardner perfc second experiment. A positive after-image in the form of tilted at 45° was induced by an electric photo-flash. A card, on a track, could be moved to an from before the subject outlines just surrounded the after-image.

. . . only the surface of the card was visible to a single eye, screen blocking the rest of the field. Mounted on each c replica of a postage stamp, half, normal, or double size. It was assumed that if the observer accepted the stamps as authentic, then judgements presumed to assess perceived after-image size would be influenced by stamp size while null-match settings would remain unaffected.

(pp.47–48)

The stimulus card was placed to the left of the subject. A size-adjustment device consisting of two black metal vanes mounted on a traverse rod on a white background was placed in front of the right eye. The background was seen as an equilateral diamond (a square tilted at 45°), i.e. of the same form as the after-image and the stimulus card. By way of a cord-and-pulley system the subject could change the size of the equilateral diamond.

An after-image was induced in the left eye of the subject. When the strobe light was removed, the subject could see the stimulus card with his left eye, and the distance of this card was adjusted until its outlines just surrounded the borders of the positive after-image. Thereafter the left eye of the subject was covered, and the right eye uncovered. The subject was told to adjust the size of the white diamond until its size matched the size of the after-image "as held in memory".

> After an initial adjustment, he was allowed to take one final look at the stimulus card; if he requested it, his right eye was covered and left eye uncovered for 5 sec, whereupon the eye coverings were reversed. Another AI was induced every 5 min.
>
> (Weintraub and Gardner, 1970, p.49)

The results of the "null-match" settings for each subject as well as for the entire group showed that physical distance and equivalent physical size of AI could be related by a linear plot as in Experiment I. It was shown also that these relationships held independent of the size of the postage stamp. In other words, the stamp replicas which were introduced as falsified cues did not effect the "null-match" settings. On the other hand, these replicas influenced the vane settings of the diamond size. "For any given stamp size vane setting increased with physical stimulus size. More important, however, the three separate functions that emerged indicated that vane settings increased as postage stamp size decreased" (pp.50–51).

Weintraub and Gardner concluded that two relationships can be formulated regarding the size of projected after-images. The first they called Emmert's Law of retinal size — an extension of optical geometry. The second they called Emmert's principle of perceived size which was allegedly linked to the classic issue of "size constancy".

The law of retinal size was confirmed by a "null-match" procedure, whereas this procedure was inadmissible for assessing perceived size.

As long as light radiates along straight lines and as long as the assumptions underlying the optical geometry of Emmert's Law is correct, the "null-match" procedure will necessarily confirm this law. Emmert may be said to have applied an approximation to this procedure. It should be stressed that the "null-match" procedure is almost the same as the procedure described by Helmholtz for the study of visual size. It, therefore, rests on the same type of specifications mentioned in Section 8.1., and the results obtained by this procedure depend on the laws relating rotations of "the visual globe" to "the field of vision".

The vane settings in Weintraub and Gardner's experiment may be said to constitute some form of indirect method. It requires that the AI is treated as an object positioned in space. The adjustment of the white diamond depended on a number of factors held in the memory of the subject. Hence the preconditions of the vane settings were essentially unknown, i.e. these settings rested on conditions that could not be specified by the researcher.

Apparent distance, it can be said, constituted one of the preconditions for the vane settings. It was, therefore, important that apparent distance remained the same for all subjects. At the same time apparent distance was at issue in the experiment, and since the subject was invited to treat the AI as an object positioned in space he is likely to take distance into account. Since distance was not specified in the introduction, the researcher could not make any assumptions about apparent distance. Nor could he take the vane setting as an indication of apparent distance; that is to say that the validity of the indirect method should be questioned.

In our opinion, therefore, the direct method is the only meaningful one. The presuppositions underlying this method can be made explicit by the researcher — they are concerned with the subject's perception of distance: in bracketing edges or in observing the coincidences of lines or points the subject is supposed to either disregard or to take for granted that the edges or lines are located at the same distance. On the other hand, the indirect method does not rest on particular assumptions regarding the subject's perception of the spatial framework. Thus it is difficult to tell in which sense we can speak of this method as a psychophysical or psychological method. In any case it is difficult to tell which is the problem or subject matter of this method. In connection with the use of the indirect method, therefore, "perceived size" should be considered as an undefined term.

Nevertheless, the researchers may speculate on possible reasons for the validity of a relationship between distance and size of the after-image as stated by Emmert's Law. One may, for example, emphasize the point that *relative* size of the retinal after-image and the retinal image of the background changes with distance. However, the change in relative size does not explain Emmert's Law unless one makes the assumption that the subject has a certain knowledge of the background, i.e. he should know that the background consists of rigid and stationary objects. Such a knowledge or understanding of the background, however, forms the minimal conditions for demonstrating empirically the valid relationship between distance and size of the after-image. But a statement of the prerequisites for the use of the method can hardly be said to provide an explanation for the relationship or law demonstrated by way of this method. Therefore, the fact that the relative size of the retinal after-image and the retinal image of the background changes with distance can hardly serve as an explanation of Emmert's Law.

9

Form

9.1 A point of view concerning perceiving activities related to form

Perception of form is probably mediated by several modalities. Thus we may be said to perceive form in touch and hearing as well as in vision. Yet form does not necessarily involve the same type of perceptual activity in these cases. It should be stressed, however, that form *per se* can hardly be considered as an intra-modal aspect in the same sense as light and colour.

This is the reason why it has been difficult to develop a psychophysics of form. It has, in other words, not been possible to define a stimulus of form in the same way as one has defined a stimulus of hue and a stimulus of pitch.

The first comprehensive studies of form, therefore, were qualitative ones. These studies belong to the Gestalt era in psychology. We have still much to learn from Wertheimer's and Koffka's early studies of form. Present-day discussions of form perception will have to take account of some of their principles and theoretical statements.

Form, they said, always constitutes an organized whole. Emergence of the whole is governed by principles of organization, the most important of which is the principle of "Prägnanz". It states that elements of the visual field are organized into the most stable units which create a minimum of stress. "Psychological organization will always be as 'good' as the prevaling conditions allow" (Koffka, 1935, p.110). Prägnanz was generally characterized by regularity, symmetry, simplicity, inclusiveness, continuity and unification. The laws of similarity, proximity, closure and good continuation were included under the principle of Prägnanz or "good" form.

Some would say that a new era in the study of form perception began under the influence of information theory at the beginning of the fifties. During these years psychologists still attached importance to the Gestalt principle of Prägnanz, but they tended to look upon it merely as an aesthetic one. It did not define "good figure" in operational terms, and moreover, it did not explain the perception of form. By the works of Attneave (1954) and Attneave and Arnoult (1956) Prägnanz was also said to be concerned with the economy and accuracy of information transmission. Attneave started the new era by violating the Gestalt principle that a form or figure as a whole cannot be analysed into separate parts, i.e. he broke up the form into a mosaic of elements. His aim was allegedly to introduce a quantitative approach, and thus to make possible a psychophysics of form.

The elements of the mosaic were given signs according to a specified figure: a bottle of ink (black, here stippled) on a table (brown, here hatched) in a blank 50 × 80 matrix of cells (see Fig. 21). The subject

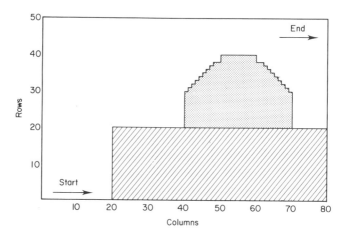

Figure 21   Figure in a matrix of cells used in Attneave's work (from Attneave, 1954).

was told to guess the colour of each cell by starting from the lower left-hand corner and completing one row at a time. The greatest number of errors was made at the points where the contour change direction most sharply. On this basis Attneave concluded that information about the figure was concentrated at these points. The question is whether the task as presented to the subject had something to do with figure or form perception. Green and Courtis (1966), in a thorough analysis of Attneave's work, answered this question in the negative. In general, an application of information theory requires an alphabet of signs with known and constant probabilities of occurrence. Such an alphabet of signs can hardly be agreed upon in cases of everyday figure perception. Green and Courtis stated that:

> Information theory is concerned with transition probabilities, while perception, whether of figures or patterns, is essentially non-sequential, or at least non-linear.   (1966, p.30)

To meet the main requirements for the application of information theory Attneave fortuitously overlooked or ignored this characteristic of form perception. In the opinion of Green and Courtis he thus happened to impose a set of conditions which were "entirely arbitrary, producing artifacts pertaining only to those conditions, rather than leading to the formulation of general principles" (p.13).

To emphasize this criticism Green and Courtis presented a number of counter-demonstrations. In one of these they showed that in the figure guessing task, errors concentrate at the corners only when a linear scanning procedure was used. When successive guesses were dispersed over the whole area in a random manner, errors did not accrue at the corners.

Furthermore, Green and Courtis reported a few other demonstrations together with a presentation of cartoon-drawing techniques to show that no parts of a physical display will necessarily contain more information than other parts. They asserted, for instance, that corners are easily predictable once information is available about other parts of the contour. Certainly, we may recognize a figure or an object by its distinctive features, and such features may be said to carry a great deal of information about the figure. The problem is how distinctive features can be defined: they need not necessarily be corners, vertices or other parts of a contour. Green and Courtis mentioned in this connection, a most illustrative example:

> . . . to discriminate between a set of snakes, it would be necessary to rely on such cues as length or girth or position of head in relation to the coils. These cues, be it noted, are not even counter cues in the simple sense; they are cues based on spatial relationships.   (1966, p.26)

In form perception, therefore, distinctive features will vary depending on the task and characteristics of the perceiver. Thus

> . . . the locus of information will be a function of the task and will change with it — not a fixed attribute completely inherent in the figure itself.   (1966, p.28)

Green and Courtis suggested that emphasis is laid on the process of perceiving, rather than the physical display. We agree with them, but we think that to use the term "process" may be unclear in this connection. Instead we prefer to speak about *the activity of perceiving*.

Actually, the discussion may be said to hve been concerned with a system of reference for the perception of form. Unfortunately this discussion does not seem to be followed up in the modern literature. Rather it is tacitly assumed that information processing of form (for a review of the literature see Zusne (1970) and Forgus and Melamed (1976)) can be studied within a metric system of reference. For example, specification of the information load of a figure (Arnoult, 1960) and the distinctive features elaborated over time by a perceiver (E. J. Gibson, 1969) are based on such a system. Even the schemata in a prototype theory of form perception are entirely specifiable with reference to a metric system.

If emphasis is laid on the activity of perceiving rather than characteristics of a physical display, we must introduce a different system of reference. A point of departure must then be taken in the behavioural possibilities of the organism in relation to a certain environment. Biological restrictions as well as contextual framework do, of course, influence the behavioural possibilities. Therefore we cannot define form, or the perceiving of form, independent of context.

On this basis, and at the present stage of theoretical development in biological psychology, it becomes difficult to formulate a research problem in the area. Thus we have no rationale at present for saying that the perceiving of form constitutes a separate type of perceptual activities. But the need for another system of reference is clear enough. An analysis of the literature in the area will show logical inconsistencies that cannot be overcome unless one introduces an entirely different system of reference for the perceiving of form. Such inconsistencies have particularly appeared in (1) studies of the complexity of forms, and (2) studies of the relation of form and orientation.

9.2 Simplicity v. complexity of form

A principle of the simplicity of a given form has been advanced in modern psychophysical literature. This principle is frequently being compared with the gestalt principle of Prägnanz: a "good" figure is also a simple figure. Simplicity is a matter of degree, and the complexity of a figure is considered as the converse of simplicity.

In general, complexity is said to be defined by the number of elements of a form or, in the case of a single figure, the number of directional changes in the contour. Using a different system of reference we may ask if perhaps complexity could be defined from the number of behavioural possibilities resulting from the figure.

Both definitions, however, need some qualification. Consider, for example the reversible-perspective pictures of Fig. 22. Each row of

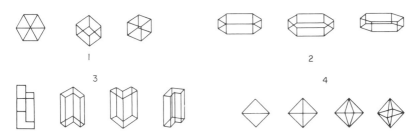

Figure 22   Different views of an object in (1)–(4) arranged in order of increasing three-dimensional appearance in each row (from Hochberg, 1978).

pictures can be described either as an arrangement of flat forms or as three-dimensional objects. Hochberg (1978) said that:

> The simpler any 2 D arrangement, the more we should tend to see that picture in 2 D; conversely, the more complex the 2 D arrangement, the more we tend to see it as 3 D (since the 3 D form must be the same and, therefore, of identical simplicity, for all views of any object). As the *number of angles*, the *number of continuous lines*, and the *average number of different angles* increase in each pattern, the tendency to see the flat arrangement decreases and the apparent tridimensionality of the form increases, although there are almost certainly other factors as well that we have not yet found.   (p.89)

Hochberg did not draw the further conclusion of this example, namely that complexity can only be estimated for a certain identity of form. Thus number of angles, number of continuous lines, and average number of different angles may determine the complexity of a *defined form*. This means that the question of what form is seen is logically prior to the question of the complexity of the form. Once a pattern is identified as a triangle one can judge its complexity. Perhaps we can also estimate the complexity of a letter, but we can hardly compare the complexity of the former with the complexity of the latter unless we make use of an arbitrary frame of reference in which the whole question of the perception of form is ruled out. Therefore, one cannot say that complexity is determined by number of elements without referring, at the same time, to some form identity. It may also be inadvisable to state that complexity is determined by the number of behavioural possibilities in relation to the figure.

Modern writers tend to think that we can compare the complexity of the forms of different objects in a direct way. Thus Forgus and Melamed (1976) maintained that a human face is more complex than a bull's eye because we can identify more features in the former — namely, hairline, eyes, nose, mouth and curvature of head — while the latter has only one feature which repeats itself. Certainly, if you had to tell someone to construct the two patterns, you would have to give more information in the case of the human face than in the case of the bull's eye. But although drawing must be related to the perception of form, one cannot merely equate the two activities. Hence the information needed to draw a pattern is not the same as the information needed to perceive a pattern.

When you instruct someone to draw, or otherwise consruct a form, you make use of a terminology and a system of reference which has turned out to be a useful one in an educational setting. The same system of reference may be applicable for the writing of computer programs for pattern recognition, but we see no reason why this system also should be applicable to the description of perceptual activities related to form.

Evidently, Forgus and Melamed assumed that the identity and complexity of a form can both be described in terms based on a metric system of reference. The identity of a form, they presumed, could be defined by reference to a spatial relationship, such as the relationship between angles or the relationship of one part to another. Thus a *square* is different from a *rectangle* because in the former the ratio of one side to another is equal to 1, whereas in the latter this ratio is different from 1.

Consequently, the identity of a form should be defined once the spatial relationship between its parts is defined. But forms sometimes appear ambiguous. Consider, for example, the form shown in Fig. 23. It may be seen in either of two ways, which might be said to constitute different form identities. Yet the spatial relationship between parts of the display remains the same.

There is also the possibility that mirror inversion of a form may influence its identity. For some observers at least d and b may be treated as different forms. In some cases, therefore, form seems to depend on locus and orientation in the behavioural space.

Thus a metric system of reference is an insufficient, and possibly an inadequate one in matters concerning the perceiving of form. One cannot define the identity of a form merely in terms of a metric system; one has at least to take into consideration some response characteristics of the observer. At the same time complexity of form must be evaluated in relation to some form identity.

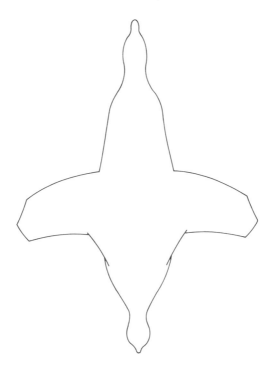

Figure 23 An ambiguous figure.

On these grounds we do not think that the prospects for modern research in the area are good. Research problems which are formulated in terms of the simplicity or complexity of forms need not necessarily be fruitful ones.

There is only one reasonable way of talking about the complexity of a form, namely the degree to which a certain behavioural or interactional possibility is a fixed or defined one. In the natural environment of many species certain figures, silhouettes, or objects may serve as innate releasers of fixed action patterns. For animals, therefore, these figures must be simple ones. On the same ground we can say that a human face need not be more complex than a bull's eye. For an infant, in a particular neurological state, the human face may constitute a simple figure, whereas other figures of perfect symmetry and regularity may be extremely complex ones.

Behavioural or interactional possibilities, however, soon become moulded by culture. Certain characteristics become important in communication about form in the culture, i.e. we acquire a language of forms which itself may be looked upon as a set of interactional possibilities. Thus a symmetrical and regular figure may be more simple than a nonsense figure because we can communicate more easily about the former.

9.3 Form and orientation

Zusne (1970) distinguished between the transpositional and transitive parameters of form. The former parameters were defined by the symmetry operations of translation, enlargement or reduction, rotation and reflection. These were called transpositional parameters because they transposed one form to another area or locus without changing the "structure" or "information content" of that form. Transposition did not affect the self-congruence of a form. On the other hand, transitive parameters were said to affect aspects of the contours such as linearity and number of turns. Hence these parameters did affect the self-congruence of a form.

Before a transpositional parameter is introduced to an experimental design for the study of the perceiving of form, it will be wise to think about the way in which the distinction between transpositional and transitive parameters has been made in the first place. The definition of transpositional changes seems to be contradicted by the possibility that forms can also depend on locus and orientation in the behavioural space. But all form, we say, does not depend on orientation. Thus transpositional changes are possible for some, perhaps many, types of forms. When we claim that a form is recognized as the same in different orientations, we are making use of an implicit definition of the form.

In studies of the effect of a transpositional change of a form, for example the rotation in a fronto-parallel plane, we have to make the assumption that our subjects are capable of using the same definition of form. If we cannot make this assumption, we may easily confound problems pertaining to the discrimination of orientation with problems pertaining to the identification of form.

9.3.1 Studies of some perceiving activities by infants

Harris and Allen (1974) have shown that these problems are confused in a number of studies on human infants' sensitivity to object orientation. We shall present a few of the studies which were discussed in their article; then we shall consider Harris and Allen's explanation of why data on orientation tend to be confounded with data on form or object identification. Lastly, we shall discuss their multi-variable design which was said to make possible a separation of the orientation and the form identity questions.

Harris and Allen started to examine an experiment by Watson (1966) in which sensitivity to form orientation by 12- to 20-week-old infants was studied. The experimenter leaned over the infant and smiled at him while his head was placed in a 0° orientation (upright position from the point of view of the infant), 180° (upside-down), 90° and 270°. Smiling behaviour of the infant was taken as the dependent measure.

It was shown that both latency and magnitude of smiling depended on the orientation of the experimenter's face. The infants smiled more intensely to the face in 0° orientation than to any other orientations. Hence it was concluded by Watson that infants, younger than 6 months, are able to discriminate orientations of a form. Harris and Allen rightly pointed out that this conclusion does not necessarily follow from the data and that an equally likely one, ". . . which has the advantage of greater parsimony, is that the infants did not recognize the non-upright faces as faces at all (absence of constancy), but saw them simply as different, and less interesting patterns". Harris and Allen also criticized Watson's view that the ability to discriminate differences of orientation and the ability to disregard such differences (i.e. object constancy) are "complementary" abilities.

McGurks (1970) study of 6- to 26-week-old infants was next to be analysed by Harris and Allen. In this study the infants underwent habituation trials with a three-dimensional model of a human face. After each habituation trial, a test trial was run with the face model rotated 180° from its original position. Decline of fixation on the model was taken as a measure of habituation. Recovery of fixation in the test trial was said to mean that the infant had noticed the change of the model.

In the first experimental condition the infants habituated to the face model labelled F_1-0 in Fig. 24 and were presented with the same face turned upside-down, F_1-180, in the test trial. On a single test trial the looking time increased considerably, therefore, McGurk concluded that the infants had noticed the change which took place when the orientation of a certain face altered by 180°.

Habituation
trials

Test
trials

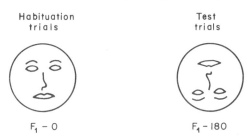

$F_1 - 0$ $F_1 - 180$

Figure 24   Face model, F_1-0, used in McGurk's study on discrimination of orientation by
infants. F_1-180 is the same face turned upside-down (from Harris and Allen, 1974).

Harris and Allen seemed to think that this conclusion was an unwarranted one. It involved, they maintained, an assumption that habituation itself was to a particular face in a particular orientation. We disagree since McGurk's conclusion said nothing about the *kind of change* which was noticed by the infant. On the other hand, McGurk's further conclusion (see McGurk, 1970, p.373) that the infants were sensitive to object orientation clearly involved such an assumption.

As part of a discussion as to whether the infants can be said to pay attention to a particular face in a particular orientation, Harris and Allen proposed four control conditions labelled 2°, 3°, 4° and 5° in Fig. 25. We may start to compare the performance of the infants in the first condition 1▲ (See Fig. 24) with the performance of two control groups. These groups should see the same upright face in the habituation trials. The one control group (given condition 2°), however, should also see this upright face in the test trial, while the other control group (3°) should see another in an upright position (F_2-0) in the test trial. Harris and Allen now reasoned that:

> Presumably, the course of habituation should continue in group 2, while, in group 3, there should be no habituation provided that the infants recognize that F_2-0 is a different face. If, however, habituation continues in group 3, then, by the usual reasoning in the habituation paradigm, one should conclude that the infants had not discriminated F_2-0 from F_1-0   (p.190)

Moreover, they maintained that such measures, if successful, would show that the infants in condition 1▲ may have attended to a particular face rather than only a face-like pattern. But Harris and Allen admitted that the measure would not show what kind of change is perceived by the infant when the face is rotated through 180° because the difference in orientation merely specifies the operation by which the change is defined by the experimenter.

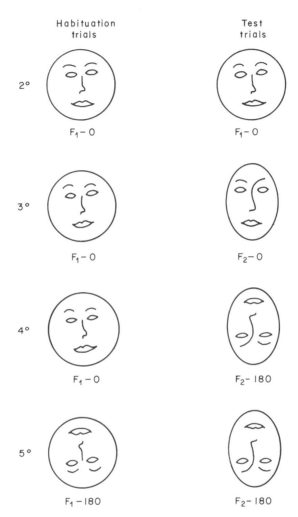

Figure 25   Face models used in proposed control conditions for the study of form identification and discrimination of orientation by infants (from Harris and Allen, 1974). For explanation, see text.

The most interesting question to ask in this connection is whether the face retains its identity for the infant when rotated through 180°. McGurk was aware of the problem, and Harris and Allen discussed whether it could be studied by the habituation paradigm. They suggested that the control group 4° would be habituated on F_1-0 and tested on a different face in an upside-down position (F_2-180) while the 5° group would be habituated on F_1-180 and tested on F_2-180. They further said that:

Our interpretation of the results from McGurk's group 1, therefore, would depend on the combination of results from groups 2 through 5. Thus the margin by which response recovery in condition 4 exceeds that in condition 1 would mark the role of the facial stimulus *per se*; the margin by which it exceeds the amount of response recovery in condition 3 would mark the role of orientation *per se*. Note that the prediction that the amount of response recovery in condition 4 would exceed that in condition 1 assumes that the infants could distinguish the two different faces when both are upside-down (oriented at 180°). This assumption, then, rests on the demonstration of response recovery in condition 5.

With this combination of results, the proper conclusion, then, would seem to be that the infants in condition 1 saw the face shown in the test trial as the same face shown in the habituation trials — a simultaneous demonstration of constancy and orientation discrimination.

(pp.191–192)

Evidently, Harris and Allen used the term "constancy" for the conservation of form identity in different orientations of the model. They soon admitted, however, that there was something wrong about their proposed conclusion. The inadequacy of the design could be clearly demonstrated when recast with the dimension colour replacing face and the dimension form replacing orientation. With the same combination of results as mentioned above, they said, one would now be led into the most peculiar sounding conclusions. The reason is that a comparison of the amount of response recovery on the test trial in the five conditions merely shows the relative contributions of the two dimensions for the resumption of the infant's attentive behaviour. It does not prove the conservation of some perceptual identity.

Harris and Allen said that they had made a logical mistake by confusing their own perspective with that of the infant. They knew that F_1-0 and F_1-180 were the same face, and so they "assumed that the infant would know it too".

As already pointed out, however, we distinguish different orientations of a form because we make use of an implicit definition of form. Therefore, if we are to study a capacity for discriminating orientation, we have to assume that our subjects are capable of using the same definition. Harris and Allen, evidently, were not willing to make this assumption, i.e. they warned against confusing the experimenter's perspective with that of the infant. The question is how discrimination of orientation can otherwise be studied.

Harris and Allen presumed that the methodological problem applied only to studies of infants, and to explain the nature of this problem they set out to analyse some experiments by Bower. We intend to show that what has been called a methodological problem in this connection is a more general problem of reference and does not only apply to studies of infants but also to studies of adults. At first, however, we shall follow Harris' and Allen's analysis of some of Bower's early experiments (Bower, 1966).

Actually Bower studied form constancy by two-month-old infants. The analysis of his experiments, therefore, pre-empts to some extent our discussion in Section 9.6. But his experiments were also concerned with the discrimination of orientation, only that now orientation referred to the slant of an object relative to a fronto-parallel plane rather than to rotation in the plane perpendicular to the line of sight.

Bower used an operant training procedure according to which the head-turns of an infant were conditioned with respect to an object at a particular distance and orientation. In his first experiment the conditional stimulus was a rectangle placed 2m away and turned 45° from the front-parallel plane. He then tested for generalization to the following objects: (1) the same rectangle placed in a different orientation (0°, i.e. in the infant's fronto-parallel plane); (2) a trapezoid in a different orientation (0°) but projecting a retinal image of equal form as the rectangle in the 45° position; and (3) the same trapezoid in the same orientation as the conditional stimulus (45°).

The conditional stimulus elicited an average of 51 responses. Test stimulus 1 (same rectangle in different orientation) elicited 45·13 responses. Test stimulus 2 elicited 28·50 responses, and test stimulus 3 elicited 21 responses. The difference between the number of responses elicited by the conditional stimulus and test stimulus 1 was not statistically significant. Since, however, test stimulus 1 differed with respect to orientation it was supposed to elicit significantly fewer responses than the conditional stimulus.

The results were said to mean that the infants had learned to respond to real form, not retinal form. Yet the results were "extremely puzzling" to Bower, since they seemed to show that infants had acquired form constancy without being able to discriminate orientation.

We would like to add at this point that Bower's puzzle was dependent on a certain preconception concerning discrimination and generalization of learning. Thus if one thinks, in agreement with Hull and Spence, that all stimulus elements of a situation become associated with the response during acquisition, and that generalization depends on the number of original elements being present in the test situation, then from the test stimulus one should elicit significantly fewer responses than from the conditional stimulus. From the position taken by Lashley, however, the puzzle would have been dissolved: learning would be selective to one or a few elements of the situation, and generalization would take place to the extent that test stimuli also contained these elements. The response may not have been associated with orientation during acquisition; therefore, a change of orientation would not necessarily influence the head-turning behaviour of the infants during test trials. However, this analysis rests on the presupposition that form and orientation can be separately attended to by an observer.

Bower modified his experiment to explain the apparent lack of orientation discrimination. Three groups of infants aged 50 to 60 days were trained and tested with different sets of stimuli. The first group was trained with a rectangle tilted 5° from the parallel position. Test stimuli were the same rectangle tilted at 15°, 30°, and 45°. For this group, therefore, the stimuli varied with respect to projective form and orientation while real form remained constant.

The second group was trained with a trapezoid in a fronto-parallel position while the test stimuli were three different trapezoids each set up in the parallel position and projectively equal to the test stimuli used for the first group. For the second group therefore the stimuli varied with respect to projective and real form.

For group 3, the same rectangles were used as for group 2 except that the rectangles were hidden behind a screen with a rectangular hole cut in it. The infant, therefore, could only see the body of the rectangles and not their edges. In this way projective form and real form remained constant ". . . the only information available on the difference between the conditioned stimulus and the test stimuli was therefore given by variations in orientation" (Bower, 1966, p.92).

Harris and Allen said that "this characterization is somewhat misleading in as much as the only source of information available to the infants would have been variations in the brightness gradient" (p.195). Nonetheless, they suggested that in a discussion of Bower's second experiment "brightness gradient" can be substituted for "orientation".

Contrary to Bower's own expectations, the infants in groups 2 and 3 showed good discrimination, whereas infants in group 1 showed the poorest discrimination. Therefore, the infants were said to be capable of discriminating orientation alone. Possibly they were also capable of discriminating projective form alone, but they were said to be unable to discriminate differences of orientation and projective form when both varied. Rather they were said to detect higher-order variables of form, while they ignored lower-order variables such as orientation.

Bower, as well as Harris and Allen, was greatly influenced by Gibson's information detection theory. Hence he preferred to speak about higher-order variables in terms of relations between simpler variables such as brightness or linear size. The form of an object, he maintained, was specified by a higher-order variable of stimulation. On the other hand, orientation could either be treated as a lower-order variable or a higher-order variable. In the former case orientation could be specified by a brightness gradient, and in the latter case by a combination of a brightness gradient and a projective form. Harris and Allen maintained that:

> Ordinarily an object's orientation in the viewer's fronto-parallel plane is specified by two factors: the object's projective shape in combination with the brightness gradient across the visible surface of the object.
> (p.196)

The test stimuli presented for group 1 in Bower's study differed with respect to brightness gradient. The higher-order variable, however, was said to be constant in the way that the combination of projective form and brightness gradient was the same for all test stimuli. Since the infants of group 1 showed the poorest discrimination, the lower-order variable must have been ignored. Constancy was said to depend on the higher-order variable. In group 3, where the rectangles were hidden behind a screen, there was no higher-order variable specifying either the orientation or the form of the object. Therefore, constancy broke down and the infants of this group responded to differences in brightness gradients.

Granted that the orientation of an object is uniquely specified by the relationship between the brightness gradient and the projective form of its contours, which is the higher variable specifying the form of an object? Is real form specified by a different higher-order variable or are real form and orientation specified by the same variable? How do we explain that infants and adults are capable of discriminating differences in the forms of objects equally orientated in relation to the observer? In other words, how did the infants in group 2 discriminate the training trapezoid from the test trapezoids? According to Harris and Allen:

> The answer is that they were perceived as different (i.e. there was no constancy) because changes in projective shape were not accompanied by changes in brightness gradient. (All trapezoids were presented in the same orientation.) Thus, Bower's conclusion that the group 2 infants had registered variations in real shape (and therefore in projective shape) is simply the conclusion that the infants had detected the varying relation between brightness-gradient and projective shape among the four trapezoids.   (p.196)

This quotation shows that Harris and Allen explained a discrimination of real form with reference to a higher-order variable that was also supposed to explain the discrimination of orientation. Therefore, they could not tell how different orientations of the same form were discriminated, nor could they tell how equally orientated forms are discriminated. The invariant and the transformation in perception were in both cases referred to one and the same higher-order variable. In this way the reasoning of Harris and Allen tended to move in a vicious circle.

We can now see how their multi-variable design was bound to fail. They aimed at a "demonstration that the infant was *simultaneously* discriminating the different orientations of what he knew to be the same object". Hence they suggested training the infant to give one response to form and another response to orientation.

> First, the infant would have to learn one response (say, head-turn) to indicate constancy (discrimination of real shape); another response (say, sucking) to indicate discrimination of orientation. This separate training would continue until the infant turns its head when the two targets are the same real shape and sucks when the two targets are in the same orientation. (p.199)

The training procedure, when successful, will hardly provide the kind of demonstration which Harris and Allen tried to set up. Such a demonstration will at least require that different stimuli can be specified for the two attributes, and that stimuli for orientation can be varied independently of stimuli for form. Thus when stimuli for orientation are varied while the stimulus for form is constant, the infants will have an opportunity to discriminate different orientations of the same form (head-turn response). Conversely, they will have an opportunity to discriminate different forms at the same orientation (sucking response). As pointed out, however, Harris and Allen were unable to specify different stimuli for form and orientation. Hence their attempt to study the discrimination of orientation independently of object form was bound to fail.

Yet we may consider for a while the possibility that either orientation or form, or both, can be specified by a combination of projective form and brightness gradient across the visible surface of the object. This combination can hardly be treated as the product of two factors, since we do not know how to transform the changes of projective form and the changes of brightness gradient to a common scale and to multiply them to determine the higher-order variable. The question is, when does the *combination* remain constant despite changes in both projective form and brightness gradient?

Harris and Allen suggested that pairs of targets be presented to infants in four different situations (see Fig. 26). The infants would have to learn the two responses to the presentation of the targets in situation 1. The pattern of responses in situations 2 to 4 would show whether the infants were able to discriminate different orientations of the same object form.

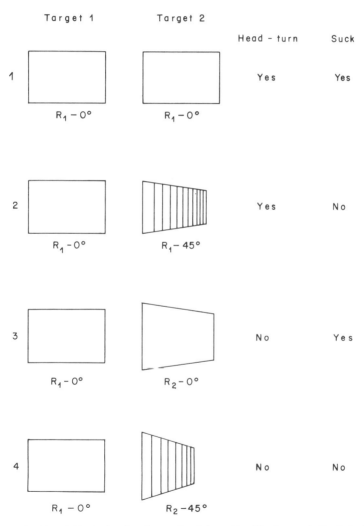

Figure 26 Multi-variable design for the study of form identification and discrimination of orientation by infants (from Harris and Allen, 1974). For explanation, see text.

Now consider situation 2 in Fig. 26. Do the two targets differ with respect to a combination of projective form and brightness gradient? In this case yes; it is quite correct for the infant not to respond by sucking (since the targets differ in orientation). But how is it possible for the infant to tell (by way of a head-turn response) that the two targets have the same form? Does the same combination of lower-order stimuli carry the information of a difference in orientation *and* an equality of form? Furthermore, we may ask how the infant is able to decide that the targets in 3 are equally oriented and that the targets in 4 differ with respect to form. Notice that no brightness gradient is present in 3.

Actually, the conception of a higher-order variable in this case involved nothing but a change in the object; either a change of form or a change of orientation. To say that the infant responds to a higher-order variable, therefore, only means to say that the infant is capable of identifying the object.

9.3.2 The form–slant invariance hypothesis

The terms slant and orientation are frequently used interchangeably. In Watson's and McGurk's studies orientation was used with reference to rotation in the fronto-parallel plane. Slant, however, tended to be used in connection with the tilt of a surface in relation to this plane (cf. the description of Bower's test objects, p.191). In the following we shall use slant with this particular meaning. We may consider slant as a type of change which is subsumed under the term orientation, or we may consider slant and orientation as different types of change. In any case both are to be considered as transpositional changes of a form.

In the following we shall discuss some classic statements and studies of the relation between slant and form of an object.

We shall start with Koffka's (1935) statement of the rule that ". . . two proximal stimuli if more than liminally different cannot produce the same effect" (p.228). Therefore, he argued that objects which had different slants in relation to the visual axis could not be seen exactly alike. He presented ellipses at different degrees of slant and his subject judged them to be equal in form. Koffka said:

> If this effect is equal in one respect it must differ in another. This other respect is easy to discover in our cases: the two ellipses which appeared of equal shape were seen in different orientation. The effect of the stimulus pattern has therefore at least two different aspects of components, viz., shape and orientation (slant).   (p.228)

Although different "proximal stimuli" were mostly judged as equal with respect to form, these stimuli were still said to produce different form-slant relationships. These considerations led to the formulation of Koffka's *form-slant invariant*, which said that a certain combination of form and slant was invariant for a given retinal image (p.233). In a footnote, however, he added a consideration of great importance for the following discussion:

> Which combination cannot be deduced, unless one either has the necessary empirical data or knows the different interacting forces. Furthermore, the invariant may depend upon total sets of conditions, and need not necessarily be the same under all circumstances.   (p.233)

Later research workers have referred to these remarks when stating that Koffka's invariant did not imply that we could say what form should be seen when the apparent slant and the retinal image was known. However, in his discussion of Eissler's (1933) and Klimpfinger's (1933) data Koffka may be said to have acknowledged a form of systematic covariation between experiences of form and slant given a fixed retinal image. Flock (1964) suggested that the covariant relation could be described as a simple product, $XY = K$, where X referred to an experience of form, Y to an experience of slant and K to the retinal projection of the form-at-a-slant. We shall refer to this as the formulation of the *form-slant invariance hypothesis*.

Contrary to Koffka's invariant this formulation is assumed to state what definite form will be seen when slant and retinal image is known, Epstein and Park (1963) asserted that several implications follow from the hypothesis. Thus the hypothesis requires that a reduction in the accuracy of slant perception should be accompanied by a reduction in the accuracy of form perception. Conversely, it was said that a correct perceiving of slant should be followed by a correct perceiving of form.

Epstein and Park suggested that these implications have been corroborated by experiments where the so-called "cues" to slant have been eliminated or partly eliminated. Monocular observation, reduction of exposure time and intensity have been shown to reduce the accuracy of form perception (Leibowitz *et al.*, 1954, 1956, 1957). In these works it was tacitly assumed that slant perception was also impaired. Langdon (1953) demonstrated considerable reduction in the accuracy of the form experiences when wire outlines were used as test objects. These objects had no surface texture and, therefore, slant may also have been incorrectly registered by the subjects.

As pointed out by Epstein and Park these experiments provided only judgements of form, no judgements of slant. Therefore, they could not be considered as a direct test of the invariance hypothesis. On the other hand, Eissler made use of both types of judgements. He reported that the form of slanted objects was to some extent seen correctly by his subjects, and yet these objects were said to appear in a "normal orientation", i.e. in a fronto-parallel position. Klimpfinger reported somewhat similar results.

Stavrianos (1945) set out specifically to test the form–slant invariance hypothesis. She presented rectangles as standard objects under three conditions of viewing: normal binocular vision, binocular vision with reduction tubes and monocular vision with reduction tubes. The subject was given two separate tasks: he was told to adjust the slant of a comparison rectangle until it appeared to have the same slant as the standard. Secondly, he was told to adjust the form of a fronto-paralleled trapezoid which had a fixed basis. The comparison objects were always viewed binocularly.

The results of Stavrianos' experiment were said to contradict the form–slant invariance hypothesis since the variability of form and slant judgements did not agree with the expectation from this hypothesis. In some preliminary experiments, however, Stavrianos found that a constant error in the form and slant judgements could be attributed to a difference in size between standard and comparison. When the data of her first experiment were corrected for these errors, she found the expected relationship between form and slant matches for some of her subjects in the monocular situation.

The question is why size should interfere with judgements of form and slant. In our opinion the answer lies in a characterization of the task. Note that the subject was told to estimate the form and slant of an object in his behavioural space. Therefore, localization must be part of the subject's task. He cannot merely disregard the size of the objects, for the localizing activity forms the whole in which judgements of slant and form are made. His implicit judgement of size forms part of the premise for his judgements of form and slant.

Stavrianos realized that a judgement of slant may be implicit in a judgement of form and vice versa, but since these types of judgements were made separately and in succession, it is not clear whether the explicitly judged form was the same as the form which was implicit in the judgement of slant.

To overcome this difficulty Beck and Gibson (1955) told their subjects to match a standard object by selecting a form-at-slant. In their own words, judgements of slant and form ". . . were made implicit in the same act of matching the standard object" (p.128). The test objects (standards) were luminous forms cut out from cardboard and fixed over a sheet of textureless ground glass in a light box. The subject was positioned 89 in. in front of the test object. He saw the object in a dark surround and with all gradients of texture density omitted. The comparison objects, however, were presented under full-cue conditions.

The experiment was carried out with two kinds of test objects: quadrilaterals and triangles:

> On half the trials O was presented with a physically slanted 10 by 8 rectangle, and on the other half with a physically frontal trapezoid equivalent to the cross-section of the light rays from the rectangle. (The latter will be referred to as the "cross-sectional trapezoid"). These two physically different but optically equivalent objects yielded the same distribution of judgments; hence we may conclude that they were indistinguishable, and that stimulation for slant had been effectively eliminated in viewing the standard. A similar procedure was used for the triangles with the same outcome. The standard slanted triangle was 10 in. base and 8 in. altitude.
>
> When the rectangle was presented, the face of the light box was inclined either floorwise or ceilingwise (top backward or top forward) at three angles of inclination, 30°, 45° and 60°. Corresponding to these six stimuli were six frontal trapezoids, half with sides converging upwards and half converging downward, at three degrees of vertical compression. Each O was thus given 12 presentations. Including the triangles he made, in all, 24 matches or judgments of shape-and-slant. There were 30 Os in the experiment. (p.128)

The standard in this experiment produced a bundle of light rays which converged to a point in the eye. Notice that the base line of the standard was always placed at a particular distance from the subject. At this distance a group of form–slant combinations could produce the same sheaf of light rays. This group was called a *transformation series*.

For each standard the experimenters had provided a set of comparison objects which were sheet-metal forms mounted at different degrees of slant on a black panel. They were positioned 30 in. from the subject and were one-third the size of the standard object. The comparison series thus constituted a number of form–slant combinations. Some of these combinations were included in the transformation series of the standard, while others were outside it.

According to Beck and Gibson, the invariance hypothesis required that the subject matched the standard by selecting a form–slant within the transformation series. In other words, this hypothesis was supported to the extent that the subject selected a comparison object which was optically equivalent to the standard.

Note that the subject selected a form–slant combination at a particular distance. But, as reasoned by Beck and Gibson, the invariance hypothesis requires an optical equivalence of standard and selected object. Therefore it would be necessary to show that the subject selects the same form–slant combinations independently of size and distance of the objects in the comparison series. *In such a case, however, the subject can be said to have matched the solid angle of light from the standard, not its form and slant.* This is to say that Beck and Gibson's design did not permit a test of the invariance hypotheses.

Is there any way of testing this hypothesis? Probably not, since a judgement of either slant or form will involve the understanding of an object in a particular position. Therefore, the two aspects cannot be independent of each other: if apparent form is known, apparent slant must also be known by the subject. Slant as well as size and distance must be implicit in a judgement of form as long as the task is specified with reference to an object.

The form–slant invariance hypothesis as formulated by Flock claims that the value of any two terms involved in the three-term interaction determines the value of the remaining term. Consequently, we should be able to "derive" projective form from estimates of the form and slant of an object. This can be done if projective form is specified as ratios or linear relationships. An absolute specification of the projection of the object on the retina or a two-dimensional picture plane in front of the retina cannot be made unless measures of size and distance are taken into account.

Epstein (1973) proposed that the value of the perspective form of an object should be "derived" from subjective estimates of form and slant, and that the "derived" and actual proximal values be compared to assess the degree to which the estimates conformed to the invariance hypothesis.

This way of reasoning involves the same difficulty as mentioned in connection with Beck and Gibson's study. It presupposes that form–slant invariance can be equated with a visual angle invariance, and that the subject is disregarding the properties of size and distance. But form-at-a-slant implies an object which, at a certain moment of observation, can only be at one distance in the subject's environment. When the subject is told to estimate its form and slant, it is tacitly assumed that he will attribute both properties to this object. In fact attention to, and the ability to make estimates of, *the same object* is a logical prerequisite underlying the formulation of the subject's task. Thus unless we assume that the subject has attended to the same object, we cannot proceed to analyse the response data.

Epstein has recently made an attempt to define the locus of a mechanism which processes form-at-a-slant (see Epstein and Hatfield, 1978). However, form-at-a-slant involves, in this connection, the identification of a particular object. Therefore, the futility of his attempt is clear enough, for such a mechanism, if it exists, must account for a complete identification of a certain object. In principle, however, we cannot say what is involved in such an identification. Hence the researcher cannot define his research task, and moreover, the form–slant relationship cannot be treated as an empirical problem in psychology.

9.4 Form, contour and object

To say that form is characterized by unification is to say that form is something limited in space. Hence form is inextricably bound to contour. Yet the relationship between form and contour is not the same as the relationship between form and orientation. The former is a kind of identity relationship which is indispensable in our conceptual scheme of the environment. The latter is conceptually separated in the way that we conceive of form as an invariant under a set of transpositional changes. For a particular object in a particular position, however, form, contour and orientation are all related by implication.

A pattern involves the repetition of elements in space and time, and may thus be said to constitute a kind of "rhythm". As such it needs not be delimited in visual space, or in other words, it is not necessarily characterized by spatial unification. Thus we are able to distinguish between form and pattern. However, since we shall not distinguish form from figure, the two terms may be used interchangeably.

We shall now say more about form and contour. Since the two are linked in our conceptual scheme, they cannot be studied independently of each other. Rubin (1915) made this point pretty clear, we think, in his demonstrations of the reversible figure–ground relationships: the contour belongs to the part which is seen as the figure. Thus if we see a vase in Fig. 27 the contour is also seen to belong to the vase, but if we see two faces, the contour belongs to these faces. On the basis of these demonstrations we shall make the following assumption: there is no perceptual activity by which the contour in perception is built up in a piecemeal fashion. Therefore, we discard Hebb's (1949) theory as well as information processing theories of contour and form perception. Rather we tend to think about contour and form as something preconceived that forms the basis of some perceptual activities.

From this point of view studies of the neural mechanisms underlying the so-called Mach-bands (Ratliff, 1965) will only be minimally relevant to problems of contour perception. The prospects are good for showing the critical mechanisms for *some* contour perception, but we

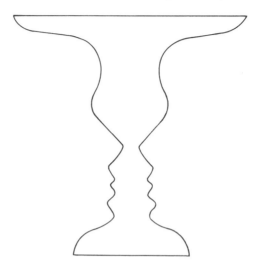

Figure 27   Figure and ground (from Rubin, 1915).

cannot infer from retinal or cortical activities related to sharp discontinuities in the distribution of luminance over a surface, *what* will be seen as contour. In general we may add that neurophysiological data cannot be related to behaviour without assuming, on behalf of the organism, a particular awareness of environmental events.

A further characterization of contour is possible. Since the contour belongs to the part which is seen as the figure, it can only have one side. In a way, therefore, the contour has no volume, and corresponds to that which Hering (1879) called a "line in the field of view". He distinguished a line from an outline trace which could be made with a stroke of a pen: differently coloured fields which adjoin each other define a non-voluminous line, while an outline trace is always to some extent voluminous. This fact means that two objects cannot be separated in a pictorial representation by only one contour. Whether they are intersecting each other or merely adjoined in the field of view of the artist, they will have to be separated by two contours in the two-dimensional representation to depict them as clearly different objects.

The one-sidedness of a contour makes it appropriate to compare it with the edge of an object. Hochberg (1978) asked whether the fact that the contour is one-sided and belongs to the part seen as the figure is the result of our past experience with the edges of objects. This possibility would neatly support Gibson's (1951) conception of form. He said that a picture-form is a form only to the extent that it specifies for the organism the form of an object. Indirectly he assumed that form identify is something which is inherent in, and is inseparably linked to, the object. He thus seemed to conceive of a unique and particular object which is the source of a certain form regardless of our interaction with that object. In this way objects are treated as the ultimate references of forms. Yet, Hochberg and Brooks (1962) showed that a child who had been raised without ever having had an opportunity to associate pictures with either objects or object names, could still identify the pictured objects shown in Fig. 28. One may say, however, that Hochberg and Brooks did not make clear the meaning of "pictured objects". Yet this work severely undermines the position taken by Gibson.

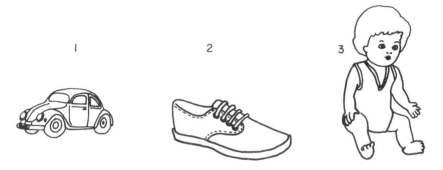

Figure 28 Pictures of object correctly identified by a child who had been raised without opportunity to associate pictures with either objects or object names (from Hochberg and Brooks, 1962).

In our opinion, form has no reference. Rather, form is an indispensable mode of understanding that underlies our interaction with objects. We cannot speak of *the* form of an object, for an object may be reacted to differently depending on task, situation and attitude of the viewer. On the other hand, the viewer may attribute form to an object, which is to say that he is involved in a particular perceptual activity. Thus object form is a shorthand description of this activity. It does not mean a form identity which is inherent in the object itself.

9.5 "Orientation detectors" and form perception

As has already been pointed out, form and contour are connected in our conceptual scheme of the environment. Thus one may ask whether the perception of form can be approached by studying the mechanisms underlying the discrimination of contour orientation. Allegedly, such a mechanism has been demonstrated by Hubel and Wiesel (1968) who recorded the excitation of single neurones in the visual projection areas of various animals. They discovered neurones that fired when a certain pattern (such as a tilted line, bar or edge) stimulated the entire field of retinal receptors, and which showed almost no response when the individual receptors were stimulated by points of light in the same retinal area. Neurones which are thus specialized to respond to particular patterns of stimulation have been called "orientation detectors".

Carpenter and Blakemore (1973) proposed that these detectors provides a basis for the perception of form and the visual recognition of objects. Thus they said that "the narrower the band of orientations to which each detector will respond, the more discriminative the system will be; and this in turn would be expected to enhance shape discrimination and pattern recognition" (p.287).

In general this way of thinking about form perception meets with a number of difficulties. Firstly, excitation of a particular "orientation detector" hardly explains the perception of orientation in behavioural space. The "complex" and "hypercomplex" cells specialized for responding to a precisely oriented bar moving in a certain direction, receives input from cells of a simpler category in the visual system. Perception of orientation, however, is a supra-modal accomplishment. Hence it is possible for a perceiver to tell what is up, down, right and left in the absence of visually distinguishable points, lines or objects. The so-called homogeneous "Ganzfield", we can say, is well structured for a perceiver who receives information from other senses. In other words, orientations in the homogeneous field are perceived without the selective stimulation of particular "orientation detectors".

Orientation of a line or an edge involves localization, and generally we distinguish between absolute and relative localization. The former probably depends on the simultaneous stimulation of several senses, while the latter may be said to be a visual or unimodal capacity. "Orientation detectors" may thus be involved in the relative localization of lines, bars and contours.

On this basis we may place Carpenter's and Blakemore's model for the orientation selectivity of cortical cells. They argued for a simple arrangement of presynaptic recurrent inhibition between orientation specific cells. Inhibitory interactions between such cells would increase the specificity of the system for signalling, for example, the orientation of a single line in the field of view.

Apparently, orientation selectivity was thought to have a bearing on contours as well as single lines, i.e. the model had a broad applicability. Yet it could only be tested for specific patterns of stimulation. Carpenter and Blakemore, therefore, more or less arbitrarily took the acute angle formed by two straight lines as their point of departure. Due to inhibitory interactions between the orientation channels, the summed distribution of excitation corresponding to these lines will have peaks that are skewed away to slightly more extreme orientations. Consequently, acute angles tend to be overestimated by the perceiver.

This leads to our next critical point: the measurement of perceptual angle expansion. Carpenter and Blakemore presented three bright lines, A, B, and C as shown in Fig. 29. A and B always met in the centre of the display to form an angle which could be systematically varied by the experimenter. The subject was told to set the orientation of C so that it appeared to be parallel to B.

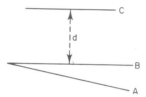

Figure 29   Stimulus lines used in the experiment of Carpenter and Blakemore (1975). C: comparison line; B: test line; A: induction line. In a separate control experiment the distance d was varied by Carpenter and Blakemore.

This procedure implies that C has been introduced as a kind of measuring device. The experimenter, therefore, should ascertain that this device does not change the perceptual event which is studied, i.e. the orientation of B.

As shown by the parallel settings of C an angle of 10° between B and A produced a considerable distortion in the perceived orientation of B. Carpenter and Blakemore, therefore, employed this angle between the two lines in a control experiment on the effect of varying the distance, d, between B and C. The distortion in perceived orientation increased up to a maximum of 2° when d was about 40 minutes of arc. Further separation between B and C produced no significant increase in measured distortion. Carpenter and Blakemore seemed to think, therefore, that when C was presented at a distance from B which exceeded 40 minutes of arc, it did not interfere with the perceptual effect which was studied.

This conclusion is tenable only for the angular separation of A and B used in Carpenter's and Blakemore's control experiment. The critical distance, dj, at which C does not interfere with the interaction effect between A and B most probably varies with the angle between the lines. Therefore, C may have interfered with the perceptual distortion effect for other angular separations between A and B. Carpenter and Blakemore varied this angle from 0° to 360°.

This means that it is hard to evaluate the role of a separate feature in the display, such as the distance between C and B, independently of the total configuration. Furthermore, the responses of the subject will always be a function of the total configuration. Hence it may be difficult to generalize the response data to apply to form perception in other situations.

It may also be difficult to derive from Carpenter's and Blakemore's data general statements concerning the discrimination of angles. The angle expansion effect demonstrated by these researchers occurs in a number of geometric illusions. Consider, for example, the straight and physically parallel lines ab and cd in Fig. 30(A). Due to an overestimation of the acute angles, these lines appear non-parallel, i.e. slightly bent towards each other at the sides of the figure. When, however, the acute angles are filled, the effect reverses. Thus in Fig. 30(B) the straight lines have been converted into contours. However, these contours appear bent in the opposite direction. The former case (Fig. 30(A)) may be attributed to angle expansion, while the latter case (Fig. 30(B)) may just as easily be attributed to angle contraction. (For a description of these and similar geometric illusions see the survey given by Hofmann, 1925, pp.112–123.)

Another point which restricts the applicability of Carpenter's and Blakemore's model is the use of lines meeting in the centre of the display to form particular angles. One may ask, for example, whether the interaction effect underlying orientation selectivity also applies to lines or line segments which do not form angles. Granted that the

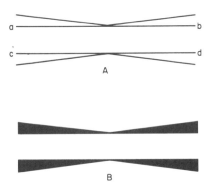

Figure 30   (A) ab and cd are physically straight and parallel lines. They appear to converge laterally in the figure. (B) When the acute angles are represented as filled triangles, parallel lines appear to diverge laterally in the figure (see text).

model applies to such displays as well as to displays which contain filled figures and contours, a vast number of stimulus situations can be set up to test the model.

It should be stressed, however, that the model requires specification of a particular task. At the same time we do not know whether the range of possible stimulus displays is compatible with the specification of one and the same discriminatory task for the subject.

The critical points that we have raised against Carpenter's and Blakemore's work apply, of course, equally well to more recent works in this tradition, such as Magnussen and Kurtenbach (1980a, b).

We have thus come to the conclusion that the attempt to relate Hubel and Wiesel's data on "orientation detectors" to the perception of form and orientation is an unfruitful one. This research tradition has given no shortcut to an understanding of object recognition and form constancy. We shall, therefore, end the chapter by reconsidering this old theme of perceptual psychology.

9.6 Constancy and the representation of form

In a study of form constancy the subject is told to match the form of a reference object by selecting one among a series of differently slanted objects. He may also be told to draw the form of the reference object (Thouless, 1931). As shown by Joynson and Newson (1962) this task is an ambiguous one, i.e. the subject may either make a "real form" judgement or a judgement of "other-than-real" form. A "real form" judgement involves an object at a particular distance and orientation. Thus again we see that the task requires a complete identification of the object, and like the other constancies, form constancy also constitutes a quasi-empirical problem of research.

However, form constancy may be said to involve an adequate communication about object shapes. Thus form itself has been treated as a form constancy factor (Campione, 1977). A rectangle, for example, can more easily be represented and communicated about than the form of an amoebic like object. Understanding and skills of representation are essential prerequisites of the constancy response.

10

Concept of stimulus in the works of Gibson and Johansson

10.1 Concept of the stimulus

There is perhaps no concept in psychology which has been more vigorously discussed than the concept of a stimulus (see Gibson, 1960; Smith, 1969). A general agreement as to the use of this concept has not been established. Yet some researchers will claim that a stimulus should be defined with reference to certain response characteristics of an observer. Moreover, the stimulus concept is generally associated with psychophysics, and in practice, it has been identified with the independent variable in psychophysics. Thus in view of our discussion in Chapter 2 it should be possible to put forward a term which can be used consistently.

The stimulus concept, however, has also been associated with dualistic and causal theories of perception. That is to say that a stimulus has been conceived of as a causal agent (cf. the distinction between *lux* and *luman* mentioned on p.10). The reason why the stimulus (independent variable) in psychophysics has been treated as a causal agent may be found in the orderly and highly predictable relationships shown by psychophysical experiments. Thus, in a certain setting, a certain wavelength always seems to produce the same hue of colour. The external stimulus in the form of a light wave, a particle, etc. is said to cause an internal event called a sensation. This conception of causal relationships in perception is a remnant of Descartes' and Locke's theory of primary and secondary qualities of sensation.

In the presentation of psychophysics in this book we have taken a different position. We have emphasized that light and sound in classical physics have been defined with reference to the sensory systems of an observer. In this way physics has been concerned with the modalities and has provided a kind of research "paradigm" for psychophysics. That is to say that the main psychophysical correspondences are given in the variables of optics and acoustics, while it has become the task of psychophysics to determine the discriminatory capacities and the limits of these correspondences. In other words, light and sound stimuli presuppose references to an observer and cannot be treated as causal events in perception.

At the same time the "paradigm" for psychophysics also states the main conditions under which the discrimination of light, colour and sound are to be considered as valid ones. For the main part these conditions involve assumptions concerning the subject's perception. In particular, therefore, the subject's awareness of the environmental setting is a prerequisite for the study of a sensory capacity. A sensation can hardly be separated from a mode of appearance, and therefore, to say that psychophysics is concerned with sensations and their immediate causes in physical energy, is probably to confuse a specification of the prerequisites for psychophysical studies with the subject matter of this science.

However, the conception that a stimulus constitutes a causal agent in perception has never been fully abandoned among psychologists. There were stimuli for the perception of brightness, hue, saturation, pitch, etc., but the perception of objects and events seemed more complex and could hardly be explained by reference to the same stimuli.

Those who thought that one could not similarly specify a set of stimuli for the perception of objects, still maintained a causal conception of sensations. But in everyday perception of objects the sensations are generally unnoticed, yet applied in subconscious inferences or judgements about the size, form or colour of objects and surfaces, we get the "cue" theories of perception.

The researchers, however, did not give up hope of finding the causes of the perception of objects. Therefore, the stimulus problem still remained the central one in the psychology of perception, but the term stimulus was used in a more loose sense than in classical psychophysics. Thus a stimulus could be any agent or event, external or internal, that caused a percept or response by the person. As explained by Stevens (1951) the stimulus problem became the main problem of psychology:

In a sense there is only one problem of psychophysics, namely, the definition of the stimulus. In this same sense there is only one problem in all of psychology — and it is the same problem. The definition of the stimulus is thus a bigger problem than it appears at first sight. The reason for equating psychology to the problem of defining stimuli can be stated thus: the complete definition of the stimulus to a given response involves the specification of all the transformations of the environment, both of internal and external that leave the response invariant. This specification of the conditions of invariance would entail, of course, a complete understanding of the factors that produce and alter responses. It is easy enough, of course, to decide upon arbitrary definitions of "stimulus objects" (e.g. a given pattern of lines, a quantity of luminous flux, an acoustic waveform, etc.), but the question is: what properties of these objects do the stimulating? Viewed in this fashion, it is evident that for no response have we yet given a complete definition of the stimulation. At best we have only partially determined the conditions and limits of invariance.   (pp.31–32)

The above quotation shows how the main tasks and problems of psychology have been specified from a particular conception of psychophysics. This conception was, in our opinion, an inadequate one, for in a sense there was no stimulus problem in classical psychophysics. Stevens, however, was not the only one who thus misinterpreted the tasks and problems of psychophysics. Gibson (1950, 1959, 1966) also seemed to think that definition of stimuli or stimulation constituted the main problem of psychophysics. But to deal with the perception of a continuous surface or an event in the natural environment one has to define, he said, a stimulus variable of a different order, i.e. a variable which includes a relationship between intensities or elements:

This variable will usually prove to be one of higher order than are the variables hitherto studied by sensory physiologists, but it is called a stimulus because it is taken to cause perception in the same way that more familiar stimuli are experimentally known to cause sensation.
(1959, p.457)

The quotation shows that Gibson may have taken the position of a dualistic-causal theorist in matters of perception. He thus fits into long standing traditions of thinking in the area, and he does not depart so radically from contemporary theories, as some of his programmatic statements seem to indicate.

By stressing that perception is a function of stimulation, Gibson not only announced a perceptual psychophysics, but he also announced *an attempt at explaining perception*. In recent years several researchers have agreed with Gibson's main position in psychology, and under the influence of many of his ideas, they have worked on problems of perceptual psychophysics. The theories thus developed have been called "information detection theories of perception". They have in common a particular view of what constitutes an explanation of perception. We shall analyse critically this view by considering some aspects of two of the theories in this group, namely Gibson's own theory and Johansson's (1968, 1974) theory. First we shall consider some of the most outstanding features of Gibson's theory.

10.2   Gibson's ecological optics

Gibson's great merit lies in his suggestion that perceptual activities should be studied in the natural habitat of man. This habitat, he said, consists of the terrestrial environment, the animate environment and the cultural environment.

He called attention to aspects of the terrestrial environment which may be of great biological significance, and to which perceptual activities are generally related. These aspects were said to be "wrinkled surfaces of rock and soil along with smooth surfaces of water". The solid terrestrial environment was structured by, for instance, "mountains and hills, trees and other vegetation, stones and sticks". It supports behaviour since it permits an organism to walk, stand or creep.

Certainly, mountains, trees and sticks are part of the physical world, and hence they may be looked upon as physical structures. However, Gibson maintained that not all physical structures are equally important for the psychologist who wants to study perception. He said that:

> . . . there is physical structure at the scale of millimicrons at one extreme and on the scale of light years at another. But surely the appropriate scale for animals is the intermediate one of millimeters to kilometers, and it is appropriate because the world and the animal are then comparable.   (Gibson, 1966, p.22)

The metric system has, of course, been applied to physical particles as well as "the animal world". In this sense the world of animals and particles may be said to constitute different levels of physical structure. However, when Gibson spoke about the world of animals or the solid terrestrial environment, he did not emphasize its measurable characteristics. Rather he spoke about the solid environment in an everyday language by stressing the immediate appearance of this environment in everyday life.

Evidently Gibson was not interested in studying the environment from the point of view of the physicist, but he wanted to consider it in relation to organisms for the purpose of developing a new branch of ecology. The result was *ecological optics* which he presented in 1961.

Unfortunately, this discipline has played a double role in Gibson's works on perception. On the one hand it referred to a system of relationships between the environment and the moving organism, and this system was supposed to make possible the generation and description of a number of independent variables in psychophysical studies of spatial perception. Although the actual choice of variables may have been influenced by theoretical considerations about space perception, ecological optics could, in principle, be developed independently of such considerations. But Gibson also assumed, more or less explicitly, that the development of ecological optics would, in itself, cast some light on perception. Thus on the other hand, he may have failed to distinguish ecology from epistemology: the principles of ecological optics were supposed to state something about the origin of our knowledge about the external world.

In his treatment of the concept of ambient light he advanced a point of view regarding this problem: the natural habitat consists of surfaces with the capacity to reflect light. From the faces or facets of a configuration of surfaces are generated a "dense interlocking network of rays". In the medium we may think of any point towards which a sheaf of rays is converging from all directions. Such a sheaf of rays "is simply an abstract mathematical statement of what is meant by ambient light". The convergence point he also called the station-point. His opinion regarding the epistemological problem, however, he discussed with consideration to what is contained in the sheaves of rays to the various station-points in a medium. He said:

> The faces and facets of the object will be "projected" to all these station-points in accordance with certain laws of projective geometry. An "aspect" of each face is obtainable anywhere in the medium. In effect, aspects of the shape and texture of the object are projected outward from it in all directions. Herein lies the truth of the figurative assertion that aspects of an object are "broadcast". Only an emitting body truly radiates energy, but a reflecting body can be said to radiate structure or information by virtue of the reverberating flux of reflected light in the medium.   (Gibson, 1966, p.15)

The problem is whether this information exists for the perceiving organism, either as potential or actually used information, or whether this information is to be looked upon as the specification of already known surfaces according to the laws of projective geometry. Gibson clearly assumed that the structure of ambient light exists as information for the organism.

Before we discuss this assumption, we shall consider more specifically how the structure of ambient light can be analysed. A useful concept in this connection is that of an optic array. Gibson said that the optic array constitutes "a pencil of rays converging to a point, and the point being the nodal point of the eye" (1961, p.225). Furthermore, the optic array is by definition structured, which means that the rays converging from different directions have different intensities. The pattern or structure appears in the way of a certain spatio-temporal energy distribution at a cross-section of the array. (This cross-section is comparable to Johansson's "picture plane", 1964.) The transition of energy from one point to another can be analysed into a set of *higher order stimulus variables*. These would always be concerned with ". . . margins, borders, contrasts, ratios, differences and textures in the array". But the variables were not copies of the environment, they merely specified surfaces and "objects" in the environment.

In one sense this is quite clear for a given physical environment and given a station-point in the medium, it will be possible to determine the structure of the array to that point. Only in this sense we can say that the array includes information about the physical environment or that this environment "projects" information about its own structure into space. But we cannot reverse this relationship, i.e. we cannot infer anything from a given structure of the array about a given environment. Consequently, the specificity of the array *alone* is zero. However, this point has generally been confused, since the researchers have smuggled in a presupposition about the environment as part of their premises, and we can, of course, infer from the structure of an array plus *some* knowledge about the environment a more specific knowledge of the environment.

A specific environment may constitute a set of rigid plane objects, like those used in Gibson and Gibson's study (1957). As an extension of this study, Hay (1966) described the mathematical correspondence between object displacement and transformation of the array, i.e. optical motions. His main problem was how many different object displacements can produce one and the same optical motion. A class of optical equivalent displacements is illustrated in Fig. 31.

Using matrix algebra Hay undertook a mapping of object displacements into optical transformations. This showed that the "optical transformation is in no way specific to the particular distance of the surface P or the length of the translatory component of D, but

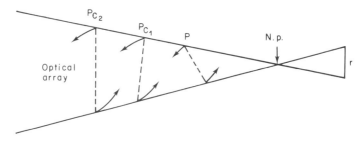

Figure 31   A class of optically equivalent displacements (from Hay, 1966).

that the optical transformation is specific to the ratio between those two quantities" (Hay, 1966, p.558). As to the information gathered about the kind of displacement (change of orientation) Hay concluded:

> . . . the optical transformation caused by displacing an object plane is specific to two alternative surface orientations, and two corresponding displacements. Thus in the general case, there is one confusable surface orientation, P_c.
>
> A one-to-one correspondence is derived from this two-to-one correspondence when the object undergoing displacement includes two or more sets of coplanar points, or when a single set of coplanar points undergoes a sequence of transformations.   (p.560)

Apparently, Hay's analysis established a high degree of specificity of optical motions to object displacements. However, this specificity was evaluated as the size of the optical equivalence class for certain kind of rigid objects undergoing certain displacements. The objects were supposed to include *one or more sets of coplanar points and the displacements did not involve changes of size and/or shape.* Certainly the size of the optical equivalence classes will be enlarged if other objects and the changes of objects are considered. If the range of possible objects is unlimited, or if the environment is in all respects unknown, the specificity of the optical motion in the array reduces to zero.

What we want to say about the relationship of the physical environment to transformations in the optic array has been most clearly stated by Johansson:

> Under specified conditions of projection, the moving and/or changing in three-dimensional space generates a unique transformation of the pattern on the picture plane. Thus we are always able to determine

from a given change in space what two-dimensional change will occur
on the picture plane and thus also on the surface of the retina.
                                                                (1964, p.183)

Changes on the picture plane can be produced without movements
or changes of objects in a three-dimensional space. Thus Johansson
generated changes in a homogeneous area of light presented in a
cathode ray tube. Starting from the information given in these two-
dimensional changes,

> . . . we immediately find that there is in fact no *specific information* . . .
> in the pattern on the picture plane, and thus in changes in the optical
> array. A two-dimensional changing pattern cannot specify both form–
> size changes of an object and at the same time its instantaneous
> localization in three-dimensional space.   (Johansson, 1964, p.183)

On the other hand, continuous transformations of a shadow pattern
(Metzger, 1934; Wallach and O'Connel, 1953; Gibson and Gibson,
1957; von Fieandt and Gibson, 1959) and transformations of a solid
angle of light (Johansson, 1964) tend to be seen as objects moving
and/or changing form in a three-dimensional space. According to
Gibson these facts show that changes in the optic array carry specific
information about the environment.

Notice that Gibson thus argued from a *psychophysical relationship*
to properties of the ambient light itself. He did not ask how it was
possible for an organism to see the transformations of a shadow pattern
as a moving object in depth. He overlooked the point that specificity
involves an organism, and that specificity does not exist merely "by
virtue of physical facts".

One may similarly question his arguments concerning proprioception: the transformation of the ambient light which follows upon a
certain locomotion of the organism has been described as an optical
expansion pattern. This pattern has unique properties which were said
to specify the velocity and direction of movements. Therefore Gibson
claimed that proprioception cannot be ascribed to proprioceptors
alone; vision also helps to inform the organism about his movements in
space.

However, specificity of the expansion pattern requires *some*
knowledge of the environment. As we have seen, Hay's demonstration
of the specificity of the optical motions depended on the assumption
that the object included one or more sets of coplanar points and that
displacements did not involve changes of size and/or shape. The
assumption was introduced by the person performing the matrix
algebra analysis.

An organism viewing an optical expansion pattern has not the same specific knowledge of object movements and their projections onto a two-dimensional screen. The question is how the organism is able to report about three-dimensional movements. To say that the expansion pattern itself carries information about these movements is to evade the question. At the same time Gibson aimed at a causal theory of perception.

The point is that the Helmholtzian position does include an answer to the question how an organism is enabled to report three-dimensional movements: if the environment is assumed to consist of rigid objects, the expansion pattern must be seen as movements in depth. Gibson purported to take the very opposite position. Therefore, he was obliged to show that his subjects did not meet the experimental viewing situations with any preconceived ideas of this kind. But, of course, the psychophysical relationships *per se* do not tell how an organism is able to respond to higher order variables. Thus Gibson did not bring about experimental facts which warranted discarding of the Helmholtzian position.

10.3   Concept of "projective interpretation" in Johansson's theory of motion perception

Like Gibson, Johansson argued against a cue-theory of perception. In particular both researchers rejected "cognitive" explanations of the perception of objects and motions in depth. Therefore, the question of what is involved in the specificity of stimulation became crucial to both writers.

Gibson started his analysis more from the distal side, while Johansson started his from the proximal side. Johansson, therefore, tended to see more clearly that optical motions alone cannot be responsible for the specificity of stimulation. Thus he once stated that "we must seek principles inherent in the perceptual process which bring about specificity" (1964, pp.183–184). Since, initially, nothing was said about what constitutes a "perceptual process", the reader may well ask whether these principles involve some sort of unconscious inferences.

However, Johansson has shown that two-dimensional transformations of (1) a solid angle of light; (2) a straight line (Johansson and Johansson, 1968); and (3) a pattern of dots (1974) are generally responded to according to a projective type of perceptual stimulus analysis. Eventually this analysis was supposed to be the perceptual process. Thus he argued for a projective type of model for three-dimensional motion perception. The simplicity of such a model should be admitted, while the question is to what extent it also serves an heuristic function. If the model is to serve as a theoretical one with a view to rendering explanations of perceptual activity, Johansson must add assumptions on how the subjects are enabled to perform the stimulus analysis in question.

To illustrate our point we shall discuss a few of Johansson's simple dot patterns. These consisted of bright spots generated in a cathode ray tube against a dark background. Figure 30 includes four different dot patterns used by Johansson. In Fig. 32(a) the two dots are moving simultaneously along parallel tracks and with the same constant velocity. The dots are seen as rigidly connected forming the endpoints of an otherwise invisible stick. Furthermore, motion takes place in the fronto-parallel plane.

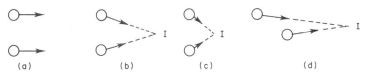

(a)   (b)   (c)   (d)

Figure 32   Dot patterns used in a study of three-dimensional motion. In (b), (c) and (d) the dots are made to "collide" at an extrapolated point I, called the "point of concurrency" (from Johansson, 1974).

In Fig. 32(b) the dot pattern is the same as in (a) except that the motion paths are now converging. Thus if the motion were allowed to continue, the dots would "collide" in an extrapolated point I, called "the point of concurrency" by Johansson. Again the dots are seen as rigidly connected. But the invisible stick is now moving in a straight track directed obliquely away from the viewer at a certain angle from the fronto-parallel plane.

In Fig. 32(c) only the directions of the tracks are changed. The dots, while seen as rigidly connected, appear to move in paths near the sagittal plane.

Johansson asserted that the spatial arrangement of the dots does not influence the perceived direction of motion. In Fig. 32(d) the motions are concurrent, relative to the point I. "Now the 'rod' is seen as moving obliquely away from the observer. Usually the direction of the 'rod' is reported as rather close to a fronto-parallel plane, but slanting on this plane" (1974, p.120).

One may ask if these examples can also serve as examples of the way unconscious inferences work in the perception of three dimensional motion. A research worker, taking a neo-Helmholtzian position, will probably explain the observed effect in the following manner: because the subject makes the assumption that the dots are all the time rigidly connected, he will be able to interpret the projective pattern as motion track concurrency in depth. The examples, however, were not intended to give support to a neo-Helmholtzian position.

Johansson ascertained that a projective interpretation of motion track concurrency took place in his experimental situations. He did not show how the subject was able to do this interpretation. We think, therefore, that Johansson has not argued successfully for an alternative model of a perceptual activity that could not, in principle at least, be equally well accounted for by a neo-Helmholtzian or cue-theoretical way of thinking.

The question is what "projective interpretation" means in Johansson's theoretical model. Eventually, this term was supposed to refer to a certain perceptual activity. We may add, therefore, that this activity takes place under a particular set of viewing conditions, and that it may rest on certain developmental conditions by the subject. Johansson did not discuss or mention any such conditions, nor did he seem to think that the model required such conditions to be specified. "Projective interpretation" thus remained an undefined term.

It should be stressed, however, that Johansson's model worked by analogy with projective geometry. But Helmholtz too reasoned from analogy. He explicitly said that we can describe perceptual activities by analogy with the inductive inferences in logic. Thus it is not clear in what respect we may speak of these models as theoretical ones capable of explaining perceptual activities.

In short, therefore, Johansson can no longer "seek principles inherent in the perceptual process which bring about specificity". The only alternative left is the saying that specificity, i.e. information of movements in depth, is inherent in the optical motion pattern *per se*. By implication, Johansson would have to go beyond a model by analogy and accept a simple dualistic-causal theory of perception.

In reviewing Gibson's and Johansson's positions, we may say that the stimulus concept has been used in a broad sense. The two researchers have tended to include in the concept methodological prerequisites of psychophysics as well as postulated causal agents in perception. Such a concept, we believe, is not a fruitful one.

The higher-order variable and the transformation pattern are merely shorthand descriptions of a number of object properties and object events. Also these descriptions rest on cultural knowledge about environmental interactions, but a system of higher-order variables includes no kind of explanation of these interactions.

10.4   Further comments on the concepts of a "higher-order variable" and a "proximal stimulus pattern"

Gibson and Johansson maintained that perception of an object's properties, and hence the perceptual constancies, can be explained by reference to higher-order variables or patterns of stimulation. The perceptual response is constant to the extent that the higher-order variable or pattern is constant despite changes in lower-order variables of stimulation. When the higher-order variable changes, the perceptual response will change too.

This attempt to explain the constancies in perception leads to a number of difficulties. Some of these difficulties we have mentioned already in a discussion of Harris and Allen's attempt to separate the question of form constancy from the question of the discrimination of orientation (see pp.162–164). Firstly we can say that we need certain rules for combining variables of so-called lower-order into variables of higher-order. These rules should enable us to tell when the higher-order variable, the combination of lower-order variables, or the pattern of stimulation is constant and when it changes.

In the case mentioned by Harris and Allen, the higher-order variable was said to constitute a combination of perspective form and a brightness gradient across the surface of the object. The problem here was to tell when the combination remained the same when perspective form and brightness gradient both change.

To avoid going round in circles the researcher must specify the higher-order variable independently of a specification of the perceptual response. In other words, he must provide a set of rules for combining variables of lower-order to form variables of higher-order independently of a particular set of perceptual response data. Gibson has not explicitly mentioned such rules. Nor has Johansson accounted for a constancy of the proximal stimulus pattern independently of a reference to the perceptual response.

Yet it must be admitted that a constancy of pattern may be ascertained independently of such a reference, and that the higher-order variable may be specified independently of particular response data from an experiment on perception. This possibility is, of course, fully understood by the two researchers, and, we can say, it provides for the premises of the Gibsonian approach.

At the same time it should be stressed that a higher-order variable can be specified in a number of ways. When taking as our point of departure a set of defined lower-order variables in classical psychophysics, we shall find that there are innumerable ways of combining them to form higher-order variables. Likewise there are innumerable ways of specifying a pattern of dots on a screen. The actual specification that is chosen is more or less arbitrary.

One may object that regardless of the particular specification of the pattern, the perceptual response remains the same under a certain transformation of the pattern. However, in so far as the researcher can ascertain that transformation *of a pattern* has taken place, he may have already presupposed a certain constancy of response.

In the second place, then, one may ask what is meant by the constancy of a response. Consider a more complex arrangement of a large number of dots on a screen, and that only the dots are visible to the subjects. A computer can be used to generate a vast number of relative movements of the dots. Each time the subject may be told to describe what he sees. One may ask which of these descriptions can be considered as a "constancy of response". Many descriptions will be of the type: "I don't know what I see, the movements are indefinite, chaotic," etc. The computer may also generate a set of relative movements of the dots which can give rise to a unanimous description by the subjects. This will, most probably, be a description of objects, i.e. objects which move in relation to the perceiver or stationary objects which serve as a kind of reference for the perceiver's own movements. The point is that the researcher will probably be able to tell in advance which are the sets of relative dot movements that can be described as object events. He knows that certain sets of relative movements can be considered as the projection onto the screen of objects moving in space or as the projection of stationary objects onto a moving screen (or a retina of a moving observer). Thus constancy of the perceptual response means a description of rigid objects or object motion.

Gibson and Johansson have both selected particular transformation patterns for studying certain aspects of motion and space perception. The selection of patterns or proximal stimulus events has not been a random selection from a universe of possible stimulus events. Rather they have selected a set of relative dot or element movements that were known, more or less in advance, to make possible a description of object events. Such knowledge, we think, is established in our culture independently of the perceptual research of Gibson and Johansson. Their experimental data may thus have been predicted on the basis of cultural knowledge in the area.

In short, therefore, Gibson and Johansson cannot merely explain perception by referring to higher-order variables or transformation patterns. Such a reference will be a reference to cultural and/or technological knowledge. On the other hand, therefore, one is tempted to ask for the origin of such knowledge. This is, however, an epistemological problem which is unrelated to a certain procedure or method. Johansson and Gibson, we think, have barely distinguished between epistemological problems of perception on the one hand and research problems of perception on the other. Therefore, it is also hard to say in which way, and to what extent, their theoretical positions differ from the positions of pioneering workers in the area.

10.5   The theoretical positions of Gibson and Johansson compared with the Helmholtzian position in the psychology of perception

In textbooks on perception Gibson has generally been credited for important theoretical innovations. Johansson has likewise been said to have given important theoretical and empirical contributions to the study of perception. Both are considered to depart radically from the Helmholtzian position.

In our opinion, the research data generated by Gibson's and Johansson's approaches can equally well be explained from a Helmholtzian position. The type of experimental data referred to in the preceding sections do not contradict the latter position. Rather they may all be taken in support of an unconscious inference model of perception. Modern research in the area has not provided an empirical basis for a choice between the type of theoretical positions taken by Gibson and Johansson on the one hand and the Helmholtzian position on the other.

We shall, therefore, start to look for similarities rather than differences between the theoretical positions mentioned. Although we are accustomed to thinking about these positions as opposite ones, there are also important similarities between them.

Firstly, psychological research problems of perception are not clearly distinguished from epistemological problems of perception. Helmholtz, as well as Gibson and Johansson, has been concerned with the sources of knowledge about the external world. Helmholtz, who was mostly occupied with the sensations of colour and sound, can hardly be said to have done experiments on object perception in the modern sense of the word. But Kilpatrick and Yttelson and other researchers who have taken a so-called neo-Helmholtzian position in psychology, have studied a number of aspects of object perception. These researchers, like Gibson and Johansson, presupposed that object perception can be investigated by the use of a general experimental method. They all seemed to think that the subject matter or the type of problems to be studied exist independently of method or procedure, and that the general experimental method used in the sciences was also fitted for their field of investigation.

However, the researchers mentioned have suggested different answers to the question of the sources of our knowledge about the external world. The researchers who stick to an Helmholtzian position will appeal to experience. Our knowledge of the external world comes from the experiences of the senses, and these experiences form the basis of particular expectations or assumptions about external objects.

The neo-Helmholtzians have spoken of an "assumptive world". For the organism the "assumptive world" constitutes the main premise or basis for responding to the stimulation of a sense organ.

Gibson has maintained that the source of knowledge about the external world is the external world itself. However, knowledge about objects is mediated by way of the ambient light, which thus serves a primary role in the causal sequence of perception. Therefore, in the cases where the Helmholtzians have related the perceptual response to an assumption made by the perceiver, Gibson has related the response to information in the optic array. Object assumptions in the perceiver and information in the optic array are given theoretical status and supposed to be independent of the particular methods used by the researchers.

Johansson first supposed that specificity must be attributed to the "perceptual process" rather that the optic array, and in this way he may have placed himself close to a Helmholtzian position (see p.184). Also, Johansson's concept of "projective interpretation" may be said to fit a Helmholtzian way of thinking. This concept, however, is part of a model which is said to simplify a theoretical treatment of motion perception. The model has been advanced as an alternative to a cue-theoretical (read Helmholtzian) interpretation of perceptual events. However, such a model may have been accepted by Helmholtz as an extension of his own treatment of spatial vision.

On the other hand, Johansson later maintained that the proximal stimulus pattern carries information about three-dimensional motion. The visual system is said to be capable of receiving and analysing this information. In this way he has taken a Gibsonian-like position in psychology.

The differences between a Helmholtzian position on the one hand and the position taken by Gibson and Johansson on the other may easily be over-emphasized. These differences, when considered in the light of perceptual development, may turn out to be negligible. Thus although Gibson ascertained that perception is a function of stimulation, he also admitted that experience is one of the main factors which determines the perceptual response. The organism, he said, is not able to register all potential information in the ambient light. By way of differentiation of the ambient light structure, however, the organism learns to detect and to respond to new properties of stimulation not previously detected. Therefore, the information that is used by the organism is a function of interactions with the environment which have already taken place.

Johansson has not similarly been occupied with problems of perceptual development, but his general position in the psychology of perception is fully compatible with the Gibsonian view on development.

In so far as Gibson considers the perceptual response to be, among other things, also a function of previous interactions with the environment, the difference between a Gibsonian and a Helmholtzian position reduces to a minimum. However, Gibson gives little place to error in perceptual behaviour. Because learning is said to take place by a process of differentiation, it will always lead to correct, however more refined, information about the external world. The result of learning will necessarily be *veridical perception*.

But perceptual activity may also be characterized as erroneous and ambivalent. Speaking of information in the ambient light, it must be admitted that sometimes this information is ambiguous — even under locomotory behaviour of the organism. The problem is how Gibson may depart from a Helmholtzian position when dealing with non-veridical and ambiguous aspects of perception.

11

A system of reference for perceptual
activities related to material objects

11.1 Previous attempts to establish a reference system

All research workers in the psychology of perception seem to have been
concerned, in one way or another, with the concept of the stimulus. As
pointed out in Chapter 2, a stimulus variable or an independent
variable in psychophysics must be defined in relation to certain
response characteristics of the organism. The stimulus or the stimulus
variable nevertheless serves as a kind of reference, according to which
the perceiving activity can be evaluated. Once we can define the
stimulus for a certain activity of perceiving, therefore, we can also
communicate efficiently about this activity.

By the defining of light, colour and sound in physics, a system of
reference for evaluating a certain type of perceptual activity was
established. This system, which also involved definitions of the
modalities, has been continuously modified and refined in physics as
well as in psychophysics to cover more subtle aspects of colour, sound,
etc. In the main, however, this system can be looked upon as a
framework of reference within which particular research problems can
be generated. Hence a research problem in psychophysics can be
formulated to the extent that adequate stimuli for the senses are
known. This is how we have come to say in a sense that there is no
stimulus problem in psychophysics. Definitions of the modalities, and
hence of the subject matter of psychophysics, make possible
specifications of the essential stimuli for the senses.

However, these specifications do not necessarily render a more
adequate definition of, for example, colour. Thus we can understand

Goethe's objections against Newton's theory of colour. But definitions of stimuli for the senses make possible a precise evaluation and more efficient communication about certain discriminatory activities. Definitions of certain colour stimuli are indispensable for an understanding of certain forms of colour blindness, and definitions of certain sound stimuli are indispensable for an understanding of certain forms of hearing loss.

The point is, however, that the stimulus problem is no research problem in the ordinary sense of the word. Rather it is concerned with the problem of providing an adequate frame of reference for studying perceptual activities. It is, so to speak, a problem which pertains to the foundation of a psychology of perception.

It should also be emphasized that the frame of reference provided in psychophysics is a limited one (cf. our discussion in Section 2.5). It permits an evaluation only of particular forms of discriminatory activities. A number of other activities — generally referred to as perceptual activities — are inadmissible for a psychophysical analysis. The study of these activities, therefore, probably requires a different system of references. The researchers who have preoccupied themselves with perceptual activities related to material objects, generally acknowledged the shortcomings of the stimulus concept in classical psychophysics. Their attempts to redefine the stimulus concept may be looked upon as attempts to introduce new systems of reference. Thus Brunswik and Koffka, in addition to the more traditional concept of a proximal stimulus, introduced the concept of a distal stimulus. The latter term involved a physical specification of a material object.

Brunswik seemed to think that a perceptual activity can be evaluated in relation to two different systems of references which he called the "intentional poles" of perception. More specifically, these "poles" were the S and A values in his constancy ratio, i.e. the stimulus match and the object match. The perceiving response R was related to S on the one side and A on the other (see p.96).

One can say that in Brunswik's system A represented the material object, and as an "intentional pole" it also served the role of a reference which was opposed to the proximal stimulus reference in psychophysics. Thus Brunswik made an attempt to give the material object a formal status in a theory of perception.

In our opinion, the reference system always prescribes a method according to which an activity can be defined. Thus if one defines an activity in relation to a proximal stimulus reference, one cannot characterize "the same activity" in relation to an entirely different system of reference. On this basis one may question the status of A, or the object, as a separate system of reference in Brunswik's theory. In so far as S and A define a scale of activities, both are considered in relation to the same system of reference. Hence Brunswik's attempt to introduce a different system of reference in order to study perceptual activities related to material objects was an unsuccessful one.

As pointed out earlier, other researchers have made similar attempts by redefining the concept of the stimulus in psychology. We have seen, for example, how Gibson redefined this concept in terms of ratios, patterns and transformations. But a different system of reference requires different methods, whereas in his studies Gibson maintained the ordinary procedures of psychophysics and hence the presuppositions underlying these methods. Like information processing theorists, Gibson included in the stimulus concept the type of perceptual awareness which may be looked upon as a methodological prerequisite. He thus tended to confuse theoretical statements of perceptual activities with statements concerning the prerequisites of methods.

11.2 Conclusions

One can say that the physical knowledge underlying the specification of stimulus variables in psychophysics has been acquired due to abstractions from material objects, and hence there is no way of studying the perception of objects with the frame of reference provided by early physics. Rather the perception of objects and the spatial framework of objects constitute *a priori* conditions for the use of psychophysical procedures. These conditions are linked with all the stimulus concepts which we have discussed. Psychophysics builds on common knowledge of objects and interactions with objects in everyday life. Taking this knowledge for granted, psychophysics has contributed to our understanding of the sensory systems and their functions, not to an understanding of the perception of objects. Therefore, the psychological study of object perception is involved in a fundamental problem of research, and this problem may in Kuhn's sense be called a "paradigmatic" one. Therefore, the psychologists will have to work for a "scientific revolution" which enables them to deal theoretically with the perception of objects in ways hitherto unknown. The aim, however, is still to evaluate precisely and to communicate efficiently about perceptual activities related to objects in the environment.

11.3 Proposals

The theme discussed in this work bears upon the foundation of the psychology of perception. Thus proposals to deal more adequately with problems of the perception of objects will have to be directed towards a "paradigm" for a perceptual science. We can further no such proposals.

However, we have repeatedly stressed in this book that perception should be considered as a form of activity. Hence perception should not be contrasted with behaviour; perceptual activity may be treated as a category of behaviour. Perhaps, in some sense, it may also be treated as a fundamental category. Eventually, a system of reference for the study of object perception should be developed more generally as a system of reference for the study of behaviour.

The sense modalities have been treated as departments of interactions with the environment. Thus vision and audition both imply forms of behaviour. However, they are studied within different systems of reference, and these systems have been developed due to abstractions from material objects. To deal with the perception of objects, the researcher cannot make use of modality-specific stimulus specifications. He must aim at a system of reference which is independent of such specifications.

In practice, psychological studies of object perception will always need to be concerned with more than one sense. Furthermore, objects will have to be specified in relation to a new system of the description of behaviour. Hence it might be useful to consider the use and function of objects in a behavioural space. Moreover, objects which support behaviour and objects which serve as tools etc., might be taken as points of departure in a description of functional interactions with the environment.

References

Akishige, Y. (1937). Experimentelle Untersuchungen über die Struktur des Wahrnehmungsraumes. *IV. Mitteilung der Juristisch-Literarischen Fakultät der Kaiserlichen Kyushu-Universität.*

Aristotle. *Metaphysics and Categories* (Oxford translations, 1908 and 1928). Oxford University Press, Oxford.

Arnoult, M. D. (1960). Prediction of perceptual responses from structural characteristics of the stimulus. *Percept. motor. Skills* 11, 261-268.

Attneave, F. (1954). Some informational aspects of visual perception. *Psychol. Rev.* 61, 183-193.

Attneave, F. and Arnoult, M. D. (1956). The quantitative study of shape and pattern perception. *Psychol. Bull.* 53, 452-471.

Barlow, H. B. and Sparrock, J. M. B. (1964). The role of afterimages in dark adaptation. *Science* 144, 1309-1314.

Beck, J. (1959). Stimulus correlates for the judged illumination of a surface. *J. exp. Psychol.* 58, 267-274.

Beck, J. (1961). Judgements of surface illumination and lightness. *J. exp. Psychol.* 61, 368-375.

Beck, J. (1971). Surface lightness and cues for the illumination. *Amer. J. Psychol.* 84, 1-11.

Beck, J. (1974). Dimensions of an achromatic surface color. *In: Perception: Essays in Honor of James J. Gibson* (R. B. MacLeod and H. L. Pick, eds), pp.166-184. Cornell University Press, Ithaca, New York.

Beck, J. and Gibson, J. J. (1955). The relation of shape to apparent slant in the perception of objects. *J. exp. Psychol.* 50, 125-133.

Bell, Ch. (1811). *Idea of a New Anatomy of the Brain* (privately printed monograph). Reprinted in *J. anat. physiol.* (1869) III (Second series, Vol. II) 147-182.

Beyrl, F. (1926). Über die Grössenauffassung bei Kindern. *Z. f. Psychol.* 100, 344-371.

Blakemore, C. (1970). The range and scope of binocular depth discrimination in man. *J. Physiol.* 211, 599-622.

Bolles, R. C. and Bailey, D. E. (1957). The importance of object recognition in size constancy. *J. exp. Psychol.* 51, 222-225.

Boring, E. G. (1940). Size-constancy and Emmert's law. *Amer. J. Psychol.* 53, 293-294.

Boring, E. G. (1942). *Sensation and Perception in the History of Experimental Psychology.* Appleton-Century-Crofts, New York.

Bouma, P. J. (1971). *Physical Aspects of Colour* (2nd edn). MacMillan, London.

Bower, T. G. R. (1966). Slant perception and shape constancy in infants. *Science* 151, 832–834.

Brindley, G. S. (1960). *Physiology of the Retina and the Visual Pathway.* Edward Arnold, London.

Broad, C. D. (1937). *The Mind and its Place in Nature.* Kegan Paul, Trench, Trübner & Co., London.

Brunswik, E. (1933). Die Zugänglichkeit von Gegenständen für die Wahrnehmung und deren quantitativen Bestimmung. *Arch. ges. Psychol.* 88, 377–418.

Brunswik, E. (1934). *Wahrnehmung und Gegenstandswelt. Grundlegung einer Psychologie vom Gegenstand her.* Franz Deuticke, Leipzig and Vienna.

Brunswik, E. (1944). Distal focusing of perception: size constancy in a representative sample of situations. *Psychol. Monogr.* No. 254.

Campione, F. (1977). Shape constancy: a systematic approach. *Perception* 6, 97–105.

Carpenter, R. H. S. and Blakemore, C. (1973). Interactions between orientations in human vision. *Exp. Brain Res.* 18, 287–303.

Cornsweet, T. N. (1970). *Visual Perception.* Academic Press, New York.

Crookes, T. G. (1959). The apparent size of afterimages. *Amer. J. Psychol.* 72, 547–553.

Cutler, C. H. (1931). Visual size and distance. *Amer. J. Psychol.* 43, 621–623.

Dennis, W. (1948). *Readings in the History of Psychology.* Appleton-Century-Crofts, New York.

Edwards, W. (1950). Emmert's law and Euclid's optics. *Amer. J. Psychol.* 63, 607–612.

Eissler, K. (1933). Die Gestaltkonstanze des Sehdinge. *Arch. ges. Psychol.* 88, 487–550.

Emmert, E. (1881). Grössenverhältnisse der Nachbilder. *Klin. Monatsbl. Augenheilkunde* 19, 443–450.

Enç, B. (1975). Numerical identity and objecthood. *Mind* 84, 10–26.

Epstein, W. and Landauer, A. A. (1969). Size and distance judgements under reduced conditions of viewing. *Percept. Psychophys.* 6, 269–275.

Epstein, W. and Park, J. N. (1963). Shape constancy: functional relationships and theoretical formulations. *Psychol. Bull.* 60 (3) 265–288.

Ettlinger, G. (1967). Analysis of cross-modal effects and their relationship to language. *In: Brain Mechanisms Underlying Speech and Language* (C. H. Millikan and F. L. Darley, eds). Proceedings of a conference held at Princeton, New Jersey, Nov. 9–12, 1965. Grune & Stratton, New York.

Evans, R. M. (1964). Variables of perceived color. *J. opt. Soc. Amer.* 54, 1467–1474.

Fechner, G. T. (1860). *Elemente der Psychophysik*, Vols 1 and 2. Breitkopf & Härtel, Leipzig. (Translated by H. E. Adler as: *Elements of Psychophysics* (1966). Holt, New York.)

Fernberger, S. W. (1941) Instructions and the psychophysical limen. *Amer. J. Psychol.* 43, 560–578.

Fieandt, K. von and Gibson, J. J. (1959). The sensitivity of the eye to two kinds of continuous transformations of of shadow pattern. *J. exp. Psychol.* 57, 344–347.

Flock, R. H. (1964). Three theoretical views of slant perception. *Psychol. Bull.* 67, 110–121.

Forgus, R. H. and Melamed, L. E. (1976). *Perception: a cognitive-stage approach.* McGraw-Hill, New York.

Gabbay, D. and Moravcsik, J. M. (1973). Sameness and individuation. *J. Philosophy* LXX, 513–526.

Geach, P. T. (1962). *Reference and Generality.* Cornell University Press, Ithaca, New York.

Gelb, A. (1929). Die "Farbenkonstanz" der Sehdinge. *In: Handbuch der normalen und pathologischen Physiologie.* Receptionsorgane II: Photoreceptoren I Teil. Springer, Berlin.

Gibson, E. J. (1969). *Principles of Perceptual Learning and Development.* Appleton-Century-Crofts, New York.

Gibson, J. J. (1950). *The Perception of the Visual World.* Houghton Mifflin, Boston, Massachusetts.

Gibson, J. J. (1951). What is form? *Psychol. Rev.* **58**, 403–412.

Gibson, J. J. (1959). Perception as a function of stimulation. *In: Psychology: A Study of a Science* (S. Koch, ed.), Vol. 1 pp.456–501. McGraw-Hill, New York.

Gibson, J. J. (1960) The concept of the stimulus in psychology. *Amer. Psychol.* **15**, 694–703.

Gibson, J. J. (1961). Ecological optics. *Vision Res.* **1**, 253–262.

Gibson, J. J. (1966). *The Senses Considered as Perceptual Systems.* Houghton Mifflin, Boston, Massachusetts.

Gibson, J. J. and Gibson, E. J. (1957). Continuous perspective transformations and the perception of rigid motion. *J. exp. Psychol.* **54**, 129–138.

Gilinsky, A. S. (1955). The effect of attitude on the perception of size. *Amer. J. Psychol.* **68**, 173–192.

Gogel, W. C. (1971). The validity of the size–distance invariance hypothesis with cue reduction. *Percept. Psychophys.* **9**, 92–94.

Grabke, H. (1924). Über die Grösse der Sehdinge im binokularen Sehraum bei ihrem Auftreten im Zusammenhang miteinander. *Arc. ges. Psychol.* **43**, 237–301.

Green, R. T. and Courtis, M. C. (1966). Information theory and figure perception: The metaphor that failed. *Acta Psychologica* **25** (1), 12–35.

Guzmán, A. (1999). Computer recognition of three-dimensional objects. Massachusetts Institute of Technology, report MAC-TR-59.

Harris, L. J. and Allen, T. W. (1974). Role of object constancy in the perception of object orientation. Some methodological considerations in studies of human infants. *Human Develop.* **17**, 187–200.

Hastorf, A. H. and Kennedy, J. L. (1957). Emmert's law and size constancy. *Amer. J. Psychol.* **70**, 114–116.

Hay, J. C. (1966). Optical motions and space perception: An extension of Gibsons analysis. *Psychol. Rev.* **73**, 550–565.

Hebb, D. O. (1949). *The organization of behavior.* Wiley, New York.

Helmholtz, von H. L. F. (1866). *Handbuch der physiologischen Optik*, Vols I, II and III. Leopold Voss, Leipzig. Second edn 1867; 3rd edn 1896. Third edn reprinted 1909–1911 with notes by von Kries. (Translated by X. X. Southhall as: *Helmholtz's Treatise on Physiological Optics,* Vols I, II and III (1962). Dover, New York.)

Hering, E. (1861). *Beiträge zur Physiologie,* I Heft: Vom Ortsinne der Netzhaut. Wilhelm Engelmann, Leipzig.

Hering, E. (1879). Der Raumsinn und die Bewegungen des Auges. *In: Handbuch der Physiologie,* III Bd. IV, Teil 4 (L. Hermann, ed.), pp.343–601. F. C. W. Vogel, Leipzig.

Hering, E. (1907). *(1907). Grundzüge der Lehre vom Lichtsinn.* Wilhelm Engelmann, Leipzig. (Translated by X. X. Hurvich and Y. Y. Jameson as: *Outlines of a Theory of the Light Sense* (1964). Harvard University Press, Cambridge, Massachusetts.)

References

Hirsberg, J. (1898). Die Optik der alten Griechen. *Z. Psychol.* 16, 321-351.

Hochberg, J. E. (1978). *Perception*, 2nd edn (Foundations of Modern Series). Prentice-Hall, Englewood Cliffs, New Jersey.

Hochberg, J. and Brooks, V. (1962). Pictorial recognition as an unlearne study of one child's performance. *Amer. J. Psychol.* 75, 624-628.

Hofmann, F. B. (1925). Die Lehre vom Raumsinn. *In: Handbuck der gesamten Augenheilkunde.* Springer, Berlin.

Holaday, B. E. (1933). Die Grössenkonstanz der Sehdinge bei Variation der inneren und äusseren Wahrnehmungsbedingungen. *Arch. ges. Psychol.* 88, 419-486.

Holway, A. H. and Boring, E. G. (1941). Determinants of apparent visual size with distance variant. *Amer. J. Psychol.* 54, 21-37.

Hsia, Y. (1943). Whiteness constancy as a function of difference in illumination. *Arch. Psychol.* No. 284.

Hubel, D. and Wiesel, T. (1968). Receptive fields and functional architecture of monkey striate cortex. *J. Physiol.* 195, 215-243.

Ingle, D., Schneider, G., Trevarthen, C. and Held, R. (1967). Locating and identifying: Two modes of visual processing. A symposium. Preface. *Psychol. Forsch.* 31, 42-43.

Jaensch, E. R. and Müller, E. R. (1920). Über die Wahrnehmung farbloser Helligkeiten und den Helligkeitskontrast. *Z. Psychol. (I)* 83, 266-341.

James, W. (1890). *The Principles of Psychology.* Holt, New York. (Republished (1950): Dover, New York.)

Johansson, G. (1964). Perception of motion and changing form. *Scand. J. Psychol.* 5, 181-208.

Johansson, G. (1974). Projective transformations as determining visual space perception. *In: Perception. Essays in honor of James J. Gibson* (R. B. MacLeod and H. L. Pick, eds), pp.117-138. Cornell University Press, Ithaca, New York and London.

Johansson, G. and Jansson, G. (1968). Perceived rotary motion from changes in a straight line. *Percept. Psychophys.* 4, 165-170.

Joynson, R. B. and Newson, L. J. (1962). The perception of shape as a function of inclination. *Brit. J. Psychol.* 53, 1-15.

Katona, G. (1925). Experimente über die Grössenkonstanz. Ansätze zu einer Analyse der Gesichtswahrnehmung. *Z. Psychol.*, 1. Abt. 97, 215-251.

Katz, D. (1911). Die Erscheinungsweisen der Farben und ihre Beeinflussung durch die individuelle Erfahrung. *Z. Psychol. Ergbd.* 7.

Katz, D. (1930). Der Aufbau der Farbwelt. *Z. Psychol. Ergbd.* 7.

Katz, D. (1935). *The World of Colour* (translated by R. B. MacLeod and C. W. Fox). Kegan Paul, Trench, Trubner & Co., London.

Kilpatrick, F. P. and Ittelson, W. H. (1953). The size-distance invariance hypothesis. *Psychol. Rev.* 60, 223-231.

Klimpfinger, S. (1933). Über den Einfluss von intentionaler Einstellung und Übung auf die Gestaltkonstanz. *Arch. ges. Psychol.* 88, 551-598.

Koffka, K. (1935). *Principles of Gestalt Psychology.* Harcourt Brace, New York.

Kohler, I. (1964). The formation and the transformation of the perceptual world. *Psychol. Issues* 3, (4).

Krekling, S. (1975). Depth matching with visible diplopic images: Stereopsis or vernier alignment. *Percept. Psychophys.* 17, 114-116.

Krüger, H. (1924). Über die Unterschiedsempfindlichkeit für Beleuchtungseindrücke. *Z. Psychol.* 96, 58-61.

Kuhn, T. (1962). *The Structure of Scientific Revolutions.* Enlarged edn (1970). University of Chicago Press: Chicago.

Langdon, J. (1953). Further studies in the perception of changing shape. *Q. J. exp. Psychol.* **7**, 19–27.

Lashley, K. S. and Wade, M. (1946). The Pavlovian theory of generalization. *Psychol. Rev.* **53**, 72–87.

Leibowitz, H. and Bourne, L. E. Jr (1956). Time and intensity as determiners of perceived shape. *J. exp. Psychol.* **51**, 227–281.

Leibowitz, H., Bussey, T. and McGuire, P. (1957). Shape and size constancy in photographic reproductions. *J. opt. Soc. Amer.* **47**, 658–661.

Leibowitz, H. and Harvey, L. O. (1967). Size matching as a function of instructions in a naturalist environment. *J. exp. Psychol.* **74**, 378–382.

Leibowitz, H., Mitchell, E. and Angrist, B. N. (1954). Exposure duration in the perception of shape. *Science* **120**, 400.

Lenneberg, E. H. (1975). The concept of language differentiation. *In: Foundations of Language Development. A Multidisciplinary Approach* (E. H. Lenneberg and E. Lenneberg, eds), Vol. 1, pp.17–33. Academic Press, New York.

Lian, A. (1976). Müller's doctrine of specific nerve energies. A re-evaluation in view of perceptual development. *Scand. J. Psychol.* **17**, 133–141.

Lie, I. (1969). Psychophysical invariants of achromatic colour vision. I. The multidimensionality of achromatic colour experience. *Scand. J. Psychol.* **10**, 167–175.

Lie, I. (1969). Psychophysical invariants of achromatic colour vision. V. Brightness as a function of inducing field luminance. *Scand. J. Psychol.* **12**, 61–64.

Lie, I. (1977). Perception of illumination. *Scand. J. Psychol.* **18**, 251–255.

Magnussen, S. and Kurtenbach, W. (1980a). Linear summation of tilt illusion and tilt after-effect. *Vision Res.* (in press).

Magnussen, S. and Kurtenbach, S. (1980b). Adapting to two orientations: disinhibition in a visual after-effect. *Science* (in press).

Martius, B. (1889). Über die scheinbare Grösse der Gegenstände und ihre Beziehung zur Grösse der Netzhautbilder. *Wundts Philos. Stud.* **5**, 601–617.

McGurk, H. (1970). The role of object orientation in infant perception. *J. exp. Child Psychol.* **9**, 363–373.

Metzger, W. (1934/35). Tiefenerscheinungen in optischen Bewegunsfeldern. *Psychol. Forsch.* **20**, 195–260.

Miller, G. A. (1969). *Psychology: the Science of Mental Life.* Penguin, Harmondsworth.

Miller, G. A. and Johnson-Laird, Ph. N. (1976). *Language and Perception.* Harvard University Press, Cambridge, Massachusetts.

Minsky, M. and Papert, S. (1972). Progress report on artificial intelligence. *M. I. T. Artificial Intelligence Lab. Memo* **252**.

Munn, N. L. (1965). *The Evolution and Growth of Human Behavior*, 2nd edn. Houghton Mifflin Co., Boston.

Müller, J. (1838). *Handbuch der Physiologie der Menschen*, II Band. J. Hölscher, Coblenz.

Piaget, J. (1972). *Psychology and Epistomology: Towards a Theory of Knowledge.* Penguin, Harmondsworth.

Poincaré, H. (1952). *Science and Hypothesis.* Dover, New York.

Ratliff, F. (1965). *Mach Bands.* Holden-Day, San Francisco, California.

Ronchi, V. (1957). *Optics: The Science of Vision* (translated by E. Rosen). New York University Press, New York.

Rubin, E. (1915). *Synsopplevede figurer. Studier i psykologisk analyse.* Gyldendalske, København.

Saugstad, P. (1977). *A Theory of Communication and Use of Language. Foundations for the Study of Psychology.* Universitetsforlaget, Oslo.

Smith, K. (1969). *Behaviour and Conscious Experience: A Conceptual Analysis*. Ohio University Press, Athens, Ohio.

Stavrianos, B. K. (1945). The relation of shape perception to explicit judgements of inclination. *Arch. Psychol.* No. 297.

Stevens, S. S. (1951). Mathematics, measurement, and psychophysics. *In: Handbook of Experimental Psychology* (S. S. Stevens, ed.), Ch. 1. Wiley, New York.

Swets, J. A. (ed.) (1964). *Signal Detection and Recognition by Human Observers. Contemporary Readings*. Wiley, New York.

Thouless, R. H. (1931). Phenomenal regression to the real object. *Brit. J. Psychol.* 21, 339-379.

Torgerson, W. S. (1958) *Theory and Methods of Scaling*. Wiley, New York.

Tversky, A. (1977). Features of similarity. *Psychology. Rev.* 84, 327-352.

Wallach, H. and O'Connell, D. N. (1953). The kinetic depth effect. *J. exp. Psychol.* 45, 207-217.

Waltz, D. (1975). Understanding line drawings of scenes with shadows. *In: The Psychology of Computer Vision* (P. H. Winston, ed.), pp.19-91. McGraw-Hill, New York.

Watson, J. S. (1966). Perception of object orientation in infants. *Merrill-Palmer Q. Behav. Develop.* 12, 73-94.

Weintraub, D. J. and Gardner, G. T. (1970). Emmert's laws: Size and constancy v. optical geometry. *Amer. J. Psychol.* 83, 40-54.

White, J. (1972). *The Birth and Rebirth of Pictorial Space*. Faber and Faber, London.

Wilson, J. A. (1973). The computer in the psychology of perception. *In: The Computer in Psychology* (M. J. Apter and G. Westby, eds). Wiley, London.

Woods, M. J. (1965). Identity and individuation. *In: Analytical Philosophy*, 2nd series, pp.120-130. Blackwell, Oxford.

Woodworth, R. S. and Schlosberg, H. (1965). *Experimental Psychology*. Methuen, London.

Wundt, W. (1862). *Beiträge zue Theorie der Sinneswahrnehmung*. C. F. Winter'sche, Leipzig.

Young, F. A. (1950). Boring's interpretation of Emmert's law. *Amer. J. Psychol.* 63, 277-280.

Zusne, L. (1970). *Visual Perception of Form*. Academic Press, New York and London.

Index